Addiction:
A Love Story

Also by Jeremy Hooker

FROM SHEARSMAN BOOKS

Upstate: A North American Journal
Openings: A European Journal
Diary of a Stroke
Ancestral Lines
Word and Stone
The Art of Seeing
Selected Poems 1965–2018
The Release

FROM OTHER PUBLISHERS

POETRY
Landscape of the Daylight Moon
Soliloquies of a Chalk Giant
Solent Shore
Englishman's Road
A View from the Source
Master of the Leaping Figures
Their Silence a Language (with Lee Grandjean)
Our Lady of Europe
Adamah
Arnolds Wood
The Cut of the Light: Poems 1965–2005
Scattered Light
Under the Quarry Wood

PROSE
Welsh Journal

CRITICISM
Poetry of Place
The Presence of the Past: Essays on Modern British and American Poetry
Writers in a Landscape
Imagining Wales: A View of Modern Welsh Writing in English
Ditch Vision

AS EDITOR:
Frances Bellerby: *Selected Stories*
Alun Lewis: *Selected Poems* (with Gweno Lewis)
At Home on Earth: A New Selection of the Later Writings of Richard Jefferies
Alun Lewis: *Inwards Where All the Battle Is: Writings from India*
Mapping Golgotha: A Selection of Wilfred Owen's Letters and Poems
Edward Thomas: *The Ship of Swallows*

Addiction:
A Love Story

Jeremy Hooker

Shearsman Books

First published in the United Kingdom in 2024 by
Shearsman Books Ltd
PO Box 4239
Swindon
SN3 9FN

Shearsman Books Ltd Registered Office
30–31 St. James Place, Mangotsfield, Bristol BS16 9JB
(this address not for correspondence)

ISBN 978-1-84861-945-6

Copyright © 2024 by Jeremy Hooker

Addiction:
A Love Story

The idea for this book began one morning in 1996 when my wife, Mieke, and I were walking in the Longleat woods near our home in Frome, in Somerset. We were both enjoying our walk, when at any moment we might see a pheasant or a deer, and talking anxiously about the subject that worried us day and night: how to help Mieke combat her alcoholism. We would collaborate on a book, we said: she would describe her experience, and I would record mine, and together we would try to understand her drinking, in order to deal with it. The idea occurred to me – as a poet, writing is what I do – and Mieke took it up eagerly. The idea excited us that morning. The collaborative work would help Mieke to combat her demon. When published, the book would help others facing a similar problem.

The idea recurred over the years. But Mieke, for all her talents, was not a writer. She was a therapist, a healer, with a great capacity for listening to troubled people, adults, but also, especially, children. But she was not good at talking about herself, or at writing searchingly about her addiction. She had written, and co-authored, studies of autism in her native language, which was Dutch. I suspected, however, that she had met the terms of the commissions by delay, and more delay, until at the deadline she had written in a fury of concentration, an alcoholic frenzy.

Mieke was a wonderful woman; to me and to many, beautiful and magical, deeply empathetic. Not just professionally, she was one of life's healers. She had healed me. She liked to say that, at our first meeting, at the reception for the Cambridge International Poetry Festival in April 1983, I was the most miserable-looking man in the room. She would also say our meeting was Destiny – as it seemed to me, too. Almost from the start we loved one another, body and soul. We spent the night talking in the study of her friend, a Swedish poet and academic, and in a grey dawn I walked through the virtually empty streets of Cambridge back to where I was staying. I felt exhilarated, and in love with the very greyness of the damp, dawn streets.

At that time, I was grieving over the unexpected break up of my first marriage and separation from my children, Joe and Emily. It hadn't occurred to me that such a thing could happen when I had taken early retirement from the university. I was going to try to be a freelance writer, while, initially, my wife supported us. When this idea collapsed with the break-up of the marriage, now, at the time of meeting Mieke, I had a vague notion of using my severance pay to buy a houseboat on the Itchen in Southampton. Dreams! Dreams!

    The truth is, I was lost.

Mieke invited me to come and live with her and her two daughters, Elin and Bethan. Having worked out my contract at Aberystwyth, I went to live with Mieke in Groningen in the Netherlands. After a time, Joe joined us, and resumed his education in a Dutch school, while Emily stayed in Winchester with her mother. Bethan went to live with her father, but remained on friendly terms with us. I settled with Mieke and Joe and Elin at 80 Korreweg, within the old, but war-damaged city. To begin with, Elin, in her teens, naturally didn't take kindly to the presence of a stranger in her home. There was friction, which we survived, and grew to love one another.

    I am ashamed to say that, in that period, which should have been so happy, and often was, I continued to be the most miserable man. As Mieke knew, I was grieving. I had been a much-married man, adoring my family, and expecting to remain married life-long. Quite suddenly, it had all fallen down around me. I missed Emily very much. I was enjoying a new life, but the wreck of the old one still held me emotionally. Over time, Mieke set me free. When we met, I had been lacking in confidence in myself, as a man and in every way. She loved me back to life, and I know now, looking back over the years before Mieke died, that she had helped to make me, as a man and as a poet, the person I was meant to be.

    We had been together for 8 years before she revealed to me, in despair, that she was an alcoholic. How blind I had been! And how well she had managed to appear to be, like me, just a person who enjoyed a few drinks as part of our comfortable way of life. Later, at Al Anon, I met an old man who said: 'When I wed my wife, I didn't know I had married two different women'. He spoke my mind exactly.

    By this time, we were living in England, where I was teaching in Bath, in the college that would become Bath Spa University. The crisis became visible when, in 1995, we returned home – we were living in Frome – from a period in America, where I had been teaching in a college in upstate New York. It had been a good period for me, with responsive students to teach, time to write, and opportunities to explore that big, beautiful country, in the company of our good American friends. What I hadn't seen, while absorbed in my work and in the new experience, was that Mieke was unhappy. Of course, she had hidden her feelings from me, because she knew how much I was benefiting from the adventure, and my new freedom to write. But, with the exception of our few American friends, she had hated the limited, self-enclosed society of professional academics, not to mention the materialistic culture. And while I had been in college, or buried in my books and writing, she had been drinking secretly.

This didn't come out until sometime after our return to Frome, when she startled me one morning by telling me she was desperate for help, so could I contact a friend, a man who was a poet and a psychiatrist. This didn't work out, but we were soon talking to our local doctor, who was a sympathetic man with a good understanding of alcoholism as an illness. (How rare such understanding is, in and outside the medical profession, I was to learn.) With his help, we managed to get Mieke admitted to the famous rehab centre, Clouds House, an easy drive for us through the Dorset countryside. Here, Mieke was offered help. Her tragedy was that she was one of life's helpers, and help was something she could not receive.

When I first went to Clouds with M. I was drawn apart into a group of fathers, mothers, spouses, children and other close relatives of the new inmates. A member of staff invited us to talk about our experience. There was silence. Then my long experience of leading seminars with shy students took over, and I started to talk. I don't remember what I said; but afterwards, I was told that others in the group had found my words helpful.

And I was ashamed, because, as a practised speaker, I had spoken. Talking about M. publicly, with the implication of understanding, I felt cheap, a hollow man. Talk was to be what I offered Mieke during our long years together. I became such a reasoner, pressing and pressing on the subject of her drinking, seeking desperately to find words – analyses, explanations – that would help her. And she let me talk; she encouraged me. She knew it was good for me, a man of words, to talk. And she listened, and agreed, and thanked me. For a time, I was hopeful. But the pattern of drinking recurred. We joked over the story of Brer Rabbit and the Tar Baby. I was Brer Rabbit becoming ever more desperately eloquent in face of the Tar Baby's silence. With time, I came to understand that M. could only talk about herself with great difficulty, and haltingly, in tears. These seemed to me the most hopeful times.

2 MAY 1996

Early May, cold & wet. This morning, I drove Mieke to Clouds House, a converted Victorian mansion in wooded country near Shaftesbury, for the beginning of her six-week treatment. It will be a hard time for her, harder than I could possibly know, but the one hope lies in this, that she has asked for help, and been admitted to a structured course that she trusts. Otherwise, she could not have gone on.

The bluebells are late this year. I glimpsed their stems in woods which are a cool lovely green, a young green, as I passed. Green leaves and white blossom, and stitchwort bringing a new delicate starry white to roadside banks.

Mieke not only talked about herself with difficulty, she could barely speak of what the origins of her alcoholism might be. Certainly, it went far back, and may have been familial, ancestral. Her father was an alcoholic. He had had a terrible time in the war, having been drafted into the German army and sent to the Eastern front. He had deserted and, with a string of horses, made his way back to the Netherlands, eating the horses as they died. Mieke adored her father; she never spoke an ill word about him. Her relationship with her mother and older sister was different. She felt belittled, and heard their voices in her head urging her to 'do normal' and putting her down. At critical moments, M. would talk about 'the pain'. I suspected some form of abuse, and at last came to think she had witnessed violence in her family, with her father and mother traumatized by the experience of the war – in hiding, going hungry, working with the resistance. I don't know what had happened when M. was very young, and I don't think she did either. But she was haunted lifelong by her childhood experience. I once saw a photo of her as an infant, which was heartbreaking, because of the misery in her face.

Shortly after 8 May, which was Mieke's 50th birthday, I wrote a poem to mark the occasion. It started from something she had said when we visited an exhibition of Native American canoes, kayaks, and other boats in upstate New York, and recalled the happiest days of her childhood, aboard her father's yacht on the Frisian waterways:

For a Woman Who Said She Could Fall in Love with a Boat

For Mieke on her fiftieth birthday

What I wish you is not a sieve
or a chugging tub
or a hulk half sunk in the mud
with ribs that clutch at the sky,
but a sound bottom,
good timbers throughout
and oceans ahead to plunge in.

Or a canoe, maybe, or a kayak
for mountain lakes and rivers,
skin or bark rider of rapids
and a wise spirit to guide you –
sickle-gleam glimpsed between cedars,
new moon drifter on dark water
              bringing peace.
Or a rowboat,
oars dripping,
crawling in creeks – where you anchor,
and lie back, head pillowed,
and dream, rocking, rocking,
watching the sailing sky.

Or else a thoroughbred yacht,
sail taut as a fin or billowing,
gull-white hull with lines
sleek as a great northern diver –
a yacht which never dives, but cuts through waves
over the crab's den and the lobster's lair,
over stones and mud where the weeds are,
under, down under, while it races over
and ocean is its pasture.

Better for you a boat like a dolphin,
a mythical craft,

part mammal and part bird.
Nose up, nose down, and the back curves
out of the water, awash and shining.
What are you then but the sea
and the sea's daughter,
waves riding waves
and spume in your hair?

Best of all though I wish you
one of your native boats.

Not a *tjalk* with a hold
full of vegetables and household stuff,
or the floating barn of a flat-bottomed *aak*,
smelling of grain and stone to mend roads.
No grandfather barge which you would care for
like a beloved elder, retired
from the work of the world.

Rather an antique sailing boat
with brass portholes and polished timbers,
stately and playful and worthy
of every weather,
canal-wise and ocean-knowing,
a boat with an engine that never fails,
and room below when you carry a fellow voyager,
and a red sail.

12 May

'Love, whose month is ever May.' But it is still cold and blowy. The colours are brighter though, green and blue, with white and pink blossoms. On the country drive, I noticed the bronze of young oak leaves, and dusky bluebells, which looked like flowers dreaming, on banks beside the road.

Walking with Mieke in the beautiful country by Clouds House, from the stone base of a former windmill on a hill, along a hillside looking down on Blackmore Vale and across at hills near Shaftesbury. Once we stood still in a deep hollow lane, blackthorn petals drifting down, sound of running water underground, and a cuckoo calling behind us.

In the big Victorian house M. introduced me to several fellow inmates. In each case it was like meeting a person without a mask, a person aware of her or his vulnerability and prepared to look another in the face. M., who had wanted to leave yesterday, was calmer and steadier than when I took her in, more herself, both in loving relation with other patients, and (what is vitally important now) in being open to her emotions. After our walk, we sat on a veranda and talked with her counsellor, a young woman called Cory. I felt the anger that has been mixed with my concern evaporate; indeed, it went with my loneliness, and in being with Mieke. I felt the reality of her need, which she is facing instead of evading, and seeking oblivion in drink, which I finally felt helpless to avert. Now, she was in the open, and we were together again.

We were happy, which was simple enough: we loved each other. And then, periodically, unhappy. Desperate. When she was drinking, I found myself reacting to her as I never dreamed I could react to any other human being. I begged, wept, shouted terrible things. I yelled that I wanted her dead. She never blamed me. Sometimes, certainly, she scarcely took it in, or immediately forgot. At rational moments, she would sometimes say, angrily, 'This isn't about you'. And that infuriated me. She knew I was prone to anxiety anyway, but the thought that her crises didn't affect me was more than I could bear. In drink, she became another woman, beyond me. I felt that if I were to fall on the floor (which, after my stroke in July 1999, did occasionally happen), she would simply step over my body. And this was the woman who loved me absolutely. Sometimes she said she drank in order to be 'not on call'. She was hypersensitive to other people, suffering with their suffering, to the point of evacuating her own sense of self. She shocked me most when, one morning during another of our walks in the Longleat woods, she confessed, almost as a matter of fact, to having no inner self, only an emptiness that her concern for others filled. How could I believe that? How could I even think that this woman, who meant everything to me, and was the most vital, individual, wonderful person I had ever known, was no one?

27 MAY

Barely time to write on a Bank Holiday Monday before returning to the essay marking which is taking almost all my time at present, and preventing me from correcting the proofs of *Writers in a Landscape* which arrived with a request for their immediate return.

I came away heavy-hearted from being with Mieke yesterday. She was very unhappy, and said she doesn't know what is real and what is illusion now. She has given so much of herself to others that she doesn't know when she is being used. I felt this applied to me, too – so much of what we call 'love' is a higher (or lower) form of egotism.

I know that her deep soul-searching is something she has to go through, and her unhappiness is a necessary part of her experience of the course. But while her unhappiness makes me miserable for her, I also have my anger, which affects me whether I withhold or express it, as I did in answering her question about how her addiction had affected our relationship: a question she is required to ask those close to her. I was tired, and impatient, and again I *talked* – but to what purpose? I understand alcoholism only with my mind – I don't live it. And therefore I *talk*, urge, even attempt to teach – all to no purpose, unless a momentary satisfaction at the words, which leaves me feeling worse, a clumsy, moralising fool.

We struggled over bottles of drink, which Mieke would smuggle into the house. I poured drink – whisky, vodka, wine – down the sink, but to little purpose. I kept a secret cache, to give her 'hair of the dog' when she was suffering, dangerously, the consequences of a binge. She had a sixth sense for where I had hidden it. I once had a special bottle of whisky, forgot about it, and when I found it and had a taste, it was full of cold tea. The tragedy had its comic moments, as I would learn, from my experience at Al Anon, is generally the case. Once, stupidly attempting normality, I accepted the offer of a case of wine for a festive occasion. The box remained in the scullery and I would note with pleasure that it stayed unopened, until one day I took a close look, and found the box had been opened from below, and was almost empty. Another Christmas, anticipating guests, I ordered some bottles of drink a few days before, and M. demolished them. I came to play Sherlock Holmes in our own home, acquiring my own sixth sense for where bottles were hidden – in the garden hedge or wall, under the sink, in a cupboard. It made me especially angry when M. drank in bed, and I would suddenly feel a bottle under the pillow.

31 May
At Clouds House to talk with M. and two counsellors, Ursula and Cory. At first, talking – but to whom? Ursula asks me. To myself, I admit, and to Mieke and you and Cory. Yes, but M. and I do have a similar intellectual problem, or psychological problem to which intellectuals are prone, of trying to work things out in our minds, whether silently (M.'s way) or aloud. But there has to be a place for this. Direct emotional expression,

which is better understood (and counsellors may prefer?) isn't all that is required. The thing is to *hear* oneself, to know when the thinking or talking has become an end in itself, which leaves others out. As at one moment I am still talking while M. is crying.

The challenge for me is to listen. When she comes out of rehab we're going to have to make a new life, and for me that means, more than anything, listening, and not being obsessed by my addiction, which is to work. And not to creative work alone, but to a way of study, a Casaubon-like amassing, which can be mistaken for work, but which doesn't work *out*. Circle within circle obsessive talking and thinking spirals in – or prepares a perfect house of thought, in which everything is in place, and there's neither window nor door.

LATER
I feel confused by what is happening to Mieke. At the back of my mind, I'm aware of the influence of reading the biography of Mary Butts which Nathalie Blondel has sent me, in typescript to comment on. In some ways, a tragic story, in Mary Butts's self-pity, which was linked to her hatred of her mother, who she felt had betrayed her over her home and inheritance. Of all emotions self-pity is perhaps the one that excites most dislike, and as I am prone to it, so I fear it. But also, as the story unfolded, I found myself responding to something heroic in Mary Butts, and wishing her the success she never really achieved in her lifetime, and may have fallen short of, ultimately, as a result of a damaged life. She experienced so much *pain* – the word Mieke uses when she talks of her childhood, and while in Mary Butts's case it was the pain of a generation, the men and women who had suffered in their minds the horror of the First World War, there is, perhaps, a kind of pain some women feel – a pain that goes with being female – if that makes sense. Men too can suffer mental torment.

Is there an agony the child who is rejected (or feels rejected) experiences; the man or woman who was that child? Or is there a kind of spiritual or psychic pain which only a woman can feel, as she does pain of childbirth or menstruation? Sometimes I feel in my ordinary selfishness as though it gives me a sort of blubber, like a seal, so that in a world that is bitingly cold to others, I swim in lukewarm water.

2 JUNE
Sunday afternoon. Sitting with Mieke in the garden at Clouds House, she talked freely in an easy way, and we passed the time together pleasantly.

Reddish-brown and white calves chewed grass in the meadow beyond the ha ha, in what had once been parkland – broad landscaped acres with a few trees planted to adorn but not obscure the view. Massive rounded cloud towers were slowly moving round. Is this why the house is so named? Probably not. But these are cloud formations that I associate with Dorset, and the very name conjures up for me.

As we sat or walked in the gardens the air around us was full of thistledown, tiny star-shapes floating up and down and from side to side, almost too light to fall. Bluebells in the sweet-scented leafy spaces under the trees are beginning to fade.

I came away from the visit easier in my mind.

I felt that Mieke with her keen mind could understand anything – except her alcoholism. I couldn't understand why she seemed unable to struggle harder. At times she did try, and she was offered help. But I suspected complacency, and sometimes accused her of it.

It was significant that when our carers at Clouds House advised – almost ordered – us to go to AA and Al Anon respectively, I began to attend Al Anon religiously, but M., after a few visits, stopped going to AA. I could see from the way she talked about the experience that she didn't feel herself to be one of 'them'. She saw herself as a therapist looking in on the group. I thought she was arrogant, and we argued.

Knowing how much she loved me, I sometimes thought she would be shaken into an effort to overcome her addiction only if I left her. She said she would die without me – which I found a burden. And I couldn't leave her. It would have been impossible after my stroke, but in any case, I needed her, as much as she needed me, and I couldn't bear the thought of her, abandoned and alone.

8 JUNE

All evening a storm presses on my skull, violent bursts of rain, lightning flashes and crashing and tearing noises of thunder, an oppressive dirty-grey light. And for now, the storm has moved off to the south, and I can hear it far away, as people on the south coast heard the guns on the Western Front during the First World War.

I tire easily in the heat, and dread the cement-grey skies which I associate now with polluted air. At times, especially at evening after a hot day, I feel a depression, a tiredness that feels like age (and may be diabetes), exhaustion of creative effort, though often enough the main effort has been marking students' papers. I frequently think of my parents, and of my brother David, and my friend Les Arnold, who died. And sometimes they seem close. At other times, simply dead, whatever that might mean: their lives ended, not here.

There's a film starring Richard Gere, not an especially good film, but with a sequence that has haunted me since I saw it in the States. Gere plays an architect, a married man who falls in love with a younger woman, and is torn between her and his wife. Speeding in his car he has an accident, and lies in hospital in a coma. In the sequence he and the young woman are swimming underwater, but gradually he moves away from her and swims into the dark, disappearing in pitch black. And we know he has died; it is obvious enough, yet memorable, haunting, as an image of utter loneliness. It is the modernity of the image too, its very lack of real imaginative distinction, that impresses: sheer secular blankness, and honesty in face of it.

9 JUNE
Outside Clouds House, sitting with M. on a wooden seat under a large, old hawthorn, within the warm earth smell of masses of white flowers, alongside a country lane. Fledgling rooks learning to fly, cawing, in the interior of tall lime trees across the lane.

How much of the pleasure of my life has been from roadside verges, in days before traffic made it dangerous and unpleasant to sit or play beside country roads. There is something magical about them, a wilderness beside the highway, a cool resting place for the hot cyclist or walker; and afterwards, places of memory, closeness to the earth recovered in an image. Memory as knowledge which the body stores, and a look at the grassy verge restores to the tips of the senses.

In another session with our counsellors, I realise more that I am part of the problem, not in causing it, but in my absorption in work (including keeping this journal) that sometimes prevents me from recognising the signs, or from hearing M. when she speaks – or fails to speak – her needs.

This is a sad story, and in some ways a repetitive one. But this impression belies the reality. We enjoyed so much together, and she told me I had taught her to appreciate the 'little' things – watching a bird, enjoying the sight of leaves growing or falling, walking in the woods. And we were so easy with each other's company. We liked to quote the words of Gabriel Oak to Bathsheba in Far from the Madding Crowd: *'Whenever you look up, there I will be. Whenever I look up, there you will be'. I wanted her to do her own professional work in Frome, and she did a little with 'the troubled and troublesome', but, mostly, resisted. She could not advertise herself. She identified closely with my work, and was a superb reader with a quick eye for mistakes, and for what worked and what did not. As my poetry became stronger, as I believe it did, Mieke was for me both critic and muse.*

16 June
Sunday outing to Wells with M., who came home on Thursday. A lovely June day with fine strands of cirrus cloud high in the blue.

In the cathedral I found myself casting a feminist eye on the sheer weight of hierarchical male figures: masters and deans and bishops in effigy or commemorated in plaques or inscriptions. High on the South Quire wall, in 14th century stained glass, Christ on a green cross. An image the iconoclasts missed or were unable to reach – left for late 20th century theologians to tie in with their new, ecologically-friendly telling of the old story. What I *saw* was M. waiting for me as she stood in shadow near the door as I returned down the south aisle from looking at Christ on the green cross.

Midsummer
In the evening M. & I drove to Avebury, where we attended a performance in Stones restaurant of our friend Philip Gross reading poems, accompanied by a singer and a group of musicians, from 'A Cast of Stones'. The collaboration also involves two painters, whose work was hung in the room.

Afterwards we walked part of the way round the circle. Western sky dying red with maps of blackish cloud. Sickle blade of a yellow, waxing moon. Grey cumulus overhead – how different night clouds are from day clouds! Somehow nearer (pressing on the heart), more darkly animate, earth-old, and bringing with them a sense of mortality. And it is the circle that reinforces it; the ancient temple with its great earth walls, ridges of bald chalk, and smell of earth at nightfall. Work of human hands that have long gone, of minds that we know nothing about, except in so far as we know ourselves, awed by night and forms of earth, feeling ourselves alone in space, knowing that we die.

On the drive home M. surprised (and pleased) me when she said that she hears two voices in my poems, a man's and a woman's.

14 July
Sunday morning, frowsy in mind and body after weeks of reading, mark-

ing, meetings, the overcast sky oppressive, airless, I set out with M. to find a breeze on Whitesheet Down. We walk away from the Neolithic and Iron Age camps on the down looking across the coombe towards Long Knoll and Little Knoll and find what might once have been a dewpond, or perhaps a ritual enclosure, a dug-out grassy space with a hawthorn in the middle of it. Outside the enclosure, one magnificent thistle. And here we do find a breeze, which cools my sweating skin.

On the slope of the down an ash grove, surrounded by a barbed wire fence, and in consequence the floor, except for animal runs, is dense with nettles, cleavers, and other plants, and has an understory of elders and hazel. Rooks roost in trees on the edge of the grove, and squabble, and moult, so that fallen black feathers stand up out of grass outside the fence. M. collects them, and I pick up feathers for her – to make a dream-trap, she says. For both of us, the grove feels like a holy place.

24 JULY
Night drive to Ramsgate. Wait for early morning boat.

Drive on grey, intermittently rainy day from Oostende to Groningen, stopping for lunch at the restaurant, by water (an arm of Ijsselmeer), where we stopped on my first visit to the Netherlands, journeying into the unknown, in 1983.

1 AUGUST
It has been a holiday of visits to family and friends. Yesterday, by train to Den Haag, where we visited the Stadshuis for Mieke to obtain a new passport. I'd noticed her old one was out of date as we waited to go through customs at Oostende. Fortunately, the officer didn't look at it closely.

In the Mauritshuis, the startling effect of Vermeer's *View of Delft*, a dark-bright moment held out of time. Here, again, were Rembrandt's *Homer* and *Saul and David* (the darkness dividing them an absolute gulf), and his great self-portraits, the young man, and the old man in the year of his death: a face conscious of creative power, proud in the young man, mildly ironic in the old. In a place of great painted portraits, it is this inner knowledge that sets Rembrandt's apart. Whereas others are seen, or revealed, his see.

What I also saw again in paintings in the Dutch tradition was the human gesture. In Roger van der Weyden's *Lamentation*; in the tender kiss in Quentin Massys' *Virgin and Child* (mother and child kissing each other, he nuzzling her hair); in Gerard ter Borch's *The Louse Hunt* (which, before I read the title, I took for a mother combing her daughter's hair). In painting after painting the human world (frozen in ringing silence in Averkamp's *Pleasure on the ice*).

That is scarcely what I saw outside the paintings, however. In Drenthe, woods and pastures, a green landscape peaceful to the mind; sky-reflecting waters. In Groningen, wide spaces, far views over fields, distant windmills, spires. One evening at Delfzijl, smell of salt water, sun shining on water and mud, tide coming in, under the Eems Hotel, where we sat over our plates of mussels and watched small flotillas of ducks making their way together, slowly, patiently, along the coast. On our way back (full moon big in the sky) we were stopped by a bridge opening to let through a long, sleek barge, *Jaguar*, on a canal cutting through the landscape.

Nature, but nature ordered to human ends. The sense of social space is also, as I felt before, very strong. People look at each other here with interest, as if to say, 'And who are you?' At first it rather offended me in my evasive Englishness, but I came to value it as something essentially friendly, though it is also true that, with the Calvinist inheritance, Dutch people have a critical spirit, and an inclination to cut others down to size. It is there in popular expressions: 'Be normal', 'Don't call attention to yourself'. Among my Dutch students, I rarely heard any stronger praise of a writer or work of art than 'quite good'.

I write this on a heavily overcast morning, at a table from which I can see, through the open door and beyond an area of grass and small trees, the white sail of a yacht on a corner of Paterswoldemeer. This has been a difficult time for me, a time of anxiety and mental exhaustion. For me, a shorter visit would have been enough. For M. too, there's a sense that nothing remains for her here – family and friends, of course, but no present life of her own. On Groningen station, remembering other arrivals and departures, I saw Joe's friend, Jan, the little boy who died, crying as the two said goodbye on the day Joe returned to England, and I went with him as far as the Hoek, and came back, and cried, too. It was a good life we had here, but we're both glad to be living elsewhere now.

2 AUGUST
High summer. Rowan berries reddening among darker green. Lammas: anniversary of the killing of William Rufus in the New Forest.

A clearer, fresher day, in atmosphere and in my mind. By narrow roads to the coast – canals, drifts of cloud, cloud-shadowed pastures, neat, brick villages – Warffum, Pieterburen. New windmills turning (acrobats gracefully performing one act), old windmills standing still in a strong, fresh wind.

To Noordpolderzijl: rushes & heavy-headed wheat swaying in wind which had cleared large, blue spaces and sculpted slowly dissolving figures among the clouds. Over the dyke, fishing boats, fishy sea smell, sand islands far out in the dark & glittering water. Horses & cattle on the grassy brink of mud & sea. Sun on a white gull, shining.

4 August
On Koningin Beatrix. We left Groningen when it was almost empty of people, in early morning light, the city at its most beautiful, and, for me, touched by memory of happy times. Mist on the motorways of Friesland, lapwings flying over, waterways opening on either side as the mist faded away. Now, in a cabin on the boat, once more on the North Sea crossing that was once so familiar to me. Sitting out on the deck a little earlier, Mieke thanked me for our holiday in Groningen. But it is I who have to thank her, for without her support, at the end of term, I could hardly have done more in my anxious state than hide in a dark corner.

6 August
Transfiguration/Hiroshima Day. At Moor Farm, Norfolk, with Lee and Kate Grandjean.

Clouded, strong wind turned, coming more from the south east. Walking with M. in the morning, downwind of two hares, big brown animals with long, black-tipped ears, on the field track in front of us, aware, but not disturbed by pheasants, and a large number of partridges, which rise noisily from the corn as we pass by. Two military jets, shaped like arrowheads, fly in wide circles overhead.

Later, alone, I watch a kestrel hovering, gliding, hunting across the wild field. The bird which stirred Hopkins' heart in hiding. I understand why, and what he means by the hidden heart (mine, too, withdrawn, deadened by anxiety). We have believed, sublimely, in a nature waiting to be restored *with* mankind. We are more likely to believe now in another story.

At dusk, watching for the barn owl. I expect it to come from the wood, but instead, turning in the opposite direction to look down the beck towards Cawston church, I see it flying towards me, low, along the line of the alders. It perches on a fence-post, drops down. I lose sight of it, but, shortly after, with Lee, see it again, hovering with rapid wingbeats. It flies towards us until we can see its heart-shaped face.

After dark, from our bedroom window: the orange half-moon, waning.

8 August
Night drive, leaving Reepham shortly before midnight, after listening with Lee to a repeat of my radio programme on David Jones. Norwich, A11, M11, M25, listening to 'Songs on Lonely Roads', the story of Ivor Gurney: poems, songs, praise of Maisemore, Gloucester, Cotswolds, ecstasy & despair of a deeply loved, older England. A country of the heart, which Gurney felt into being, but based on elements my father and mother knew, before the noise of roads penetrated almost everywhere. M. driving, fast & well, me a tense, nervous passenger, unable to take my eyes off the road, peering into the dark we were hurtling into.

12 August
A day with our American friends, David & Kim. We took them to Mells for lunch at The Talbot, and visited the church and churchyard, which M. finds so peaceful. I suppose I do, too, but for me it is a peace after the turbulence of war – the First World War, which overshadows all the earlier centuries. Or seems to, in the memorials & inscriptions & Flanders crosses. In the grave of brave, tormented Siegfried Sassoon, who lies near his friend Ronald Knox, 'hidden in Christ'.

From Mells we drove by twisting country roads to Wells and the cathedral, which delighted our friends. And for us they were delightful company.

Thinking about our time with them in North America, with a teaching schedule that made it almost a holiday for me, reminds me what a strain my life in college has been for me during parts of this year. Like all strain, it reduces the mind to the prison of present circumstances, shutting out memories that might be liberating and painting the future in its own grey anxious colours. As I sit at my desk now, hanging leafy branches of the birch waving in a pleasant breeze, I know that I *must* come out of this.

14 September
Today, we walked from Worth Maltravers to St Aldhelm's Head, chalk dust powdering our shoes. Past a quarry below us, and suddenly, over the dry-stone wall, a view of Portland across the sea. Between stubble fields, by a field of rough clods, stubble ploughed in. Knapweed on grassy

bank between track and ploughed field, some purple flowers, but mostly clusters of shining stars where the flowers had been.

A landscape that calls to my mind the Powys brothers, walking together, or alone. Llewelyn lying in his shelter looking up at the stars. Before I mentioned the thought, M. told me she had seen a Lee Grandjean figure in her mind, elongated, bending forward as he moved across the land. This is Powys landscape, one they felt and imagined: cliff-top fields, the great line of cliffs from St Aldhelm's Head to White Nose – more waves than a line, sea-sculpted, time-shaped. Grey limestone, white chalk, blue sea. Chesil Beach fine as a yellow straw. Old Harry rocks, like chunky pieces of a child's jig saw, and, across the water, West Wight, the other end of the shattered chalk bridge.

Swallows turning quick over the fields, a few bright butterflies. Then the interior of the small Norman chapel, named for St Aldhelm, but, surely, built some centuries after him. So here, again, myth is the poetry of time. Now and then. A specific human presence investing the place, because people with the power of belief or imagination walked here, and other people saw them in the landscape, to which, in a building or a vision, they gave an image or a shape.

Seen from the cliff-top the sea vibrated, twinkled with light, dark blue against limestone. This Dorset coast is sublime. My heart leaps at the sight of the cliffs to the west, cliffs which, for all their solidity, are made of leaping, curving waves. Natural beauty that delights the mind and heart has nothing to do with one's self or little story. Knowing that is partly what delights.

My critical involvement with Powys writings, M. says, is a love affair. But what I fear as a poet is worked-out ground. The poetic attitude I admire is William Carlos Williams', who heard in his people's language the new. For an English poet in this old country, is poetry wedded to the old?

What I should tell myself – and do – is: *The poetry of earth is never dead*. Provided one can distinguish it from escape into dead traditions, into isolation. To think, then; to see through, but also to be moved by what one is moved by – earth & air & wind & rain, harebell hanging on its thread-like stem, gull floating on the sea; to reveal life in its hiddenness.

21 S<small>EPTEMBER</small>

In the evening we were in Winchester to hear Matthew Francis read at the launch of his Faber book of poems at the Guildhall. Beforehand, walking with M. from the passageway where we had had a meal at Pierre Victoire, I turned angrily on a drunk man who accosted us and told him to go away. I've felt bad about it since. He was friendly, but all I saw was someone forcing himself upon us. I wish I could go back and play the scene again. Mieke turned to him with a smile, which pleased him.

Now, as I sit at my desk and look out of the window, I see the dulled-green birch leaves, with yellowing leaves among them, hanging down and waving, with a listless look – and it is the end of summer, the beginning of another academic year, and I have consumed my time with worry. I see the drunk man with his dark curly hair, his foolish friendliness, and my stupid, stone face.

24 October

Leaves turning yellow & gold on horse-chestnuts, yellow on the birch, leaves falling, but not yet the constant fall. One morning, a bright rainbow & its fainter double in front of me as I drove into work. Yesterday, a most beautiful pale blue sky with puffs & drifts & islands of white cloud – shores of time constantly changing & wearing away – and suddenly, through the mellow blue, a flock of black birds.

One night Mieke woke up crying because she had dreamed I had died.

10 November

A dry-stone wall, green fields to a cliff edge and the sea. In the fields an old farmer is destroying mushrooms by knocking them over and beating them to pieces with a walking stick handle. Mieke protests against his destruction of what would give other people pleasure. He seizes hold of her and drags her off to an old stone farmhouse. I try, ineffectually, to intervene, but am next in the living room of the farmhouse with a woman and her two grown-up sons. We talk about the old man and his violence and possessiveness and the family supports me in my proposal to call in the police.

Where does it come from? Waking from deep sleep, I can only wonder.

11 November

Speaking to Gerard Casey on the phone, he had said he hoped Mieke would be with me when I visit him. He told me that he feels her healing presence. It is true, and I am witness to it, and many know it. She has had a great struggle since coming out of Clouds – and before, of course – but this includes the effort not to drink, not to dull pain or seek oblivion. She talks more about her feelings and past experiences. She looks better too, and breathes more easily. But still, it is a struggle – more than I can know.

A year ago, my father was dying. I have missed going down to see him, sitting with him, feeding him, talking a little. He and mother are often present to me, in the sense that I am strongly aware of them as themselves. The past is truly astonishing: the living that *was*.

On the radio this morning I heard Stephen Jay Gould talking about bacteria as the most successful species. Scientists seem at times to exult in the loss of human uniqueness – by which they seem to mean species dominance. And I find myself thinking, impatiently, *nonsense*. It is one thing for humans to be humbled as a species, and something to be grateful for, as one comes closer to life in all its manifestations, wondering at and valuing it. But it is quite another for thought to dismiss personhood – or lose it by default, because the thinker is operating at a level of abstraction that discounts the reality of the unique being of each person one loves, and can know in oneself, if one dares. There lies the challenge: to know that which, in being unique, destroys all categories, all abstractions, and *faces* us with the radical question. There itself is meaning, in the face of the loved one, or looking out of our own eyes, if we choose to see.

5 FEBRUARY 1997

Mieke has had a relapse recently. She was very frightened last night when I found an almost empty bottle of whisky among clothes in the washing basket. She had no memory of having bought and drunk it. She's afraid she's going out of her mind, and said she would like to be 'locked up', in case she buys more drink without knowing what she's doing. No lectures this time. I realise how useless they are, and am tired of the sound of my own voice. I tried to comfort her, without diminishing the danger; perhaps fear is necessary, but not panic or terror, which may become a roundabout justification for drinking. It has to be a matter of picking oneself up and moving on one step at a time. Trying to help alone, I almost despair. Immediately I feel anger, then impatience, frustration, which make me self-righteous. But I have come to recognise that this is a disease. My underlying feeling is fear – that M. will harm herself irreparably, that I will lose her, and worthless anxieties over appearances & social shame.

It is a fine, soft morning as I write these words. Already little birds are more active, flitting about the gardens and among the silver birch twigs swaying in a breeze. If only Mieke had some of my egoism! I find so much pleasure simply in living. Even this morning, glimpsing blue tits in the tree outside my study window, seeing earth freshly turned, and usually in writing too, observing, or trying to find words to see by. In all, so much pleasure, the pleasure Wordsworth named, which there is in life itself.

In my mind, a picture of Mieke holding up a sunflower, two faces side by side, hers smiling. But, often, what she utters is pain – in her words, and in her voice. Pain of abuse when she was a child, and tapes playing in her head, denying her. And, with the repetition, desire for oblivion. Not death (hope lies there), but oblivion to the pain & the voices. What people see is a woman who gives life, who heals, and sustains, and is herself a life force. This is the woman I know, so well that it's taken me years to recognise the pull downwards. Because life flows differently in me, I find it difficult to understand the disease. Impossible, but I must know that it is a disease. Without her, what would I be? Not a man who sits at his desk writing in the security of love.

Woman with a Sunflower

Here are two faces
side by side, one smiling
for the warmth that fills both.

Dearest, no one draws you down
to the cruel and narrow place
that was your childhood once.

It is not I alone who call you back.
It is these faces shining
full of the light of the sun.

We were settled, in Frome, in an old house that we loved. It had meant a lot to me to get a job in England, towards the south, if not in my native Hampshire, where I had wanted for years to return to live and work. From my study window at the top of the house, when a leaf moved on a birch tree in the garden, I could see the Westbury White Horse, and clumps of trees on the edge of the Wiltshire Downs, and, with a short drive, we could be on Whitesheet Hill looking down on Blackmore Vale, or at Stourhead. From the other side of the house, we could see Cranmore Tower in the Mendips.

As Mieke had introduced me to her land, which I had come to love, so I was delighted to be able to introduce her to my special places. She had held an important position in Groningen, but the pressures of work were killing her, so I didn't feel guilty when she joined me in England. Unfortunately, since she wouldn't advertise herself and gain the work she undoubtedly would have done, she found herself in something of a vacuum.

10 MARCH
Warm & sunny after early fog. Many brimstones fluttering in Dorset lanes. Celandines out on banks.

Our last counselling session, with Ursula, at Clouds. She asked us each how useful we had found them. Initially, I'd felt some resentment at being treated as part of what I regarded as 'Mieke's problem'. This was my misapprehension, however, and I hope I learnt to become less defensive, and perhaps less conceited. Speaking to or in front of a counsellor made me relax the rigid division I maintain between private experience and public disclosure. I was made aware of my tendency to think in abstract terms about fairness and truth, instead of responding to the concrete situation. M. & I are both inclined to intellectualise. I urge her not to think she can work everything out in the circle of her own consciousness; but I often try to do the same.

It was when we drove back in mid-morning sunshine that we saw the butterflies, one, then another, and another. It was as if they had all hatched in the same hour, perhaps they had.

Later, in college, I gave a talk about 'poetry of encounter' to my poetry class and read them Christopher Middleton's wonderful 'Wild Horse'.

13 MARCH
A bad night. Mieke has a heavy cold which is making it difficult for her to breathe. The day after Ursula warned her of the consequences of drinking, she bought and drank a bottle of brandy and took a large number of hedex. Afterwards she was panicky and ill, about two weeks after drinking herself unconscious, and feeling so ill the next day she said she had learned. But it doesn't work like that. It frightens me to see her hurt herself, but it makes me angry too. In Clouds, structure imposed discipline. Outside, there is none; but no one can survive without self-discipline. Anxious, and tired after a night of broken sleep, I have spoken out again this morning, but feel at my wit's end. This is an adversary that I seem to grapple with, but each time it slips out of my grasp. The addiction is so alien to me. It is alien to

all reason, and drives towards the opposite of life and health. By contrast, I feel myself to be a cheery simpleton, ignorant of life's complexity.

As I write, M. is with a psychotherapist delving into her childhood. But I have become sceptical that this helps her. I'm no longer convinced that psychological talk helps her not to drink. I would like to believe she is being helped, but I can't overcome the fear that, in her case, returning to the past drags her down.

17 March

The difference a week can make! On Monday, I was assessing what I have learned from counselling, and shortly afterwards I was looking critically at M. Now I know that I am with her, and she with me. There is nowhere I can be apart, except when I draw away to my own harm.

Work helps me to keep going. I think of it as my motivating force, but I know that at all times Mieke sustains me; her love, our love for one another.

20 March

In my dream last night, I seemed to be experiencing someone else's life, as a member of the family. Fishing in a lake, my line is suddenly drawn out tight, hooked to a net in which a boy is pulling a little girl across the water. He drags the net under; Mieke, with other people, dive in to save the little girl, but she is lost. M. is washed up, almost drowned. The parents grieve; then I am travelling with them, part of their caravan. We are in Arizona; I am walking barefoot up a rocky hillside covered in loose stones, watching out for scorpions. We are going to Mexico City, which I look at on a map, but, briefly, I am on the summit of a high mountain, looking down sheer sides at the Red Sea, far down, a wedge of red water. I am seized by vertigo. We are then on a wide shore, beating forward into snow and trapping some kind of animal, but being opposed by other people who want the animals for themselves. In all this itinerary, which includes stages I have forgotten, years are passing and the adventurous journey is somehow someone else's life.

23 March

Palm Sunday. My 56th birthday. Mother used to tell me I was born on a Mothering Sunday, during an air raid.

Up before dawn and out in the garden, hoping to see the comet, but cloud obscured the sky. After breakfast, M. drove us out into the country, and we walked at Tellisford, by a ruined mill, over a bridge, the river dark green, black & silver, whorled & rippled under wind. Two pillboxes made of concrete & yellow stone in a meadow by the river, where two boys were fooling about and fishing. Elders in leaf; reddish-brown catkins on grey alders, their lower branches burdened with flotsam washed there by floods. *Flotsam* is a good word, which I first learned to use of wartime debris strewn on the shore in Warsash. Celandines near the river, blue ground ivy & early cuckoo flowers at the edge of a wood. White violets sheltered by a bramble patch.

As we walked away from the weir and the loud noise of falling water diminished, we heard a blackbird singing from a treetop. I remembered my father saying, near the end of his life, when he was blind, that he would like to live to see one more Spring. Back at home, I revised my poem for Gillian Clarke, for a book of tributes to be handed to her on her 60th birthday.

9 MAY
The day after Mieke's birthday, which we were able to celebrate properly this year, with Elin, who decorated the breakfast table in festive style, Mieke worked herself into a state over an application for a post in psychology at the college where I work. It is puzzling to see this complete lack of confidence in someone so able, who is good at helping others who lack belief in themselves. But this is almost a norm among people I know. I am aware in myself of a trait that I share with my father, who did too little with his 'gift of seeing', contenting himself with success as an artist on a small scale, in a local sphere. He was proud; and he was afraid. Fear is what shaped his life. In one form or another, it's the greatest obstacle I meet, sometimes as an external check, but invariably as something within myself. One thing we fearing ones must do is realize its potential virtue. Moral virtue in respecting boundaries, but also as a feature of creative energy, which springs from struggle with one's bad angel.

18 MAY
Sunday afternoon walk with M. & Bethan & Ard in the Great Elm woods. Onion smell from masses of bristling, white ramsons. Rich vegetation of early summer, including red campions, yellow archangel, and late bluebells. Hart's tongue ferns have risen up now; in winter, they lie flat on the ground, like tongues fallen slack from dead mouths. Liquid birdsong, but no cuckoo. River swollen with rain, with light gleaming on fast-

flowing, earth-brown water. How good to see it after the dry early spring, and to walk in a sweet breeze, clouded skies broken, thunder heads driven back to the horizon.

25 MAY
Walking in Longleat woods with M. Scent of fading bluebells, and different smells of sawn timber – pine, oak, birch. Sunlight shining on and through leaves undulating in a breeze, which also moves ferns on the forest floor. *Play* of light and shadow, we say; *dance* of a pair of brown butterflies turning round and round each other as they rise and fall. And it is hard not to feel a life in all things resembling our own, at the same time as all around, animate and inanimate, is completely non-human. Yellowy green oak leaves, fallen in small clusters on broken off twigs, leaf tissue damp and soft to touch. Large and smaller deer slots going side by side on a muddy path, presumably doe and fawn. Out of the woods, views open of the Mendips and the Wiltshire Downs. But still no cuckoo.

26 MAY
In the shade of Asham woods on a hot day. Patches of 'Godlight', as my mother said her grandfather said.

Casualties: tiny dead creatures covered in black flies; a young crow, unable to fly, fluttering along the path in front of us; all the deaths & lives we are too big or too clumsy to see. Tiny green caterpillars with black heads work down on silk threads from hazels, swinging in a breeze too light for us to feel.

As we come out of the woods into the sun, and stand on the quarry edge looking across at Cley Hill and high ground from Salisbury Plain to Longleat and Stourhead and Alfred's Tower, all hazy blue, *cuckoo, cuckoo* sounds among trees on our side of the quarry. It is a shock emerging from cool green shade to exposed heaps of rock, grey, red-veined quartz glittering, with young trees growing out of rock & dross & hard ground. Below us, the empty quarry, a scattering of green plants growing back through the grey floor.

'There's something magical about it,' M. says. 'Weird'. 'The destruction people leave behind – the stillness, the deadness, which is also part of magic'. 'It's very powerful,' she says. 'The lack of life, yet everything coming through it.'

Where we stand, at the edge, there are tiny white wild strawberry flowers. The cuckoo is still calling loudly as we walk back into the wood, where the young crow flutters away from us, and manages to fly up onto a tree stump, where it sits eyeing us.

2 JUNE
Driving into work this morning, I passed a young man in a blue suit, with his back to me, and, for an instant, it was Dave, on leave from the RAF, full of hope for the future. And for that moment, instead of being a grown man driving a car, I was a boy, thrilled because my exciting eldest brother had come home.

As I recall the past, I realize this will sound like a story with a 'plot', a beginning, middle, and end. If that is so, it isn't what I intend. Our relationship was one of complete intimacy. Certainly, she knew me through and through. What I felt with her was the central mystery – a feeling increased by the mystery of alcoholism, which we came to understand in terms of demonic metaphor, as if it were a person, the very Devil. I felt with M. that we came to the lifelong dividing wall no emotion or thought or word could penetrate. I recall a passage in John Cowper Powys's Wolf Solent, *in which lovers, a man and a woman, lie side by side, each in a completely separate universe. In another novel, Powys speaks of the paradisal division between men and women, cause of both ecstasy and inbuilt frustration. How can we truly know another person? How can we know ourselves? These are questions that my temperament would incline me to ask anyway. With Mieke's 'escapes' into oblivion, and with the strangeness of her compulsion, the questions became especially acute for me.*

26 JULY
A morning when it seems green rain is running off trees in a neighbouring garden and slanting across dark green leaves. A darkness in my mind too, as I limp around on a tender foot, and M. lies downstairs with a black eye and bruised cheekbone after a relapse and a fall the other night. Yesterday I finished teaching on the Ohio university summer school, an experience of mixed pleasures, intellectual and sensual, including the response of beautiful young women. But here I am definitely an older man, no longer on the young side of middle age, and feeling it, whatever fantasies of youth I still entertain.

28 JULY
Does Mieke drink because she is ill, to alleviate pain, or is she ill because she drinks?

I have a sense of her darkness of soul, the irrational compulsion that drives her to do what she knows will harm her. At times, I feel that I don't know M. at all, though we are bound to one another. Is it true that the more one knows another person the more mysterious they become? Familiarity is the ultimate confinement. I think I have always known this, periodically glimpsing the strangeness of life through the mental walls we construct to contain the real mystery, and make a superficial order that is easier to deal with.

There's no pleasure for her in drinking. It's as though when she's feeling well a voice inside asks her what right she has to be healthy – the same voice that questions her right to achieve anything. When she describes the sickness in this way, I feel I can understand. But how help her to ignore the voice and avoid self-harm?

It is no good anyone living through or for another. We have been two together, but increasingly in the last months this has changed, so that at times it seems that I am keeping Mieke alive.

What is she afraid of? I asked myself last night, as I walked out in the dusk. Is this, perhaps, the question? And this morning I wondered if I am actually bad for her, and whether she wouldn't actually die without me, as she says she would, but find an inner being, a reason within herself to live.

29 August

With use of 'she' in 'Groundwork' poems I am conscious of organising materials with what I think of as a woman's sensibility, which is of course part of myself. I want to use that other voice M. says she hears in my poems, but not just to say what I already know. Some pieces have come almost from nowhere – for example, M. getting up in the dark just before dawn, saying the day was 'unstable'. Sometimes all I need is one word – which may disappear in the image it releases.

31 August

The very houses seemed stunned as I looked out at them this morning, after hearing of the death of Diana, Princess of Wales. A wind was blowing the leafy birch branches back and forth, and behind, the misty autumnal high ground had a look of land for which there could never be anything new. She was the most loved public figure of my time, a bright, warm person, by all accounts, who must now become even more of a fairy-tale princess, exchanging her celebrated image for myth. 'Poor kid', M. said, when I had taken her the news. It is like a medieval morality, as we wake up to the intervention of Death, who has interrupted the festivities and taken the fairest and brightest one.

13 September
M. was feeling ill today, but, late in the afternoon, I persuaded her to come with me to Millfield school for the private view of Peter Randall-Page's exhibition of drawings, 'In Mind of Botany', and it did her good to get out. Randall-Page writes: 'I think we have much closer connection with other living things, both flora and fauna, than we realise. We are all part of the same biological system and my desire is not only to know this intellectually but to feel it in my bones'.

That was what Mother said – she felt in her bones that she wouldn't die – and it made a deep impression on me. Knowledge felt in the bones is certainly what any artist who responds to nature needs. Without it, we will not draw on the life we share with nature. And, of course, in drawing on that life we create forms, rather than copying forms that already exist. To break our taste (as Lee says) requires us not to reproduce what we see, but to use that other imaginative organ, by which we know nature from the inside.

21 September
Late afternoon, on a still, warm day, we walked to Cranmore Tower in Mendip Forest, uphill along a green lane between high hedges, hazel nuts, small green catkins, & autumn fruits on the bushes – black elderberries, sloes, hips. Comma butterflies sucking sweetness from blackberries, and a few spidery seeds of rosebay willow herb on a light breeze, which we felt as we climbed higher. Nearing the Folly we could see Frome in the distance, and just make out where our house is; beyond it, the Westbury White Horse. Blue haze over the land below. Looking at an old beech, M. said: 'once upon a time I would be up there, sitting in the hollow all day'. Small groups of shaggy ink cap toadstools under trees by the path. Suddenly a buzzard glided over with a crow diving down at its back and harrying it from the sides.

Back at home, when I walk from the side of the house where I have been sitting at my desk, I can see the sun lowering over a long ridge of the Mendips where Cranmore Tower stands up, reduced by distance to a size smaller than a child's brick.

2 October
Late afternoon: with M. at Orchardleigh. Gnats dancing – gold bits – in warm sunshine. Blinding eyes of light on the lake, which was stained yellow-gold and green by reflections of turning horse-chestnut leaves. A yaffle started up close to us and we watched its broad, yellow-green back as it flew away calling alarm, like laughter.

In the graveyard at St Mary's, the 'green chapel', a grey squirrel sitting up by a tomb looked like grey stone, and, until it moved, we took it for an ornament. From the time-haunted, abandoned parkland, and the mound covering the remains of the old house, we walked back on the other side of the lake in full view of the Duckworth house, at the bottom of the sloping grounds cleared for its prospect. We talked about the social feeling inseparable from 'big' houses in England, how one will see them with an owner's or a servant's eye, even perhaps with some of the deference my grandfather, who had worked at Blenheim as a boy, showed towards the families. For M., who sometimes lived in grand houses when she was a child, it is different, and she sees them without either guilt or resentment.

Everything about the day hinted at opulence: colours, warmth, peace, seclusion, memories of vanished privilege. Underfoot the ground was hard, after a long period without rain; but I can't say I really thought about drought, or much about social conditions. For I have always loved places like this, and was, from childhood, free to enjoy them, at Newlands Manor, Walhampton, and elsewhere. Contrary to the Raymond Williams view, I suspect that it wasn't unlike that for servants and estate workers, especially in places where they were well treated. My grandfather, at Blenheim, courting, would probably have felt he belonged to the place, although knowing full well he owned no part of it. It isn't his world that I feel is far away when I walk in the grounds at Orchardleigh, but a former owner's, the poet Henry Newbolt, with his public-school values, and imperial, masculine ideals. That too one knows as a memory of the great divide, which appears in the most peaceful places as shades of young men – 'It seemed that out of battle I escaped'.

15 November
As we walked on a track through the Longleat woods, a small brown fawn got up from vegetation on one side, crossed over and slipped away among the trees. Behind us as we climbed, deciduous woods rose above conifers – gold-brown, almost dark red, against cloud. Looking again at the place from which the fawn had emerged I realized that everything one

says about nature is untrue. I had spoken of 'vegetation', but now saw the 'tangle' of many different plants, but only a tangle to the human eye – in reality, an interaction of growing things, a hiding place for deer and birds, a habitat for insects and small mammals – one small part of a world that no one could describe exhaustively.

Talking about this led us back to the idea of a 'Higher Power' which we have often spoken about recently, and which for M. is a stumbling-block at the first 'step'. Now she said: 'Somehow I've been looking for God all my life. But expecting something shattering, like a burning bush. Not looking for the small signs'. As she spoke, we were looking at a beech tree which was indeed 'burning', like yellow flame. But she meant, rather, meeting people, or opening a magazine or book, and unexpectedly finding something that speaks to her.

We talked again about 'our book', and again I was running ahead anticipating the finished product, while we know that what matters is to write, step by step. I feel how deep M's lack of self-confidence goes, in effect, her self-obstruction, the compulsion to put obstacles in her own way. But surely, this doesn't betoken absence of self, but self that won't open to admit any Higher Power, or some failure of faith in life, though to those who know her M. is herself a life-force. As she dwells on the first step, without any prompting, I feel hope, for I'm sure the problem lies deep, in an obstruction planted in her in childhood. And I realize we can't remove it by our own unaided wills, and she too realizes this. It is as she opens her mind and heart that I feel hope.

3 December

A colder night, the Christmas tree glittering pleasantly in the centre of Trowbridge. I have a friendly feeling towards the old church with its bulky stonework and tall spire, as if it embodies a knowing about life and death from its position in the community. As I walk, with slight unease, across the graveyard, I always remember, possibly because of my destination, my father's story about the old drunkard who came to at the foot of a gleaming white stone angel in a graveyard, and got such a fright he never touched another drop.

There was a lot of laughter at Al Anon tonight; there often is in this group, some of it at stories about 'our alcoholics'. It expresses tension released, and is never unkind. One thing that does make me uneasy is the talk about 'them'. I understand that it expresses the group's 'us' and enables detachment, but it makes me uneasy because I don't think of M. in that way. I feel that I may have allowed myself to get too involved, and that our close talks and readings are a mistake, since they somehow normalise the situation and permit drinking. Wouldn't there be more hope if she were left alone to suffer the consequences of her alcoholism, and really reach 'rock bottom'? I find the idea of not sharing with her very hard, and the thought of her loneliness unendurable.

In the meeting we talked, among other things, about staying healthy. It isn't uncommon for the person living with the alcoholic to break down or become ill in some other way, as a result of the stress of the situation. It may even be the alcoholic who survives.

Later

Even as I was writing the above Mieke was under the influence of drink. Again, I accepted that she wasn't feeling well. Then suspected, and found a glass with a mixture of vodka & juice hidden in the bedroom. I shouted, I demanded that she produce the bottle. She denied there was one. I shouted more, and she produced it while I was out of the kitchen searching in another room.

This shouting is folly. I *know* she can't help herself. But sometimes it's only mental knowing, more theoretical than actual. It's hard not to blame an alcoholic, not to see alcoholism as monstrous selfishness. But it was I who at the meeting said 'addiction is beyond reason. We can't deal with it with our reason. The alcoholic can't overcome or control it with reason'. Then, what?

18 December

Mieke is ill this morning after a bad week. Twice at night she has fallen heavily, once in the bedroom and once in the bathroom. The first time I saw it happen. She blundered out of bed, apparently unconscious, and, before I could prevent it, went down blindly, headlong, unable to attempt to break her fall. It was horrifying, and throughout the day, in class, the noise of her fall echoed in my head.

The falls were the worst of the week: the complete lack of control, almost nonhuman in its unconsciousness, like a heavy inanimate object (the proverbial sack of potatoes) going over, and the possibility of serious hurt – to which people under the influence seem immune, but one can't take that for granted. And once, beginning to recover, M. said to me: 'Why is it I want to die so much? I just don't understand it, it's so strong'. She went on to liken her inner world to a Bosch nightmare, saying how sorry she was to have let me into it. *As if she should have showed me only what she thought I wanted to see!*

Part of my response is anger. Not with M., but with what I perceive as a foul, life-denying antagonist, something that is the bitter enemy of all that I hold dear.

28 December
This morning, I feel empty, sick of all the talk, my talk, disillusioned by the hope dashed again, disgusted at what drink does to Mieke. I want it to stop, not only because of what it is doing to her, which I worry about over & over, but because of this monomania, and the deception, the secrecy, the erosion of our equal partnership. The thing I am struggling with, as I have learnt from Al Anon meetings, is the negative bond, or the influence of living with an alcoholic on my mind & spirit. It challenges everything I believe in, not at an intellectual level, at which I can find detachment, but in daily living, in being who I am or seek to be. This is intimately involved in M. periodically becoming another person, in effect a no person, all her brightness, her intelligence, her life force quenched. Again & again, I pit myself against the antagonist, the state of mind or spirit that compels her to make this happen, and realise again that I am combating an addiction, an illness, which is a kind of wrestling with Proteus, as though, grasping at armfuls of seawater, one could somehow hold the sea.

The truth is that, for all my involvement, I am discounted. Not Mieke, but her addiction sets me aside. None of my words or approaches make any difference. Nor, it seems, does love. It is love that we expect to hold, to be, somehow, saving. But addiction seems stronger than love. This is what ultimately bewilders me, the more so in that I have seen Mieke as all love; seen her as I should not have done, since I have seen her in terms of my needs, although also as she presents herself. But this is what we are now trying to grapple with: her identity, her needs, apart from her giving, her mode of being towards others, without regard for her inner being.

29 December
At times, in the immediacy of feeling, I say things that are only partly true, or which appear, when I look at them again, a lie. The problem has intensified since I have thought about M. as an 'alcoholic', which has been influenced by the language of Al Anon, such as 'the alcoholics in our lives'. But, as I have tried to say to the group, this way of speaking troubles me, since Mieke is not a category to me, but a person, with all the depth of

mystery that implies, and the woman with whom I share my life.

At once, with sobriety, I know what M. means to me, absolutely.

I can't put this into words; the underlying reality of our lives is beyond words. And the trouble with words is that they obscure or distort. Life isn't so much what we can't see, as what (sometimes) we do see, but can't say.

The beauty of a woman, her deep goodness, is difficult for a man to speak of. Difficult in our world of reticence and irony, but also because of male needs and sexual conventions, which distort the truth and hinder its expression. One of the things I admire in George Oppen is the way he speaks of his wife, Mary. I know that whatever I say about Mieke is a lie, when, in describing her alcoholism or my reaction to it, I have forgotten the beauty that humbles me.

15 February 1998
A hazy morning in the Longleat woods. A sign of spring – two male pheasants fighting, then scuttling off separately, across the path and up the hillside. When I kick a log hewn from a tree trunk M. laughs and describes the action as 'typically male' – something to do with 'marking territory'. I feel it rather as a gesture of affection: appreciation for the solidity of the thing.

Late March
A week with M. in Sweden at the invitation of Professor Harald Fawkener. I lectured and read my poems and joined in discussion with Harald and his students and colleagues at Stockholm University. Afterwards we stayed with Harald and his wife Pia at their home in the country, at Falköping, more than an hour by fast train from Stockholm, and he took us to visit medieval and ancient sites in the area. Of the many marvels Harald introduced us to, the most marvellous were the cranes. Thousands of cranes, elegant, pearl-grey birds, their cries less harsh than peacocks', a honking, a muttering. In flight they are a sign of ancient wisdom. Landing, they touch down with stately control. Our journeys took us to high places with far views over forest and farmland, skylarks singing overhead. At Skara we went into the cathedral, where the ground, Harald said, consisted of 'layers and layers of monks': a thousand years during which monks had lived and died and been buried.

When it seemed impossible that we could see more, Harald brought us to an area of ancient passage graves, stone circles and standing stones. There is a power about such places – a power springing from belief. It is almost as if one expects the stones to move. What is this place? It seems always to be on the point of answering. And its answer is *no answer,* echoing down the stone centuries.

At the university, after I had given my talk ('The Dearness of Common Things'), I was astonished when several students marched in, singing, and gave three cheers for me, and a very kind lady who is the English department secretary, produced a marvellous cake. The day had been so full, I had forgotten it was my birthday. I have never known a week so full. The welcome we received in Sweden was more than I expected. For Mieke, too, it was a week in which she was full of energy, walking round Stockholm, fully involved, completely well.

10 May
M. is suffering; she has a pain in her lower bowel, which she has had for two years and only recently admitted to, and went to the doctor, who is making a hospital appointment. We are anxious but she insists on not looking forward, on taking life a day at a time, and enjoying those when the pain is less. Without her wisdom, I tell myself stories about what might happen.

The swallows have returned, and a blackbird sings from somewhere hidden among leaves on top of the birch, filling the space around with song, as the air is filled with windblown green leaves.

22 May
I'm just back from visiting M. at the RUH, Bath. After collapsing from great pain, badly bruising her foot in the fall, she was taken into hospital two nights ago. Colitis has been diagnosed – painful, but not as serious as pancreatitis, which the doctor who visited her in the middle of the night feared. There will be further tests, but she is more comfortable today.

The interim, after a night virtually without sleep, sitting beside her on a hard wooden chair in Casualty, has been dreamlike for me. Initially, very alarming; less anxious after my visits. Back at home now, I'll see if I can keep awake enough to mark some student poetry scripts.

Later
At 11, I met Elin off the train at Bath station. She remarked on what I feel acutely – the emptiness of the house without M. here to greet us.

1 June
I brought M. home from hospital today, weak, but with a positive diagnosis. On the first day of June the first June roses were hanging from hedges on long sprays.

6 June
First outing for M. since she went into hospital. A short walk in Nockatt Coppice near Heaven's Gate, looking down on the Safari Park. Rainwater on fern leaves. Fullness of the June grasses, with foxgloves, red campion, sweet-smelling wild roses. Resinous smell under pines; cuckoo calling on the far side of the woods.

A day for remembering. As we set out, I was singing one of my father's songs – 'Sea Fever' – but not as he would have sung it. As we returned to the car a heavy shower began, wind lashing shrubs & trees.

14 June
Rain falling on our heads and pattering on leaves as we walk in the woods. Then a break in storm cloud, bright sun, a little steam rising from pine needles on the woodland floor.

Twittering, a blackbird's lyrical notes, a pheasant, woodpigeons cooing: voices of an aftermath, between the season of mating, nesting, bringing up their young and midsummer silence.

We bring with us another 'world', more the one in which we live, as we talk about the politics of 'language' writing, which seems to require every kind of fracture & dissolution – unmaking the entire Western 'narrative' (reason, patriarchy, self, etc.); all that is seen as complicit in 'late capitalism'.

I am both drawn to the theory and find it unsettling. M. says she sympathises with furious rejections of consumerism. My feelings towards the thought-world of 'language' poetry are more ambivalent, and more personal, since it makes me more aware of how bound up with certain traditions I am. What I reject is the authority of materialistic ideologies, which theorists of this poetry seem to operate entirely within.

I am in a fog, where lights flicker that may be will-o'-the-wisp. I am aware of strong attachments, some of which have a perplexing doubleness, such as my feeling for earth, land, and the pastoral aura that may cloud it. I have to work in the fog.

27 June
Rain has been pelting down, and now, looking out, I can see leaves shining with wetness, dark cloud moving away towards the east.

M. is having a bad day and is resting. She's had neither complete diagnosis nor significant remission since coming out of hospital, only some days & nights are better than others, when she has less pain. Joe may be at the Glastonbury Festival; in which case he will be getting wet and muddy for the second year running.

Work helps me to keep going. I think of it as my motivating force, but then I know that at all times M. sustains me; her love, our love for one another.

9 July
Another bad day for M. At lunchtime I discovered she had been drinking, in spite of what the specialist at the hospital had said. I was frightened, and angry, and felt a sense of hopelessness.

In the evening we talked, or I talked at her. It is so clear to me that she must not drink, but she finds ways of permitting herself to; even after Clouds, she hasn't fully admitted her alcoholism to herself.

As it's clear, so I spell it out. And feel better for talking, and convince us both. But I know that for M. it will take more than words.

19 July
After several days of acute pain, M. could walk a little this morning, so we drove to a track on the downs above Upton Scudamore, where we had a short walk.

Such rich variety of wild flowers on banks beside the track – knapweed, scabious, agrimony, sainfoin, and many more. Nearby Army ranges help to preserve flowers that have gone with meadows & wild verges in other areas.

Harebells blowing in a fresh breeze. Red berry clusters of cuckoo-pint in undergrowth, hard green berries on thorn bushes. A kestrel, holding itself against the wind, hovering; letting itself go, it speeds across the sky. A heavier, slower buzzard mews.

I feel as though I have missed the summer this year. Now, sunlight already looks 'old'; but I love that too. In an indoor life I am bound to miss the many subtle changes, and M.'s health this year has meant that I've seen less than usual. But work has had a lot to do with keeping me in, and rain.

21 July

Dying of alcoholic poisoning, Jack Spicer's last words were: 'My vocabulary did this to me'. Behind his words, there may have been a Wittgensteinian idea about the limits of one's language being the limits of one's world. But it is a visceral sensation, which must have been terrible for a dying man – limitations incarnate in words, and felt as part of his very flesh. I first intuited this when thinking about Lionel Johnson, how his poetry was, in a way, the death of him. The things he had a passion for – Winchester, the old school, youthful friendships & ideals – held him in their grip. And with Johnson the drink too was in some way integral to the passion: a living on the past, which drained life from the source.

    Life knows nothing of closure. An individual life ends: last words, last thoughts, an end to consciousness. But continues in genes, in influence on other lives. Possibly, in spirit: no one living will ever know. We are capable of making suffocating prisons for ourselves with our vocabularies, and dying of words. But it is possible to speak and write differently. And ultimately, perhaps, words have the capacity to reveal, in the fraction of life we know, the living moment: now, always, at the flood.

25 July

Last night I dreamed that I had AIDS and was dying. I was confined in the caravan in the garden at Brynbeidog, lying in bed and drifting slowly towards complete unconsciousness. The worst thing, it seemed, was that my work wasn't going to live beyond me. All the journals, all my published writings, were somehow contaminated by the disease, and were going to be destroyed.

    With M. ill in bed, the weekend was dark, and on Sunday, as I discovered in the evening, she bought a bottle of vodka and drank half of it. Does she drink because she is ill, to alleviate the pain, or is she ill because she drinks?

    This morning I let myself go, and raged: 'It's my life too'. In recent weeks I seem to have lost my sense of purpose. I have a sense too of Mieke's darkness of soul, the irrational compulsion that drives her to do what she knows will harm her. Whether in kindness or in rage, I talk too much. I have a useless kind of knowledge, and eloquence that breaks out whether in rage or in an attempt to understand; and I watch the words vanish.

    At times I feel I don't know M. at all, though we are bound closely to one another. Is it true, I wonder, that the more one knows another person the more mysterious they become? Familiarity is the ultimate confinement. I think I have always known this, periodically glimpsing the strangeness of life through the mental walls we construct to contain the real mystery.

It is almost mid-day; the leaves on the birch have a worn look and are now quivering, now still, under an overcast sky. I feel the need of someone to talk to.

31 July

M. felt well enough to go out this morning, so we drove to Corsley. A few days ago, looking out of my study window, I noticed a church tower, with a flag flying from it, which can be seen in the middle distance. So, this morning we went in search of it, and found it beside the lane between Chapmanslade and Corsley, a lane that in places is a deep hollow way. The church, St Margaret of Antioch, stands in an overgrown graveyard, a wild garden, where old tombstones are partially hidden among long grasses, purple & yellow thistles. Since a lady was opening the building just as we arrived, we got to look inside, and found the interior, without aisles, remarkably spacious. But it was the exterior that impressed us most – from a tall, dark-barked pine (also just visible from my study), with lower limbs lopped off, standing near the gate, to the wild graveyard (red-berried cuckoo pint by the wall) and the flag blowing in a breeze. Next to the church, on one side, a Tudor Manor Farm, and, on the other, in a hedgerow tree, a goldfinch & a greenfinch. Yesterday the area was a darkness within the view. Today it is visible as actual fields & buildings & woodlands (remnants of ancient Selwood Forest).

2 August

A walk with M. on a warm Sunday morning of patchwork cloud and blue sky. From Egford: nettles, thistles, and a leaning Sarsen stone in hummocky cow pasture – site of a pre-Saxon settlement on an ancient trackway from the Mendips. Magnificent teazels touched with purple; green elder berries, reddening haws, and clusters of hazel nuts in hedgerows. The track led to the remains of medieval Vallis Manor, partly built into a new house, partly heaps of stones.

Returning downhill, we followed a muddy path beside the Egford brook. The path took us past abandoned quarries, rock grounds, cliff-faces of tilted limestone strata. Past limekilns, where vegetation has begun to loosen the stones. On one side of us the river, old sluices, on the other rock walls, mossed & ferny, branches overhead. Damp, shadowy places, where we sensed other geological ages. Comfrey, snails on hogweed, where once were cycads & giant dragonflies in forest swamp, once crinoid & Bellerophon on the seafloor.

5 AUGUST
Mother's birthday. M. and I both said we miss her, as we walked in Bath on a cloudless, hot morning.

Among other things, I miss her stories. She provided a sense of connection with the family, with living members, and with some long-dead. If, now, as I look out of the window towards the edge of Salisbury Plain, it isn't only landscape I see, it is because of her. She gave me my sense of connection to the land.

The life we can't see is also the life others have given us. No concept or words are adequate to describe the sense of a more than personal source on which one draws. This, I realise, is one meaning I ascribe to *quickness*: when, in a simple perception, one feels both the life of nature and the life-stream, which includes the dead on whom one's existence &, to some extent, one's apprehension depend.

9 AUGUST
A restless night, during which I had a humourless dream about being due to give a lecture on humour in English poetry at a conference (Terry Eagleton was there!), and being unable to prepare it and, when the time came, standing up and mouthing dreadful platitudes – 'Chaucer is full of humour' – garnished with pretentious blathering about self-conscious humour in Tennyson!

After breakfast on another hot day, we drove up to the Westbury White Horse and walked in a cooling breeze. I stood on the Neolithic long barrow, land below stretching into haze. Later, Emily drove over, and after taking her and M. to Mells for Sunday lunch, we sat in the garden playing scrabble.

One sunny day last week, which began in hope, ended badly, when it became obvious M. had been drinking. There was a cloud in her face, a darkening that seemed to emerge from within, which is one of the tell-tale signs. I felt she has given in and no longer wills herself to get better. But it isn't so simple. A day or less passes and she is again buoyant. And she is always so good to me that I may notice states less than I should.

5 September

Even now, I'm not certain publishing my *Welsh Journal* will be a good idea. I conceived of it as a book of 'openings', but now realize it repeatedly opens inwards, with my states of mind as the subject. It isn't that I have any objection to autobiography; it's more that I'm not sure this kind of 'life' is one I want to make public. The *Welsh Journal* is self-centred, as I feel the best of my poems are not.

M., with whom I've discussed this wearisomely – if anxious, obsessive reiteration can be called discussion – says the journal is inherently interesting. That's what I want to hear.

She has been in good heart for the past two weeks – until yesterday. Today, the cloud is in her face again: a physical & spiritual illness. There's no pleasure for her in drinking; it's a kind of self-punishment. It's as though when she's feeling well an inner voice asks her what right she has to be healthy – the same voice that questions her right to achieve anything. When she describes the sickness in this way I feel I can understand. But how help her to ignore the voice?

Selfishly, I sometimes try to imagine life without her. But I can't; it opens such an abyss, such a blank emptiness. Our life together is a good one for both of us, and I know that this is mainly due to her.

10 September

At Moor Farm. Evening. Elin's birthday. I spoke to her on the phone; then to Mieke, who is with our friends in Tilburg. Elin, in tears, told me M. had been drinking. She had found a bottle of vodka under her bed.

Talked about the situation with Lee & Kate. Then, at dusk, walked to the moor to watch for the barn owl, but it didn't appear.

Later

Lee has an acute sense that each of us is alone, and has to be self-responsible; that we can't live other people's lives for them, and shouldn't be required to, or try. I know this is something I have to face; that M. and I have to confront. We have been two together for much of the time, but, increasingly in past months, this has changed, so that at times it seems I am keeping her alive.

What is she afraid of? I asked myself, as I walked out in the dusk. Is this, perhaps, *the* question?

I wonder whether I am actually bad for her, and whether, without me, she wouldn't die, as she says she would, but find an inner being, a reason within herself to live. On the phone, she said she missed me terribly. But I don't want that; I want her to be for herself.

21 SEPTEMBER
Monday morning. M. came in from shopping with a half-bottle of vodka, which I poured down the sink. She must confront this. I can't be a haven for her in which she destroys herself. I have told her she must seek help, and must choose between drinking and our life together.

Ironically, I had come back from Moor Farm with a new 'militancy', which had immediately evaporated when M. returned from the Netherlands buoyant and energetic. But now, a few days later, the terrible thing, which I thought we had under control, re-emerges in the most mundane way possible, as if the first act of the week had to be self-harm.

30 SEPTEMBER
After days of weeping mist, equinoctial winds. Leaves embrowning, yellowing, on hedgerows & trees in Dorset lanes, as we noticed on our drive to Clouds.

Our meeting with Ursula & Pippa was at my request & with Mieke's consent. But I didn't feel the urgency today I had felt when making the appointment. After a crisis, as M. virtually knocks herself out, feels ill, and gradually recovers, everything is fine to the point when I almost forget, and come to believe the crisis was the last. But now we both recognise the need to seek help again.

One night I dreamed she had left me, and gone off with a sculptor! I was left in a strange land crying out her name. When I woke up and told her, we both laughed about it.

10 OCTOBER
National Poetry Day has come and gone with a terrific emphasis upon *fun*. I feel po-faced in saying it, but it makes me feel weary & snappish. The logo of a smiling egg-face comes to mind – something to stamp on poems & poetry books.

11 OCTOBER
At Great Elm, M. feeding bread to ducks, several canny ones on the bridge parapet, a multitude on the pool below. Along the stream, leaves borne on the current or washed up on rocky islands. Dark shadows under the leafy canopy & damp-gleaming rock-face. Old rockfalls across the path, large,

squarish limestone boulders, like temple ruins in a jungle.

'You can see that strong forces have been working here,' M. said. In fallen rocks with cracked surfaces, in rocks pushed up vertically, in twisted trees. 'Something has been working from inside the earth.' She sees it as 'a prime example of how nature rights itself after people have worked in it'. It isn't a comfortable place, this valley where cloth and iron industries once made use of the natural resources. The bare downs have an appearance of serenity that is absent here. It is really the passage of time we are seeing: thousands of years that have smoothed over marks of early settlement & burials on Salisbury Plain, recent centuries of industrial labour in the Mendip valley.

Somewhere out of sight, in sky between cliff and woods, a buzzard mewing.

18 OCTOBER
At Al Anon during the week I talked about Joe's problem with drugs, and found myself speaking about my feeling of failure as a father. But I feel that I don't want to say much. The group is extremely supportive of one another; for some, perhaps, it is a family, the one place they can really be themselves. I welcome their friendship and counsel, but I don't feel it's a matter of survival for me, as the group may be for others. I need them for their understanding, because each one knows what it is like to live with an alcoholic, and therefore understands my fears, frustration, rage. They say only one who has had the experience can understand, and even most doctors can't.

I found the expression used in the Third Step – 'Made a decision to turn our will and our lives over to the care of God as we understand Him' – slightly odd, even comical. On reflection, I can see that it isn't all that different from the idea of St Thomas Aquinas, of which R.S. Thomas in his Autobiographies reminds us: that God reveals himself to us according to our capacities. Except that it seems to be shadowed by the notion that our understanding comes first, God second – if we decide to believe in him at all.

The leader of our group was looking at me intently as he explained the meaning of this Step. I thought he was expecting me to raise some objection, to say that I wanted to leave God out of it; or perhaps he was looking for assent. In fact, I only nodded. It wasn't an occasion for theology! Otherwise, I might have said something like, 'What's my understanding of God compared to God, and to God's understanding of us?'

22 October

Autumn winds were blowing strongly as I sat with colleagues at a departmental meeting. Now it is quieter, on a wet, grey afternoon, though leafy branches outside my window are seething. M. is in bed, lying in a darkened room. She has eaten little for several days, but has been drinking every day. This is exhaustion, despair.

I too am very tired. We talked this morning before I went into college, and cried a little. I felt both were good signs. She is so secretive, and often silent. I am learning to talk less, now that I realise the uselessness of a mental & verbal 'control'. She spoke about having been the little girl who hid under the table, and of her mother 'hammering' into her mind that she was nothing, nothing, nothing.

It is as if there is something possessing her, or imprisoning her spirit. I feel it in the heavy silence, in her mind turning and turning without release. At these times, it is as if she has resigned her life. She says she stays in bed to avoid 'attention-seeking', but knows she is thereby the centre of attention, and her sickness dominates the lives of those who care about her. Again, reason doesn't meet the case.

In their voices, as much as in what they say, I know my fellows at Al Anon have lived in a similar situation for years. Often, I feel I am far more fortunate because M. has supported me since we first met, and still does when she is well. On good days I feel a fraud for being a member of the group. Then come days like these, reminding me how far back M.'s sickness goes.

For some time, my great fear is that she will die. And her living voice and smile fill my being, her love kindles me, a look, a few words, a touch bring me out of my dark burrow. I must help her to *come out*.

23 October

After a bad day & a bad night, Mieke is weak & ill today. Is this rock bottom?

In spite of the circumstances, there's a certain pleasure in my weekly attendance at the group in Trowbridge. There's the feeling of acceptance of oneself and one's problem, which is known to the others, and understood. The sharing even produces a certain sense of belonging, which attaches to my night walks across the town and through the churchyard (mindful of Parson Crabbe and my pilgrimage with Les Arnold to the poet's church), to the building and room in which we meet, sounds of bell-ringing practice reaching us through closed windows. I am aware of the irony that it takes crisis, an unavoidable confrontation with pain, to enable us to break through our shells of superficial contact – the social world increasingly given to us courtesy of Murdoch media & consumerist culture – to meet as suffering, *thinking* beings. Again & again in my life, this knowing of people, of the inner being of another, has shaken me out of false consciousness.

25 OCTOBER
After gales & floods, it was warm in the sun as we walked in Bradford on Avon or sat beside the plane trees, river running high & brown.

On the high ground near Leigh Farm, a sweet smell of decaying leaves, wind fresh but not cold, the chalk hills from Roundway to Longleat shining. We opened the gate into Arnolds Wood: a green path between hazels, long grass growing between the various trees. 'Could do with the sheep in,' M. said. Blue sky, clouds flying over, Christchurch bells ringing. The trees we planted in memory of Les are small, but high enough to hide much of the outer landscape. Images of Les, and his words, came back as we walked in his wood. I could see him, in happy mood, on steps outside the back door, pulling the cork out of a bottle of red wine. How hard it is to think of him belonging to the long centuries.

30 OCTOBER
Following news of Ted Hughes's death, a line came into my mind when I looked out at the dawn sky this morning: 'This house has been far out at sea all night'. At the back of Cley Hill a storm sky with a crack of fiery light. Clouds above the furnace changing colour – grey, purple, orange, a stain of mustard yellow, and beyond the cloud a metal-blue sky. 'Fierce', M. said. And again, I thought of power: poetic power, and nature's turbulent dynamic energy, human life and its persistence and violence.

Ted Hughes was a complete poet – he wrote as he had to; he developed his poetic gift to its fullest extent. In consequence, the death that now leaves us with a sense of loss, and of emptiness as though some feature of the land like a Dartmoor tor has gone, will in time produce a feeling of completeness. This seems to me what all poets should aspire to - besides which all disappointments, such as lack of recognition or hostile criticism, are chaff.

2 NOVEMBER
To Clouds with M. on a grey morning to talk with Pippa. Light drizzle.

Burnt gold leaves on the beeches at Stourhead.

Since the crisis two weeks ago things have been better for both of us. M. frightened herself; but the main reason for improvement is that we are sharing more. Al Anon has helped me: I know now that I can't order our lives according to my wishes, and with a good deal of talk, which is really wasted breath.

7 NOVEMBER

After two good weeks Mieke relapsed yesterday. An anaesthetic at the dentist seems to have precipitated it. Afterwards she attempted to shoplift a silk scarf but was caught, and let off with a warning. Then she bought two bottles of drink, in Bath, and brought them home, driving recklessly.

Now, as I sit at my desk, it is Saturday afternoon with a benign, clouded sky overhead and over the clear line of the downs, and a mild wind shaking the yellow leaves on the birch-tree. As though I have learnt nothing, I have been *battering* (her word) M. with talk, although at times she has talked to me about her recent nightmare. It is when she speaks of not wanting to live that I meet something I can't face, and react to with horror and rage. It isn't the whole truth about her, but it is part of the truth, and associated with that absence of self, and giving her life to others. Despite my experience of depression, this is utterly foreign to me, partly because I have a strong sense of self, and partly because I love life. And that is what most of my thinking turns on: the river of desire

As I sit here, it is the yellow of the leaves on the tree that seems to be the light I see by. November: my father's birth month and his death month, and a time when, as the leaves thin, I seem to see colours more acutely. In association with him, perhaps, or because, as leaves fall and the landscape opens out, colours stand out in starker contrast.

8 NOVEMBER

Sunday morning walk with M. over rain-wet, fallen leaves in the Stourhead woods near Alfred's Tower. Gleams of sunlight in mist among pine trees below us. We broke small, crisp-tasting chestnuts from their prickly shells. Few sounds – occasional tinkling or twittering notes of small birds, prickling of water dripping from trees, a throaty croaking which we thought at first was a pheasant, then perhaps a raven. Tired after yesterday, after anxiety & talk, M. was herself again, laughing at mud underfoot, delighting in the mild air, enjoying life.

9 NOVEMBER
'We admitted we were powerless over alcohol – that our lives had become unmanageable'. It seems to me that Mieke hasn't taken this first Step. I could hardly believe it when I realised, yesterday evening, she had been drinking again. But my surprise is the surprising thing. Each time, I really believe we are starting again – and this was reinforced when, on Saturday, she said with bitter longing that she wanted the last fortnight back again.

So, another weekend has passed. And I know this morning that our lives have become unmanageable. The word stares at me from inside my head, and is written in what I see – now, the yellow leaves shaking in a light wind.

Our lives: for it is obvious M. cannot manage hers; and this inevitably affects our lives together. There is no end to humility, T. S. Eliot said. No end to the lessons of humility, as, each time I think I have learnt something that enables me to manage the situation, I find myself helpless. In one way not, however: I will *not* allow my creative mind to be destroyed. I too have a selfhood to defend, which entails the recognition of every self and the life by which we all live.

11 NOVEMBER
Came home from work. No light on in the house, which is almost dark. M. startles me, coming out of the bedroom. Denies she has been in bed. Sits at the kitchen table saying nothing. In a cupboard under the sink, I find a bottle of vodka, which is almost empty. I don't say anything; there's no point.

I was talking again in the middle of the night, asking M. why she can't turn her stubbornness *against* drink, instead of against herself. We have a joke which began when Elin called her, affectionately, 'old goat'. It goes with a facial expression, and a whole-body language, when she is set on doing or not doing something. Formidable!

Two days ago, we had a really good talk, when she told me about the 'black thing' she says she can feel crouching on her left shoulder. She was aware that this is a medieval image: a devil-figure or bad angel, which we would describe now as a mental projection. But this is how she perceives it, as a black thing.

At the time, I felt we had gone some way towards dispelling it, with laughter, and with analysis. But the day after, she was drinking again. This afternoon I returned again to a dark house, M. in bed, where, she said, she was keeping herself 'safe' – which I have often heard when it means the opposite.

At Al Anon I hear stories that make me feel how lucky I am – terrible stories of drink that completely alienates one person from another; injuries; bitter blame heaped by the alcoholic upon the partner. Comparisons are pointless; each 'case' is different; but I realise that we have a close and loving relationship, that M. never blames me – on the contrary, she is endlessly generous in her praise of me. And it is because there is so much good in our lives that I find her self-destructive behaviour so hard to bear and to understand.

EARLY EVENING
While I was writing the above M. went back to bed. She can barely speak, says she is 'withdrawing' and feels very sick. I suspect she is dead drunk. What should I do? Probably, nothing. Just see she doesn't fall and hurt herself.

13 NOVEMBER
Why are you doing this? The question rushes into my mind. Last night she was semi-conscious, or asleep; lying very still. Seeing her like this, my heart catches, until I know she is breathing.

I don't know whether it does any good talking about a 'black thing'. By externalising the addiction it might make it less resistible; or it might provide an idea of an 'enemy' that can be resisted.

Getting into bed I accidentally find an empty vodka bottle under a pillow. M. says it was from the day before; she had forgotten it was there.

22 NOVEMBER
Sun behind cloud, gleaming on the brook in Vallis Vale. Water a beautiful clear, greeny-grey.

In the first quarry: great blocks of limestone, strata dipping down, damp-stained blocks where the sun seldom reaches. Graffiti high on the rock-face: STONED HENGE 86! and WE NEED MORE DRUGS. Small trees growing out of crevices. A dry crabapple leaf with a long red petiole came off in my hand.

'The Earth feels powerful here', M. said. 'Angry. You could see the force if you were to speed up time. It would be very explosive.' She spoke of the 'male stone counterpart to rolling hills further on', comparing this area, where water runs off the surface, with the chalk, which is absorbent.

This place was in my mind when I turned to writing poems for *Arnolds Wood* – scarcely a beginning yet. At the back of my mind: stone wall country, which I associate with Les. And the need to ground my imagination with touch of earth or stone.

3 December
Came home from work to find Mieke had had a relapse. For once, I was able to persuade her to show me where the bottle was – empty, in the rubbish bin.

A colder night; the Christmas Tree glittering pleasantly in the centre of Trowbridge. I have a friendly feeling towards the old church with its bulky stonework and tall spire, as if it embodies a knowing about life and death from its position in the community. It is a feeling rather than a thought, as I walk, with slight unease, past the walls and across the graveyard.

There was a lot of laughter at the Al Anon meeting tonight; there often is, some of it at stories about 'our alcoholics. It is a laughter of tension released and never unkind. One thing that does make me uneasy is the talk about 'them'. I understand that it expresses the group 'us', and enables detachment. But I don't think of M. in that way. Since our lives first became united we have been 'we'; and we talk about everything closely, including M.'s alcoholism. This, indeed, is one reason why I have found it so difficult to understand, for one day we can be so intimate, and in agreement, and the next (or sometimes the same day) she can be beyond communication, stupefied.

Later. Even when I was writing the above Mieke was under the influence. I suspected, and found a glass with a mixture of vodka & juice hidden in the bedroom. I shouted, I demanded she produce the bottle. She denied there was one. I shouted more, and she produced it while I was out of the kitchen searching in another room. This shouting is folly. I *know* she can't help herself. But sometimes knowing isn't enough, and it's hard not to blame an alcoholic, and see the addiction as monstrous selfishness. And it was I who at the meeting last night said, 'addiction is beyond reason. We can't deal with it with our reason. The alcoholic can't overcome or control it with reason.' Then, what?

13 December
Last week ended badly. On Friday, I went with Mieke to Devizes for her to attend an AA meeting, but we got stuck in a traffic jam, and when we got to the Meeting House the door was closed. Late in the afternoon, I

felt M. wasn't quite herself, and found a vodka bottle, three quarters empty, behind a picture propped against a wall. In a way, this was more disillusioning than usual, since I felt she had chosen to drink. It seemed wilful, as though, after the disappointment of missing the meeting, she'd said to herself, 'O hell, I might as well have a drink'.

18 December
Mieke is ill this morning after a bad week. Twice at night she has fallen heavily, once in the bedroom and once in the bathroom. The first time I saw it happen. She blundered out of bed, apparently unconscious, and, before I could prevent it, went down blindly, headlong, unable to attempt to break her fall. It was horrifying, and throughout the day, in class, the noise of her fall echoed in my head.

Once, beginning to feel better, M. said to me: 'Why is it I want to die so much? I just don't understand it; it's so strong'. She went on to liken her inner world to a Bosch nightmare, saying how sorry she was to have let me into it. *As if she should have showed me only what she thought I wanted to see!*

19 December
Leafless days are here now. I look out on the silvery white-skinned birch, stained green, each twig with buds like tiny, pointing fingers. Behind it, evergreens, and, far in the background, a rounded clump of beeches on the edge of Salisbury Plain. I feel more and more that I have to go on alone, not separating myself from M. or Joe or anyone I am close to, but drawing on my inner resources, and continuing to live my life whatever happens. For me, this means work: developing as a poet, teaching, writing criticism. It means also what I am doing now: taking pleasure in light on the birch bark, on twigs, and, beyond them, evergreen leaves shivering in wind; in all that comes to the eye in this way – a magpie landing on a branch in a neighbouring garden, washing shaking on a line. And, at the back of my field of vision, the downs, clouds, blue sky.

21 December
Patches of ice on Dorset lanes, frosty grass stiff by roadsides, as we drove to Clouds in bright sunlight.

Pippa says recovery for M. will be a long, gradual process; the danger is that she will do herself irreparable harm in one of her drinking bouts. Once again there is hope. Days of sobriety lie ahead. Once recently she called her increased drinking over the past 10 weeks a kind of leave-taking from alcohol. It's an odd idea, which could easily be self-deception. Yet I do feel a change is occurring, with more of M.'s problem out in the open.

From Clouds we drove to Shaftesbury for Christmas shopping. Home in the dark.

CHRISTMAS DAY
Outside, a dreary, wet day; inside, warm & seasonal with decorations & lit candles, as M. loves to make it. Joe, alone in London, was feeling hopeless and crying when I spoke to him, and at the same time apologising for his self-pity. He could have spent the day with us.

28 DECEMBER
Since Christmas, Mieke has been drinking. This morning I feel empty, sick of all my talk, disillusioned by hope dashed again, disgusted at what drink does to her. I want it to stop, not only because of what it is doing to her, but because of the monomania & its effects upon me, and because of the secrecy, the erosion of our equal partnership. There are times when I feel I could just go away, if I had anywhere to go to, but I know that, wherever I was, I would be thinking about her, worrying about her health. Living with an alcoholic challenges everything I believe in, not at an intellectual level, where I can find detachment, but in daily living, in being who I am or seek to be. Again and again, I pit myself against the antagonist that quenches all her brightness, making her become a no-person, and realise again I am combatting an addiction, an illness, which is a kind of wrestling with Proteus, as though, grasping at armfuls of seawater, one could somehow hold the sea.

It is love that we expect to hold, to be, somehow, saving. But addiction seems stronger than love. This is what ultimately bewilders me. Thinking about M. as an alcoholic, influenced by the language of Al Anon such as 'the alcoholics in our lives', has become part of the problem. As I have said to the group, M. for me isn't a category but a person, with all the depth of mystery that implies, and the woman with whom I share my life.

I can't put this into words; the underlying reality of our lives is beyond words. And the trouble with words is that they obscure or distort it. Life isn't so much what we can't see, as what (sometimes) we do see, but can't say.

The beauty of a woman, her deep goodness, is difficult for a man to speak of. Difficult in our world of reticence & irony, but also because of male needs, which distort the truth and hinder its expression. I know that whatever I say about Mieke is a lie, when, in describing her alcoholism or my reaction to it, I have forgotten the beauty that humbles me.

New Year's Day 1999

Still sleepy after a late night seeing in the new year with friends, we set out in the morning to drive to the south coast. Over Cranborne Chase down to the New Forest, through New Milton and along the coast to Milford. Lunch at The Smugglers Inn, the pub formerly The Crown, craftily renamed for the tourist industry. Years ago, I would drink in a Milford pub until dawn with Jim Insole and his group of musicians, at the invitation of the landlord, our friend Sandy Tullis, a charming, generous man who had been a fighter pilot during the war. After lunch, starting from Saltgrass Lane, we climbed Hurst shingle spit. Blue sky, bright sun, fresh wind off the sea, which was choppy, greenish-grey with a dazzling suntrack. Luminous haze off the Island shore, the down with the point of the Tennyson Memorial humped up dark. Breakers creamy white on orange shingle. I got a shoeful of water. Behind us, on estuary water between mud-flats, hundreds of brent geese & a few swans, the larger birds pushing gulls back onto the salt marsh. Back in the lane, we looked at people walking singly or in couples along the spine of the shingle bank towards Hurst – small, dark figures – and the white of swans & gulls echoing the bright, white-washed lighthouse.

Afterwards to Lepe: the same journey made on another New Year's Day, but in very different circumstances, when Joe was a little boy. Where all is so familiar, it was strange to think this was our only visit in many months. Stranger that, for the first time in my life, I have no base in the area where I feel I belong. I was careful, though, to control the surge of nostalgia, which would close me in on myself, apart from M. I want to begin this year with a renewed sense of purpose, which means living where we are. In the past year I feel I have learned something, borne of M.'s addiction – something to do with caring but not managing or controlling, loving *in spite of*. In some ways, my designs have been broken.

4 January

Home from a day in Bath to find the house in semi-darkness, M. in bed asleep, an empty vodka bottle in the pedal-bin. Alarmed, I shook her awake. She denied having been drinking – always the first response.

5 January
I felt no compassion this morning, only fury borne of frustration. I was afraid that Mieke could have killed herself. I tell her I can't go on like this much longer. She says she will go back to the Netherlands. But she has nowhere to go, and, alone would not look after herself. It amazes me that I can think like this. Only yesterday, we were close companions. Soon, we will be again. But now this *thing* comes between us, this corpse of love.

6 January
The situation became worse yesterday when M. slipped out and bought more drink. At the time she was ill and barely able to communicate. In the evening, when I thought she was in bed, I was surprised to find her coming downstairs from my study, where she had been searching for bottles. By this time I was really frightened. But she fell asleep, and slept peacefully all night. As I realised later, and as she admitted, the immediate cause of this behaviour was her fear of a job interview, and her fear of rejection. She was actually trying to make herself so ill she wouldn't be able to attend it.

8 January
M. has just left for the AA meeting in Devizes. I am ready to begin work: checking Les's *Shaker City* against the typescript, starting to mark student essays. Outside, it is a damp, warm day.

The last few days have been bad. Last night, in a detective spirit that has become second nature to me, I noticed the absence of a particular glass from the cupboard and recalled the noise of a drawer closing, which I had heard earlier. This time, it was a bottle of port, which had followed the vodka & a large quantity of whisky, the rest of which I poured down the sink. I had also found another empty bottle. The truth is that, in recent months, Mieke has been drinking more, more often, and this week I have been more afraid.

Again, I almost didn't go to Al Anon, since I was concerned about leaving her. But I did go, and found relief in talking about our situation with people who understand. Everything was reassuring: the paving stones pitted with puddles of dark rainwater, lights in the windows of the large, old church, the climb upstairs to the meeting room, the voices & faces of my friends, warm in their greetings, and anxious because I was late. Then the talk, jokes & laughter, the readings. I feel I have learnt to talk more freely at Al Anon, to be more fully myself, so that I was able to share not only something of my experience, but also my dark perception that alcohol is stronger than love, and counter-perception that it isn't the person who ceases to love, but the drink which temporarily annihilates him or her.

In another way, I still have a lot to learn, especially when I recognise a nasty self-righteousness in how I speak to M., when she sobers up after a spell of drinking. There's a pharasaism about my condemnation, a petulance, and what I now realize is frustration, because life has been out of my control. Yet, there's a lesson here for me to learn: that I am not arbiter or manager, that living isn't what I say it shall be. Earlier, I stood on my dignity, wanting to deny that alcoholism is the sort of thing that happened in my family! Even when I first went to Al Anon, I assumed that I was there for Mieke, not myself. The subsequent experience has been humanizing, and I have confessed my vulnerability. From boyhood, I have had a stoicism, but, from the first, M. saw behind my mask.

9 January
Last night saw the end (if it is the end) of Mieke's worst bout of drinking. She had bought more drink on the way back from her AA meeting in Devizes, as I discovered in the evening.

When I went to see her in bed she looked near to death. Much older, ominously still, with an expression I can't describe – exhausted, defeated – in wide open eyes. She can come back from this. On another occasion, she might not. We speak of drink talking; we might also describe it as killing, without the will of the victim.

This morning, appalled at what she had done, she spoke of being afraid of dying. This rang truer than her talk of wanting to die, which comes, I think, from the part of her the drink affects. I saw it as the most hopeful sign she has shown for some time.

19 January
Dawn at the end of a bad night: blackbird singing from the top of the old plum tree in a neighbouring garden.

21 January
In our group meeting, I had been talking about acceptance, learning to adapt oneself to what happens, instead of predicting events and our reactions. This morning, in a fury, I have spoken violent & ugly words to M., who was probably too drunk to take them in. She has been ill for several days with what she has said is 'flu. This morning, she got up at 6.30

saying she was going to make us a cup of tea. I fell asleep, and when she came up with the tea, after 8, she could barely stand, and fell back into bed saying how tired she was. At the time, I thought this was the illness, and she should sleep as much as possible. A little later, I realized the truth, which casts everything into doubt. I simply don't know when she is lying to me.

It's a foggy morning, the world outside muffled, beads of moisture hanging on twigs & branches. I have made an excuse not to go into work, in fact, told a lie. I should have gone, but I can't leave M. when she's in this state, just in case. There's no one else in a position to look after her.

Last night, after several days when we had been close, I spoke calmly, philosophically. This morning, I was all but cursing her. I don't even want to think about it; if I write, I want to write about something else, describe other things than this sad and sordid round. For that's what it feels like: round we go and around. Sober days when we are together, talking intelligently, hopefully, making plans, then down, down… What is rock bottom?

I had a strange dream last night. I was walking with a companion away from a storm, the sky at our backs growing darker and more threatening. We were walking towards woods and I was aware of the danger of sheltering under trees from a storm but felt that if we could get into the wood we probably would be safe. At the entrance to the wood were three or four old oaks, leafless, and, among them, some kind of electricity box, which, obviously, would attract lightning. I wasn't aware of lightning striking, but now the trees were red and somehow ruckled, and inside the wood it was the same: a place of broken, burnt-red trees & branches that was also some kind of ancient ruined civilization with fragments of statuary among the fallen branches. My companion picked up a piece like a helmeted or maned head that was his 'emblem'. Afterwards, I was reading his novel, or he was reading it to me, or we were in it: a gothic story of sex and magical powers. My impression (which I have had in dreams before) was of being in a story that has been or was being written or told.

A wise, older man in our group insisted: *we must never lose hope.* Another man feels certain the only end of his wife's drinking will be death. I spoke of acceptance as something that is neither hope or despair. We are not in control of our lives: I have learnt that. What, then, can we do except adapt to what happens? Easy enough to say, but not to practise. Others speak of sinking our will in the will of God. I don't really know what that means. I understand much better learning to use what life brings. So much is outside our control. No one knows what will happen from day to day, hour to hour, or can predict the next moment with absolute certainty. But this doesn't mean we can't direct our lives – shape them so as to meet events as they occur. Remaining open even to the loss of our selves? Not predicting even death?

24 January
We have gone back to the First Step together, M. with more emotional conviction than I have seen in her before. 'Utter defeat' are the words burning into us: which is what I have witnessed, and what I have felt. In-between looking after her, I have marked folders of MA work, and read again in *Lyrical Ballads* and in Berdyaev in preparation for talks I shall be giving next month.

7 February
In *The Big Issue,* a photograph of Richey Edwards, singer with the Manic Street Preachers who mutilated himself and disappeared in 1995. It was a picture of him as a boy, and it reminded me strongly of a photograph of Joe at about the time he came to live with us in Groningen. It wasn't only the two young men that I couldn't stop seeing, but the alert, fresh, intelligent look, the expectancy in their faces, the promise of a world.

Outing with M. on a cold, bright morning to see the snowdrops by the river at Great Elm. Catkins in hedges and over the water. New grass risen through winter soil. In the sky, a waning half-moon, and a puff of fast-moving cloud.

8 February
The day began with a thin rain of snowflakes criss-crossing, spiralling down. Later the fall gradually thickened, until large, feathery flakes were falling slowly, and beginning to settle. As the day progressed, M. was moved watching the state funeral of King Hussein of Jordan on TV – with the death of a peacemaker, enemies gather, pay tribute, and for a time a new age of peace seems possible. I assessed work downloaded from the on-line Creative Writing MA, wrote reports, looked out at falling snow.

13 February
In Bath, in a restaurant with a friend, I told him something about M.'s addiction, and he told me he was the son of an alcoholic, who died when he was a boy. I'm not sure that I should have spoken. It's difficult sometimes

to balance my need to talk to friends and what I think M.'s wishes might be. On some occasions this means that I say nothing, and in consequence have to edit my life drastically in order to communicate. But this isn't a complaint. I feel that our relationship has deepened in recent months, partly as a matter of respect, as I've become more aware of how much pain she suffers, and how bravely she copes with it. But any word, even love, seems cold in this context. When I talk about acceptance, I know that something doesn't quite ring true, because I don't want any other life.

18 FEBRUARY
At my desk for the first time this week. Came home from Bath on Sunday feeling ill, and went to bed with a cold which turned into a chesty cough. On Tuesday afternoon I got up, and M. drove me into Bath, where, with some physical difficulty, I gave my talk on J. C. Powys & Nicholas Berdyaev at the Bath Royal Literary & Scientific Institute. Yesterday followed a similar pattern: in bed all day, until I went out in the evening to Al Anon. For once, I said almost nothing, which may have been what prompted an older member to tell me, at the end, I looked 'like a ghost'. He seemed to regret it immediately, perhaps thinking he had upset me, but it was a pretty good description of how I felt.

28 FEBRUARY
I wouldn't have thought it possible, but this morning Mieke walked with me in the Longleat woods. Luminous morning, white sunlight in mist, and a strong wind blowing against us. Celandines & primroses still a rare sight, with only green plants in the woods, ground spiky with bluebell leaves. Male chaffinch excitedly singing and listening, which came boldly towards us from branch to branch of a small tree. It probably didn't even see us, a bird made incautious by sexual longing.

23 MARCH
58 today. Shaky after talking, talking, last night & again this morning, I have just returned from a short walk with M. at East Woodlands. Crisis again: late yesterday afternoon I thought M. was dying. Later, feeling a little better, she got up. The painful symptoms are physical, but we both now believe the underlying cause is a disposition formed in childhood. What is there to do, then, except unlearn, relearn?

I feel I must help – there are only we two alone together; medical assistance, so far, hasn't amounted to much. But how could it, if this is self-inflicted? It is as if she needs to learn to live, or learn the functions that enable life. I must say this now, though often she has been for me life itself, and I have been the one she has helped to learn.

We walked a few steps in the woods – she was feeling faint – and listened in the stillness to birds singing – twittering, chirping, squeaking, a caw, a few lovely, lyrical phrases – songs, scattered throughout the woods, that seemed to be voices of all the hidden life, which the trees, standing apart, could give no sign of.

Later, my brother Tony rang to wish me a happy birthday. 'We can't keep people alive', he said, and 'we mustn't paint the devil's face on the wall'. It was good to hear his voice, and to know everything we share, a spirit, a way of seeing and feeling, deeper than our differences.

On my desk, smiling a wonderful smile, sits a little fat Buddha which M. gave me today. He is gold-painted and the broad smile creases his face. He seems to be full up with wisdom, his belly rounded with it. He sees a cosmic joke, which I, not being enlightened, don't share. Looking at him, I can't help smiling, my face creases. He sees the larger joke. And I see the small one, and now the burden is leaf-light, and has gone.

28 MARCH
Walking with M. in the woods on a bright, fresh morning, I tried to explain to her what had gone through my mind at the phrase 'bluebell wood': that it had called up the dead who loved such places; that, now, the very idea was an aspect of sentimental pastoral. For her the words have no such associations, and she is free, here, of the burden of social history that I carry. We talked about 'the culture of resentment'. Leaning on a gate, and watching butterflies crossing a meadow, we talked about the end of the world, agreeing that humankind don't deserve to survive. This on one hand, and on the other my conviction that we are only at the beginning. There was nothing apocalyptic, no death-wish or misanthropy in this talk, only a sense of the contrast between human power and its abuses and the life of nature. Out of sight overhead, a buzzard uttered its piercing call. Across the path, a dead fox, belly eaten out, brush trailing, flat to the ground.

31 MARCH
Fell asleep after a restless night and dreamed again of returning to Southampton University and walking through the familiar rooms, where there was no one I knew. Woke late, as Mieke was coming into the room,

and having told her about the dream in a state of depression, went on to talk about my failure in every respect. In a black mood, failure seems real & absolute, unchangeable. In another mood, I see it as a version of my life-story, which I harm myself by telling. Its best version is the story of life and work unfinished, in which even what one has done is subject to modification by later use.

Easter Monday
Morning walk with M. at Great Elm, scrambling over muddy rocks by the stream, across the quarry railway track and uphill to a path at the top, which brought us back along the edge of the wooded valley to the car. Blackthorn in flower. Windflowers in the woods. White and blue violets growing on a mossy tree stump. Hazels in tiny leaf. (How evocative Robert Browning's word in 'Home Thoughts, from Abroad'!) Sudden big noise of a bumble-bee. Fresh, quickening leaf-sprays, buds, pussy willows: a sense of soil moving (we can almost see it, as in a film) as plants push up. If I could consider going away to live on another continent, it wouldn't be now.

14 April
Snow falling, settling, weighing down new green leaves & flowers, white blossom barely distinguishable from snow on hedges.

Snow among bluebells in the woods, when, on a cold afternoon, we drove to Clouds for a counselling session with Pippa. Alcohol hasn't loomed so large in my mind recently, but I'm aware of the danger of complacency. We spoke of the possibility that Mieke's illness – her fibromyalgia – has replaced her drinking, which she might turn to again if the pain that is taking up so much of her energy is alleviated. I feel she has been happier recently, more hopeful, in spite of the pain. There's no comparison with the latter half of last year, when we both thought she might die.

At Al Anon in the evening, our subject was the Fourth Step. I said little. It had been a long day.

17 April
At East Woodlands with M., after a day when I had read too much, choking my mind. This is the most wonderful time out of doors, between the bare branches of March and the full-leaved trees of May. Now, at the edge of woods, we can look in, through new leaves, and still see primroses among windflowers and bluebells. In all, a new life, which I will never be able to describe.

After the losses of recent years, I have lived on because Mieke has taught me to live with loss, and because we love each other. When I have the sense to see it, I know our time together is the fullness of life.

25 April

On the way back from Brecon after the Vaughan colloquium, I stopped by the church at Llansantfraed to show Mieke the grave of Henry Vaughan. I think one would feel this to be a sacred place in any case but Vaughan's poetry and the humble words on his beautiful tombstone, green-stained with lichen under the yew, make it more sacred. Today it was the dandelions too, bright faces in sunlight, and cuckoo flowers in damp places by the church walls. A great hill sweeps up above the church, inducing a sensation coinciding with the hope that Henry Vaughan did ascend, that all his passionate yearning for God was not in vain. But what is 'vain' in the light of a life completely, passionately given?

We drove home past bluebell woods where I used to stop and walk with Joe when he was a little boy. We agreed that it would be good to live in Wales – that old dream of a cottage in the country, which I once realized, and, ironically, M. had during the same period when I was living at Brynbeidog.

29 April

All downstairs lights in the house were off and Mieke was in bed when I came home from Al Anon last night. This morning I found an empty cider bottle and two empty half bottles of vodka, confirming what I was sure of anyway, not least because she was ill. Forgetting every lesson, I lost my temper and accused her of still denying that she has a problem, since she doesn't go to AA, and weeks pass when she seems to forget all about the Steps. The truth is, I forget too, despite attending Al Anon, where I often speak with a detachment that makes it seem as though I have wisdom to offer those who are in a crisis. Again, it is the sickness that frightens me. At present, M. seems to recover within a day or a night, but the threat is always present, on top of her fibromyalgia. She speaks of her 'demons' and of remaining silent in order to protect me from them. This makes me angrier, since watching her harm herself and living with the consequences of her addiction are hardly protection. What I see in her is refusal of her own creativity, she to whom many people are indebted for *their* being. So, I reason, futilely. And of course, reason doesn't meet the case. Each time, I come back to the first Step.

I hear many stories that are worse than ours. Is it only human beings who can refuse life? And doesn't that mean refusal of creativity? When I hear of people whose whole lives are dedicated to alcohol, who spend their days & nights virtually alone with a bottle, despite being married and having children, it seems to me a rejection of life.

At the same time as I reason, or afterwards, I am aware of the power that makes me powerless. And, paradoxically, it is good for me to realise this. Not good for M. that she should be at the mercy of forces out of her control, but good for me to be reminded that all my words and ideas are no more than driftwood which I cling to in a stormy sea.

'Seeing' Mieke, I look at life, which means I do not see, but realise the distance between all my means of expression and her reality, her being. And this is why I write, really, attempting to reach into the space between my impoverished resources and the richness & strangeness of living being, unique and at the same time bearing life.

8 MAY
Mieke's birthday. A dark day. She has been drinking over the past ten days, and now felt too shaky to go out for the meal we had been looking forward to, and we had to cancel the booking.

We talked about the vicious circle and her inability to break out of it. While she doesn't blame me for her alcoholism, she does blame other people for what they did or did not do in the past. She sees clearly that to break the circle she will have to take responsibility for herself. But there lies the problem: a form of behaviour that has become embedded. Relating to other people as the one who gives and helps, she finds it hard to acknowledge her need. The psychological mechanism makes me feel we are playing a sort of game: like chess, where there are many possible moves, but all are within the same game.

So, around we go and around, and in and out, but always within the game, which is a desperate and potentially fatal one, until I see that it is only another power that can break in, and show M. her powerlessness. But unless she lets it... Yet I know it *could* happen, and although I become desperate at seeing her repeatedly hurt herself, I have not despaired.

9 MAY
Mieke's dreams:
She is in a skyscraper with Elin as a baby, and the skyscraper is on fire, but she doesn't know it. Then she is above the building, and sees it being

enveloped in flames, and is unable to do anything to save the baby which she knows is still inside.

She is in a woman's ward in a hospital. Her friend Lizzie comes in as a patient, and she gives Lizzie her best silk scarf. She doesn't know why. Mieke then realises that her own leg is covered with suppurating sores, and she is concealing it under her nightgown. She is the only woman in the ward hiding what is wrong with her. When she goes back to bed, she finds a half bottle of whisky hidden under the pillow.

She is in the corner of a field watching a big white horse trying to get over a dyke. A shepherd is urging the horse on and his dog is running in circles. Mieke is afraid *of* the horse and afraid *for* it. The horse runs at the wall of the dyke but cannot get over.

When she tells me about the dream and we talk about it, she agrees that she is *everything* in it: the fearful onlooker, the shepherd & his dog, the horse, the dyke...

I raise my voice in complaint, fear, analysis. But why do I never say what *fun* we have together, in laughter, in talk, in companionship, in loving? This is the selfish cause of my fear: that I have never been as close to anyone as I am to M., or as completely known and understood, so that the life I live now is our life, and I dread the thought of being without her.

2 May

I feel how irrelevant my words are. Although I mean to help, and hope to understand, sounding 'wise' about M.'s drinking makes me feel I have made a trivial remark. In herself, and in what she means to me, she is infinitely more than anything I can say or write. Being comes before language: this is what I 'see'; this is the recognition in which I am true to myself. Whatever philosophical complications follow, and whatever objections are raised, this is where my sense of things begins and ends. It comes, I think, from first things felt in love; some mother-wit, perhaps the 'language' of mother and child. But I don't know anything about it; it is more what I 'know' with, by unknowing.

13 May

Grey-green days, wet & leafy, with a heavy atmosphere. To Clouds with M. to see Pippa yesterday. I felt low, dispirited, but as we talked I realized the situation has been better this year, and for M. her birthdays are distressing occasions, so I should have predicted how she would react. There seems little hope she will stop drinking completely in the near future but – thank God! – the awful drives to oblivion have ceased.

After the meeting I went into Bath and attended a reading at Waterstone's at which three of our creative writing students read from their novels which have just been published.

15 May
Driving Simon Trewin, the literary agent, to the station, after our CW Open Forum Day, I took the opportunity to talk to him about our Addiction 'book' and he said he would like to see a portion of it. M. is eager to start work on this, and then going on to edit it. We both think this worth doing, irrespective of whether it leads to publication. I have a rather superstitious feeling (which I once had with *Welsh Journal*), that what has been written shouldn't be changed at all. With M.'s help, I dealt with this by realizing the words were mine, and I had the right to 'shape' them better, not to falsify, but to clarify, past ideas and emotions. As long as we maintain integrity, there's no reason why our experience shouldn't have a part to play in the public sphere.

16 May
To Freshford in the evening for a surprise visit, which Colin Edwards had arranged, for Ros's 50th birthday. M. had spent all day wrapping up fifty small presents.
    At dusk, in a narrow country lane between high banks and hedges, a badger crossed in front of us, just like a small bear.

21 May
Angry with M. for drinking, and anxious at the prospect of reading at the relaunch of the Michael Tippett Centre in college, I told her I didn't want her to attend, so that I wouldn't have to worry about her as well as the reading. In the event, dry-mouthed, but apparently confident, even relaxed, I stared into the lights, not seeing my audience, and read Les's 'Brassrubbing' poem and poems from *Arnolds Wood*.

24 May
Home from Cardiff after a night away, I found the door locked, with the key in the lock on the inside (which I have urged Mieke never to do), and it took some ringing and knocking before she came down to let me in. After so much recent furious preaching, I had come home in a mood of reconciliation, but now I was in a rage, caused by fear. Again, after a while, I reasoned, talking on and on, and asking M. to talk to me. And she would not, or could not.

As well as being really worrying, this is *boring*. The same dulled round, M. obstinate in a cocoon of silence, periodically disabling herself. Yet it passes, and the light comes back into her eyes. But this preaching, this reasoning, all the fury of words, the effort to persuade, *it does no good*.

Detach, detach.

31 May

At East Woodlands with M. after a day reading & working on the word processor. Cool & refreshing under leafy trees, among foxglove spires, overall the strong lyrical voice of a blackbird.

Stepping out of the woods on the far side, from far off, just audible, *cuckoo, cuckoo*. This is what we had come to hear, on the last day of May. While we were standing still, a fawn walked out of the woods, saw me move, and bounded back in. Walking back, we heard the cuckoo again, closer, louder – in fact, two cuckoos, casting a spell over the land.

25 June

At Al Anon I said how important it was for us to tell our stories, for honest telling increases understanding, without which, there is the danger of becoming trapped inside oneself, brooding on what may well be a false version, and sinking into depression. How well I know! And now I can say things that sometimes help others, but I can't always act on them myself.

27 June

Late in the afternoon, in strong wind & bright clear sunlight, we walked on a path between Longleat beech woods and open ploughland. Following the path, which became sandier, with deer slots among bootprints & pawprints, we came to an exposed space, where the wind blew refreshingly against us, and foxgloves were whiplashing. By the lane, another tall, purplish flower, which we later learnt was hedge woundwort. Healing plants, and all the richness of ditches: grasses, reeds, ox-eye daisies, golden-yellow birds-foot trefoil.

'Chequered shade' under trees – old words, not always defunct, sometimes linking us to the dead who used them. Out in fresh air, talking, in love & trust, or just looking, words regain substance, as one sees (with touch) *wheat, beech, honeysuckle.*

4 JULY

After a month of sobriety Mieke has been drinking again. Twice in recent days she hasn't been able to come out with me to events she would normally have enjoyed. On a desolate evening my mind went over & over the pattern. It was as her arm was beginning to heal, after a fall, that she deliberately disabled herself – as it seemed to me. It is as if she doesn't want to live. I don't mean she wants to die, but to live an active life, fulfilling her gifts. Last night, I felt her sickness.

Again this morning, I *talked*, reasoning, trying to break through. Twice in the past year this has seemed possible: when we walked in the woods and M. spoke of her difficulty in conceiving a Higher Power, and when we went back to the First Step and felt our powerlessness over alcohol. But most of the time she is, in a sense, unreachable: loving & giving & apparently the most open person, but in fact turned towards others, away from any self-disclosure.

What verbal wounding can compare with the harm she is doing to her health, and to her life? That talking doesn't do me any good is all too clear. I dislike the man I become, or reveal myself to be. But I don't aim to wound, but to shake her awake.

This is what I should have learnt is impossible. It is one of the main messages of Al Anon: only the alcoholic can save herself/himself. And suppose I am right in thinking Mieke's self-harm springs from a deep psychological wound, ultimately a spiritual lack arising from her inability to recognise any Higher Power, which could breach the walls she has built around herself, with a suffocating self-sufficiency? For M., there is no God's-eye view ... But if there isn't that or the equivalent, how can we enlarge and transform ourselves?

I am no longer inhibited in writing about these things from fear of being disloyal to Mieke. I write in order to understand, so that if possible I may help. And I write to help myself.

One night in July, without warning, I suffered a stroke. This resulted in a period of hospitalization, at first in Bath and later in Frome, as I slowly recovered enough to be able to walk with the aid of sticks. I was well enough to return home in August, where I continued to convalesce before returning to work at Bath Spa University. My convalescence was in some ways a happy time. It was good to be home again with Mieke, and to be able in time to climb the stairs to my study, or to sit out in the garden. Most days, we took short walks together round our immediate home area, where I delighted in noticing many small things I had overlooked in my more vigorous days. Mieke took good care of me, and only on rare occasions was I aware of her drinking. After some 6 months I was able to return to work at the university, and after a time an unexpected opportunity arose which led me to apply for and get a new job, at the University of Glamorgan. I subsequently wrote about this period of sickness and convalescence in *Diary of a Stroke*. It was a happy time partly because drink played a small part in it, and we seemed in consequence to gain a new, untroubled intimacy. Unfortunately, as summer passed and autumn came on our lives began to resume the old pattern.

As I turn again to my journal to tell the story of our last months in Frome and our years in Wales that followed, what I feel acutely is that life escapes – my life, but most of all Mieke's, which was so much more than episodes of drink. She is present to me now, and always will be: a complex living woman, subtly intelligent and wise, but with a wisdom she could not apply to herself. As I write, I feel her as a critical presence, aware of the inadequacy of my portrayal of her and of our life together. Still, she would urge me to write. She knew that I had to.

6 OCTOBER

While I was writing in my journal, M. came in from the local shop with a half-bottle of vodka. I heard it clink in her pocket, and took it and emptied it down the sink. The same shortly after with a bottle of beer. So here I am playing detective again and appointing myself judge & jury. It was a blessed time when there wasn't any need for this. And by what right do I do it? Shouldn't a person be allowed to drink? Members of my Al Anon group would point out the futility of my action. But I *cannot* watch her harm and possibly destroy herself without trying to prevent it.

I really did think the pattern had been broken. In recent weeks, it seems to have been re-establishing itself. Happy autumn! Happy winter! Welcome back the old merry-go-round, which goes spinning round & round until the old figures totter and fall off.

23 OCTOBER

Jane Garbutt came to lunch, during which I realized Mieke had been drinking, vodka & painkillers. Afterwards she went to lie down, and I talked to Jane, who said that, whatever M. might do, I had to live my own life / look after myself. I countered by saying we depend upon one another. But I know Jane is right: no one can live another person's life or should try. If I am not in and for myself, I do not live. If I do not live, I have nothing to give anyone else.

I poured the vodka down the sink.

27 October
Our wedding anniversary. In the evening M. talked a little, with difficulty, about her addiction. (She had been drinking in the middle of the day.) She could name her qualities, but somehow her feeling of being worthless (which speaks with her mother's and sister's voices) outweighs them. It is terribly hard for her to speak about herself, her inner life. The struggle shows physically, with long silences, tears, few words.

Wouldn't it be better to let the subject rest? Can we fight obsession with obsession?

I'm not a healer, but I do know something about mental illness. For me, it means a long struggle towards wholeness. In M., I see how her very goodness relates to her lack of a sense of self-worth.

29 October
Blue tits in the birch tree, yellow as leaves, blue as the sky seen between leaves.

The Third Step is the crux: 'Made a decision to turn our will and our lives over to the care of God *as we understand Him*.' Naturally, M. strongly resists the idea of bowing before God (in whom she does not believe), or *any* Power. But she is a healer, and she is in touch with a great power. She will not use it for herself, however – it is the same resistance as that to advertising as a therapist and to asking a fee for her work. She can only give with ease.

There is a thought-knot here, which I believe we have begun to unpick. First, she does have a sense of a Higher Power – stronger than most people's; she has been in touch with it all her life. Secondly, to draw upon it for herself is not to exploit it for selfish ends, any more than we think of using food or air in that way.

One intellectual problem has been her reaction against a narrow version of feminism – basically, leave-the-man-and-become-a-Lesbian – which she has identified with the movement as a whole. She met this among women in the Netherlands, and, as a woman who loves men, and a woman with a strong attachment to her family, she reacted against it with anger. In consequence, she cut herself off from the very stream of thought & feeling about women's healing power of which she herself is living proof.

10 November
Mieke got up early this morning and drank a bottle of white wine. She had

come back from a counselling session with Pippa with a new justification. Drinking is something she needs to do periodically in order to be not 'on call', to switch off from her responsibilities. Taking my morning walk alone, I found myself getting angrier and angrier. As if we weren't equal partners, and as if I hadn't carried the burden of her self-harm for the past few years, and even been made to feel, at times, responsible for carrying her life. And it infuriates me that she uses a counselling to justify the very thing that is hurting her. It is also, of course, that I don't want to feel a burden, or that everything she does, she does *only* for me.

2 December
After several days of feeling ill and exhausted, Mieke has been drinking today. I have been ill with the same virus, though not as bad, and it hasn't stopped me working. Fearing she would make herself worse, I spoke angrily to her, and she told me to 'fuck off' – which is fair enough. As well as fear, the idea of self-inflicted sickness brings out a puritanical disgust in me.

February 2000
The cycle of drinking & illness continues. Today, Mieke was wiped out, and I went into college with a heavy heart, leaving her in bed. In the evening she spoke a little of her despair. It seems to me to come with or after the drinking, not to cause it. What I see is evasion. Semi-conscious from drinking, M. can't address the problem. Sober, she doesn't want to.

Is the cause genetic? I suspect that it has something to do with her father and her feelings for him. Evidently a tough, hard-drinking man, deeply affected by terrible war experiences, and, afterwards, restless, devil-may-care. Sometimes he had money and they lived well; sometimes, none. Sometimes he left his family and went off with other women. But never, never, has Mieke spoken a word against him, or mentioned him except with love. Her mother, on the other hand, she speaks of very critically, and *blames*. Somehow, I think, she identifies living with her father; as he was, generous, risk-taking, is the way to be.

In a way, I understand. All my life I have been drawn to outlaws – generous-spirited people careless of their own welfare, non-conformists. Even as a boy I was drawn to children who were outsiders. It's life that draws me, in M. and in all those I love or have loved. A generosity with life that doesn't count the cost. Not as a gesture only, but because that is what the person is. I think the creative impulse springs from this – which we need to channel, to control in the discipline of an art, which is the very thing the outlaw rejects, or only partially accepts. I protect myself more. I love the generous giver, but avoid the wildness, or carelessness, that wastes.

22 FEBRUARY
When I arrived home from college, I found that Mieke had made herself ill. Frightened at the prospect of going back to AA, she had been drinking. But she did go; a fellow woman member picked her up in her car and took her to the meeting in Warminster. This showed real courage, and desperation. Recent drinking resulted in a feeling of shame. Strange to say, nothing is more welcome in the circumstances. It is only when M. *feels* what she's doing, suffers it in body & mind, that there's hope. And it's only then that she seeks help, without which it's very doubtful that any alcoholic will be able to stop. It's such a humbling disease, but until the addict is humbled, no resolution or effort will work.

25 FEBRUARY
To Salisbury with M. in the afternoon. Parking in the centre near the war memorial, I saw the name W.R. Mould among the fallen of the Great War. He must have been a member of Mother's family; she would have known who he was. Afterwards we booked into a small hotel on Mill Lane, left the car there and walked back along the river into the centre, on our right the water-meadows, in front of us the cathedral, as in Constable's famous painting. Dad would have been thrilled by this view, which, no doubt, he knew well. I was tired from the walk but we found a Turkish restaurant and had a good meal, after which, revived, we walked on to a Friends' Meeting House, where I gave a talk on 'Poetry and the Sacred' to members of the Salisbury Poetry Circle.

9 MARCH
Having attended AA the night before last, and said how beneficial she found it, M. was drinking again yesterday. Later, when we were able to talk about it, she said she didn't have a choice, the compulsion was too strong. But how can this be? She chose to go to AA, made herself go despite initial resistance, and went willingly the second time. And she could, surely, have chosen to ring a friend from AA when she felt she might give in. And what about alcoholics who resist the temptation, isn't it as difficult for them?

I deeply distrust this talk of 'compulsion'. Certainly, my knowledge is limited, because I'm not subject to it; but I suspect that in this instance M.

is using her psychological subtlety to make things difficult for herself – or to make it easier to give in. I don't say there is no compulsion, but I have to believe there is choice, for both our sakes.

After recent optimism, this repeated the fortnightly pattern. And M. said – again – she had felt so good; too good, as though she had no right to health. Nothing enrages me more, though I know rage is futile. But this seems to be the voice that makes it happen, perhaps a voice she has internalized since childhood, which has become a sick kind of reasoning. I rage because I fear it; it's a voice that justifies lack of a sense of self-worth, self-harm, oblivion, and would justify death.

After a while she broke down and cried. And though seeing her suffer is the last thing I want, that's where hope lies.

Probably that's true for all of us. I'm not a judge in this case, even if sometimes, when enraged, I talk like one to M. I have too great a sense of my own need. All I do or say with any value springs from it.

10 MARCH

How at times like this I long for normality: the postman's cheery greeting, Jenny stopping me in the road to ask how I am, and telling me about herself – busy doing the cleaning in six houses, feeling well after severe ill health (breast cancer) in recent years, the man behind the counter in the post office making a joke about the price of stamps. Just to be out in the air is a relief. Fresh air, hedges touched with green leaves, the glorious daffodils.

Indoors, we are locked into the problem together. No one else knows how sick she is – and what could they do if they did? Talking again, I feel that I become the mad reasoner, though what I am doing is pleading for common-sense: only see the connection between this morning's illness and recent drinking. Only *see*...

What a situation this is: the healer who turns from offering help and wise advice, says goodbye in a friendly, encouraging voice to a client and, coming back into the room, virtually collapses, all energy spent, nothing for it but to rest, and endure. And, maybe, when I am out of the house or in my study, slip out to the corner shop for a bottle of vodka.

The alcoholic's love seems strange love, since by hurting herself she must hurt the ones she loves. But I know Mieke loves me, and my life is stable because of her. Even a smile tells me that all is well with us, in what is eternal in our relationship.

And when I can, in these critical periods, I go on with my work. Not only because there's nothing else to do, but because I want to. Come what may, I have to use my mind.

15 March

Back home early from college, I found Mieke feeling better. On Monday, I had called the doctor in to see her, and had sent my apologies to Bristol University, where I was due, as external examiner, to attend the Board for the Certificate in Creative Writing.

In my dream last night, I had mislaid my stick and was walking vigorously without one. After lunch today, with M. at East Woodlands, I climbed the stile and walked down through the woods, to where they open on the meadow that looks towards Alfred's Tower on the hill above Stourhead. In the woods we could hear traffic on a distant road, and firing from the Army Ranges on Salisbury Plain, but there was also a distinctive hush, with occasional small voices of birds in tree-tops. Underfoot, new growth. It is so simple, being startled by the appearance of a flower – violets, for example – but at that moment I know instinctively what Winifred Nicholson meant when she said flowers are the secret of the universe.

25 March

Desperate, I talked with Elin on the phone last night. She said things have been getting 'darker', which is true.

This morning, exasperated & afraid, I told M. I would go to Wales by myself, that I wouldn't let her drag me down with her. I have begun to think the unthinkable, in these weeks when it seems something in her has determined not to accept help.

Last night, she told me the drinking began in earnest in America, where I had a job and she didn't. But if it is only these last few years that she has had the illness, doesn't that mean she could be cured? Only if she wants to be. And this is what I can't now see any sign of, when every instance of hope is followed by drink and debility.

Could I really leave her? I have felt that, come what may, I would see it through. But that doesn't take into account how terrible it can be to witness a person's ruin. How utterly dispiriting the recurrent lapses, hope dashed from day to day. How frightening. And the thing is like an evil spirit that has made its home with us and is expanding to fill the whole space of our lives.

I remember a man at Al Anon saying there were times he hoped his alcoholic wife would fall down the stairs and break her neck. These are the possible infections, when the sickness spreads beyond the alcoholic to those closest to him or her. Then one becomes poisoned, and any sick thought is possible, which causes damage even when it is fleeting – a momentary ugly fantasy.

Of course, I shouldn't issue ultimatums that I don't intend to carry out. But it's fear that speaks in me when I do. At these times I am face to face with the thing itself, and it is utterly unyielding, deaf and blind to reason or compromise. The only promise it makes is that it will go on to the bitter end and all I can do is watch, if I want to: 'Take it or leave it, death is what I intend'.

If we have made any progress during the past five years it has been to expose the strength of the addiction, or 'madness', as M. calls it. And the exposure has occurred through the dashing of one hope after another. When I look back on earlier hopes I appear to myself like a very child. Nobody can know the first thing about addiction if they haven't lived with it.

In the garden, among damp greens, shocks of bright yellow forsythia. Could I go on alone? If I had to, I would. But how we see and feel the life in things when we are alive to one another! Then, the world kindles. We seem to be joined in feeling to its life, the same flame that is in our eyes, flickering in the things we see. Sharing has always meant almost everything to me.

6 April

M. drank half a bottle of red wine in the early hours of the morning. I asked her what she would do if she were me. 'Take me for three months to some place where there's no alcohol.' A space shuttle orbiting the globe? Even in the Australian outback or the Arctic Circle it would be possible to obtain alcohol. I thought the prospect of moving to Wales would make a difference; the idea of a new life for both of us, that would inspire M. not to drink, was my main motive in applying for the job. Staying here while the pattern repeated itself, down to the final act, seemed insupportable.

The whole thing is a terrible enigma. And she is sacrificing everything: health, looks, hope. No one who is not an addict can understand this. And the addict can't understand it either.

7 April

M. has talked a little today. She says that while she has always thought she is not afraid of dying, this may be untrue. Perhaps her flirting with death expresses fear.

The obsession was with me as soon as I woke up. Sometimes I seem to myself the crazier, always looking for signs of drinking, my first thought entering rooms in the house being where a bottle might be hidden.

But we have talked today – M. has talked – and that's a cause for hope.

During the day I wrote a rough draft of the final chapter of my book, *Imagining Wales*. I doubt that I shall change it from my earlier intention, but something has changed: when I planned it, it was retrospective; now I was writing it in the anticipation of going back to Wales.

8 APRIL

Another bright morning, dandelions in shady places opening at the approach of the sun.

As we walked round the bungalows, Mieke carrying my stick, we spoke to an old lady who was standing in the doorway of the last one. 87 years old, with a painful knee that makes walking difficult, kindness in her face. She said she had often watched me as I walked round the green in front of the bungalows, and had seen how well I was doing.

Every day now leaves & new blossoms are appearing. For all the global changes we are aware of, and the coming changes we fear, spring is still spring. I never felt April was the cruellest month although I know depression can be blacker in contrast to the rise of sap & unfolding of leaves, the stasis more wretchedly spiritless. Even in the heart of a grown man there's something that skips like a lamb at the touch of the spring sun.

Mieke's deep hidden life, which at times seems a burden to her, is wonderful to me. How understand this? The truth is, we know so little of what lies within another person. The mind can be a hell, yet the person contain deep resources of goodness. We see faces – even the face of a dandelion doesn't tell us what the flower is. Even in intimacy, we live with surfaces. Mieke is a wonder to me; sometimes I feel I don't know her at all. And, sometimes, when she is locked into addiction, that feeling is hellish. And sometimes it is joyful, and I am deeply grateful.

15 APRIL

More snow overnight. Now, Cley Hill & the hills above Longleat are mottled white. Having gone out to post a copy of 'Imagining Wales' to University of Wales Press, and to fetch Mieke's medication, I saw her walking back from the corner shop. She has been in pain from rheumatism for several days, and I thought her unable to leave the house. Following her in, I found an unopened bottle of vodka hastily concealed in the waste bin. I have told her that if this goes on, I won't have any choice – it will be my compulsion – and I shall be going to Wales alone. I can't watch her destroy herself, and I don't intend her addiction to kill me.

God knows, I didn't want to think any of this, or to say it. But the degradation this year has been terrible: not just the suffering she inflicts upon herself, but the lying, and the stubborn refusal to face the problem. Sometimes it seems to me our relationship has been undermined through the downward spiral since last November. Yet I know that, when the shadow lifts, all is good again.

Can one live without hope? Can a marriage survive hopelessness? It is different, I think, when a person is mortally sick, when, with love – and, no doubt, in some instances without it – the partner offers unqualified support. What makes this different, though it is a sickness, is the erosion of values on which a relationship is based, and the suspicion that in Mieke's drinking there's moral choice. And it is all so remorseless – in the face of the stress that contributed to my stroke; the deception; the shabby subterfuges; misery on misery.

Well, it's no use whining. I have talked more than enough today, disliking myself for what I was saying, but driven to it.

16 APRIL

M. last night, in bed, asleep or semi-conscious, with a glass of warm whisky clasped in her hands, and having taken painkillers. I kept watch until about 1 in the morning, when I was fairly sure she was going to be all right.

And she doesn't *see* this – except in the picture I paint for her, scaring her, as I had been scared. It is all concealment. There had, of course, been another bottle, which I hadn't found. If she goes on clasping her secret, as she held the glass, she will surely die.

We have to open our hearts to one another. She taught me that – there's the terrible irony. We have to talk in mutual trust, letting our emotions flow. Without this, the heart is stifled; instead of being a safe retreat, the inner place in which we hide becomes a prison, where we die.

Another day, cloud and blue sky. Birch twigs & plum blossom waving in a breeze. When I look closely, I see there are a few tiny green leaves on the birch.

After the crises, when I am completely alone, and after the immediate reaction when I write in fear and angry frustration, I know that M. & I will be companions until the end.

Easter Saturday

A drive with M. through the New Forest – trees coming into leaf, all the varied greens – and through Lymington. Lymore, the road to Keyhaven, where the Island humps into view and everything changes. At Saltgrass Lane, where high tide had covered the road, a strong smell of seaweed. We climbed the shingle-bank, which I couldn't have thought of doing until recently. Again, from one world to another – swans on the estuary behind us, Island ahead, waves lapping on shingle, breeze off the water and a healing air. It's not the sea surface only – glittering, wind-etched – but the movement – the whole sea moving – that rests the mind.

1 May

Bluebells are out now. Flowers drenched with colour, for which there is no likeness. Seeing a few together, wet after rain, I have thought them deep-sea blue. But in the woods on a sunny, breezy day, as we saw them at East woodlands today, they are more sky-colour, an airy, hazy blue.

Turning at the gap into the field, we were greeted by a young man and a young woman out walking with their dog, who said they never met anyone here, to which we responded in kind. The man said the church in the woods would be a good one to get married in, implying that was how they judged churches. Not a bad way.

Coming out of the bluebell-scented woods, we entered the churchyard, where the breeze had brought a smell of manure from a tractor spreading muck on a field. Inside St Katherine's, sitting down at the back, I looked up at Christ crucified in the stained-glass window over the altar. It seemed incredible that the figure had generated such intensity of feeling, not love or reverence alone, but hatred between people. In the empty church, I was more conscious of a loneliness about the figure, pictured in a dated style that has little meaning now. But what image can live, unless it comes from a body of belief, and is felt as a focus of human need?

19 May

A visit to Wales where, at lunch today, we received a warm welcome from new colleagues at the University of Glamorgan. Initially, M. was possibly the more enthusiastic about the forthcoming move – or the less ambivalent

– but now we both have good feelings about it. Typically unselfish, it was M. who saw the post as being far better for me, and I feel she was right. I note among new colleagues a tendency to welcome my return to Wales as a homecoming. I am grateful for this, and at the same time regard it with some irony.

25 May

Mieke has been drinking again, and has retreated into almost total silence. Yesterday she said: 'I want to die'.

Elin sent me a long email yesterday. She was distressed because an acquaintance in the Hague had told her Mieke had told him she was dying of stomach cancer. M. denies having said any such thing to Hans. She was indignant at the accusation, which (after I had reassured Elin) I discovered to be true.

In fear and anger, I lash out with my tongue. She will not seek help; the help she has been given, she has misused. Trying to get her to talk to me is like talking to a wall – except she is a sick woman, and I can never be sure how sick, and whether I should be calling in medical help. Perhaps I should let be; only what I'm aware of is the pressure of the unspoken, the prison she makes of her mind, in which she believes she can resolve the problem. But she can't; the problem lies somewhere in the imprisoned self.

In her sickness she creates an atmosphere of sickness around her. She harms herself and hurts those who are closest to her. She tells lies and makes it impossible for me to know what the truth is. She can't be trusted or relied on, and she makes the future horribly uncertain.

M. says to me: 'be patient'. I feel that I'm waiting for the end.

Reading over what I have written under the influence of fear & anger, I realise how sordid the effects of alcoholism are – more than I am able or care to reveal. It is a kind of anti-life which narrows the world to a dark tunnel and destroys the human personality. Yet, this isn't how I see M. At worst, she refuses to be, resigning all responsibility for herself, which is terrible. But this is not M., and, behind the wall, I know the person she really is, the one she has temporarily shut out.

27 May

On not hearing the cuckoo – yet. At East Woodlands, wet underfoot, after the rainy days of Spring have become the rainy days of early Summer. White petals of the rich, sweet-scented may are beginning to embrown.

Mieke ventured out fragilely. But she is up and about. Awake at dawn, I had a horrible vision of future possibilities: moving house, going to a new job, and having to do it alone, while M. is incapacitated. And she is the one who has always impressed on me the folly of thinking 'If...' Friends compliment me on my strength and toughness, which appeals to my vanity, but may also help me to find strength. But at dawn today I felt I might break.

14 JUNE
After M. had been to the shop, I took a bottle of vodka from the car boot and poured the contents down the sink. But I can't stop her drinking.

Elin rang in the evening and we had a long talk. What I realise is that, with M., there's nothing left for me to say. The fact that I've tried to *say* anything shows how little I've understood. The bewildering thing about alcoholism is that there's nothing so precious the alcoholic won't sacrifice in order to drink. So, there can be no moral covenant between an alcoholic and other people? In effect no marriage, in the sense that marriage involves mutual responsibilities? I don't believe it, yet the possibility is staring me in the face. It is as if periodically a different perspective made of distrust & lies swims sickeningly behind our companionship. For days, our life together is settled firmly in place, then again the ground begins to shift and shake.

16 JUNE
Mieke collapsed this morning. Inevitably. She had been drinking day & night. She tells me my bottle of malt whisky, which I thought I had cleverly hidden upstairs, is full of cold tea. I have found several empty bottles in the house and in the garden.

This morning, Joan, our neighbour, brought over her lovely nine-month-old granddaughter and initially M. was all smiles & attention. When Joan had gone, I got her to lie across several chairs and placed cushions under her head, and called the doctor. When Dr Ellis came, she was able to walk to the sofa in the front room. He was sympathetic and concerned, but could do little, giving M. a prescription for more medicine and saying he would contact social services.

Joan had spoken angrily and understandingly to Mieke yesterday, and this, together with a sober period and a feeling of shame & general wretchedness, made her more open to talking about her condition. But she also said there was no hope for her in view of her family's history of alcoholism, which of course I countered strongly.

This morning, she seemed ready to make a new start. What I didn't know then was that she had already been drinking.

When she collapsed, I felt she wanted to be hospitalized. There was perhaps some degree of manipulation: she wouldn't rouse herself for me to help her onto the sofa, but when Dr Ellis came, she got up, at his encouragement, and walked there by herself. And now she became more coherent too.

26 JUNE
Henry Gee, writing in a *Guardian* supplement, predicts: 'Genomic organisation will allow us to fashion the human form into any conceivable shape. We will have extra limbs, if we want them – maybe even wings to fly, accessories enough to benefit a self-made angel'. When I read this and his other predictions to M. (who has read a lot of science fiction), she sighed and said she would like to live in a hut in the woods with a cat and a dog, gathering berries and nuts and going for walks with me.

2 JULY
Walking with M. this morning, the sight of Cley Hill across the fields reminded me of when I first saw it – not then knowing its name – from the train on that ecstatic journey south, after I had got the job at Bath College. Certainly, that was one of the happiest days of my life.

But I will not now look at this landscape with regret. We have lived here, and now it is time to move on. For me, indeed, a new lease of life, which I couldn't possibly have foreseen last July, or until a few months ago.

14 JULY
Four weeks today since Mieke last had a drink. She has overcome crises with determination and the help of medication. We take nothing for granted, but we both feel the change.

The summer continues wet and clouded. There are bright poppies growing against grey stone, smoky blue cranesbill. But as usual at this time of year, I am lethargic, and sit around watching cricket on TV (weather permitting), mentally in the doldrums. Typing up my diary/autobiography, I oscillate between pleasurable surprise and embarrassment, now feeling there may be something in it worth publishing, now thinking the whole effort misguided.

'These are the dog days, Fortunatus.'

16 July
A year ago, I was taken into hospital. Today we held a going-away party with friends from the college and the area. It was sunny, but cool in the shade of the birch-tree and we were able to sit out in the garden until evening. Barry Cooper brought us one of his paintings. Paul Edwards gave us a copy of his wonderful book on the life and work of Wyndham Lewis.

It is hard for me to take in the difference that a year has made. The fact that we are leaving is perhaps the most surprising part of it. I don't feel sad, because the change will mean a new opening; but it will not be easy to leave here, or these friends & neighbours. Yet perhaps the fact of my illness and convalescence will make it easier than it would otherwise have been. These somehow make change welcome – the fact of survival, the conviction that things must go on just-so, followed by the unexpected gift of a new possibility.

31 July
In the company of a young woman from a letting agency, we visited several houses available to rent in and around Caerphilly, and decided to take one on an estate at Machen, alongside woodland and the river Rhymney. Back in Pontypridd on a warm afternoon, we walked round the town and the market.

Partly no doubt as a result of the ensuing fatigue, I woke up in the night feeling despondent, and talked blackly to M., saying I had made a mistake leaving Bath Spa University, and taking a job for which I shall have to devise and teach new courses, and in leaving our home in Somerset, in easy reach of the New Forest & the coast, and so on… A miserable, depressing recital, such as I'm prone to, and in which (M. listening patiently & sympathetically), I seem to incite myself, eventually running out of things to complain about, and, mind cleared, falling asleep.

6 August
There is a male romanticism, and it has dominated most of my life, like an emotional haze in which the woman is partially concealed, or an ideal figure that replaces her reality. Only with M. have I had a chance of knowing more; and, paradoxically, this has not come about because of my empathy & attentiveness, but because of the needs she has been forced to reveal.

What I'm trying to say is – I have the chance.

8 August
'What kills alcoholics is pride.' Our social worker, speaking from long experience. Yes; and it is also true to say: *What kills is pride.*

Something has happened to M. in the past two months: she is both open and in control now. And she has done this for herself.

9 August
Evening: last meeting for me with the Al Anon group in Trowbridge. Following convalescence, I couldn't have had a warmer welcome back from my old friends. I was able to tell them about Mieke's recovery – with all due caution, of course – and they were so pleased for her & for me.

When we moved from Frome, I left my Al Anon group. Being with them once a week or so, in Trowbridge, had been one of my life's most rewarding experiences. I have never quite known the equivalent with any other group of people. They were exceptional individuals, but there was also the link formed through common understanding of a problem which only those who have lived with it can truly understand. Not even the most understanding outsider, including professionals, can know the emotional experience of living with an alcoholic – the fear, anxiety, mixture of anger & pity, recurrent sense of hopelessness, the whole bewildering mixture of emotions. So, there was a very strong bond in the group, which enabled emotional expression & relief, & laughter. I became very fond of several members, especially the older, slow-spoken man who led the group, and an old woman whose son was an alcoholic. He once came to speak to our group, a man who hadn't had a drink for fifteen years, but who knew that he was an alcoholic. I forget exactly what he said, but his inner strength and empathy made a deep impression on me. And of course, I could talk! More than that, I found with the group something I had been looking for life-long: a sense of community. I had had it with friends as a youth, but my principal adult experience was of being on the outside, as a poet in the academic world, as an Englishman living in a Welsh village, as a man longing for what he felt – probably quite wrongly – his ancestors had enjoyed, a sense of belonging. It was the friendliness, the sense of sharing a predicament, and the emotional openness of the Al Anon group that meant so much to me.

19 August
At 20 Chestnut Close, Machen
Mieke calls the estate 'toy town', but it is pleasant enough here, while we wait to find somewhere permanent to live. In the night, I find myself thinking about Old Schoolhouse, going over the rooms and the garden in

my mind, and about Frome and the life we have left behind us. Inevitably, there will be sadness for both of us; and the memory is still strong in my mind of how, a year ago, having come out of hospital, I climbed the stairs to the room with my father's paintings on the wall and the view of the Mendips from the window, and how I sat out in the garden with the rose of Sharon at my back. It was there that I regained energy & the ability to move on. Life is hardly new for someone who is nearly sixty, yet it has been renewed for me, and I have the chance, in a new place, of further renewal.

Old Schoolhouse

Today, I recall the old house
where my mother died
and I convalesced, and you
who taught me to grieve
revealed to me your wound.
I remember the limestone walls
pitted with fossils, the cellar
like a dungeon of sweating stone.
From the attic, looking one way
we could see the Mendips
and in the other, a clump of trees
on the edge of Salisbury Plain.
How much before us the old house contained.
We too are now part of that history,
our happiness and our despair,
all that we cared for so much,
which to old walls means as little
as a mouse squeak or web of dust.
If there were ghosts, they were felt
not seen or heard – generations of children,
a memory deep in the fabric
where you listened, longing to heal
all who suffered or were lost,
unable to find healing for your wound.

30 August

Over our evening meal at a pub in Draethen, I asked Mieke what it was that first attracted her to Wales. She spoke of her feeling of being ill at ease in the flatlands, a feeling she related to the Puritan culture in which people are made to sense the eyes of God are everywhere observing them. By contrast, the mountainous Welsh landscape, with all its hidden places, made her feel invisible. From her first visits to Wales as a young woman, she was drawn to the landscape and the people, and felt she belonged among them.

2 September
To Manorbier on a warm sunny day, the great castle, where Gerald of Wales was born, looking down on a freshwater stream running through rocks & sand to the sea. Afterwards, with no particular destination in view, we drove along narrow coast roads, and came eventually to Laugharne, where, on a beautiful evening, we walked as far as the famous Boathouse. Tide out in the broad estuary between wooded headlands, the river & lesser streams snaking through an expanse of ripple-marked sand. Cries of seabirds – gulls, pipers, a curlew – emphasising the stillness & peace. Beside and over red & purple rocks, marked with mustard-yellow lichen, we climbed to the garage which Dylan Thomas had used as a writing room. Through the window we could see his chair askew in front of the desk, as if he had just got up and left the room, papers on the desk and screwed into balls on the floor. We walked on along the path above the boathouse, looking across the estuary at a hilly, pastoral landscape with white-washed farms, three yachts resting on their sides on the sand; the trees at our backs cast shadows across the river and onto the sand. I could imagine the poet here – on this quiet evening, the place had a magical quality, which was partly something he had interpreted, and partly a colouring of his words.

4 September
Woke shaking from violent anxiety dreams. Perhaps I'm more apprehensive about this new job than I realise.

On a lovely afternoon, a smell of autumn beginning under the trees, I walked by the river to the post office on the main road, to post a letter to Green Books about my proposed selection of Richard Jefferies' writings. I felt my walking to be slow, laborious, and used the new, red acacia stick M. had bought me in Narberth. Several older women, some with sticks, greeted me with a friendly word. In Narberth, an old man from whom we bought tickets for the small museum, had asked us whether we were pensioners, which took me aback. But there it is; as I labour about the campus or make an expedition to post a letter, I realise I'm not the youth who was inducted into the university at Aberystwyth thirty-five years ago. And with the realisation comes the perception that it's absurd for me to be approaching this new job like a man with no confidence in himself.

10 SEPTEMBER
Sunday. A glorious late summer/early autumn morning. Climbing Mynydd Machen on the opposite side of the valley, we heard the clock of St John's church strike 12. I have a strong sense here, among the people we meet, in the woods where charcoal-burners used to work, and in quiet places where few industrial remains are now to be seen, of the lives of the generations. It arises in part from the idea first put into my mind when living in Llangwyryfon, that the old life was still going on, and was the reality of the place.

Our conversation related directly to this, and to 'the enigma of death' (Uncle Kolya in *Dr Zhivago*). I had been thinking again of the feeling I had had at Moor Farm, of the near-presence yet complete absence of the dead, which, one day, we too would share. M. asked me whether the feeling bothered me, and said that, far from troubling her, she accepted the idea of making a contribution, and being remembered for a time by those whose lives she had touched. This led to her wondering whether the need to leave a mark was a male need, arising from an insecure sense of identity. And so, we talked.

23 SEPTEMBER
This is now, this is here. On a warm, sunny day at Maenllwyd Inn, Rudry, where Kay is treating us to a meal. We sit outside on the terrace, below us green fields, and in the distance landscaped spoilheaps on the mountains above Bedwas. Kay, who knows about Mieke's recovery, says of our recent move & changes in our lives, that we have 'risen from the ashes'. M. echoes her, speaking of a second chance. There's a promise of newness in their confidence, in the warm and mellow day, the beauty of the surroundings, and our pleasure in one another's company.

21 OCTOBER
Stephen Batty rang me this morning to tell me Gerard Casey has died. At the time we were sitting up in bed talking emotionally about M.'s drinking in recent days. Gerard was a strong man, tormented by illness and pain in his later years. As I write these words, I can see the front room of the house in Mappowder – empty now – which was like a simple, austere,

but highly cultured monk's cell. It was my great good fortune to meet Gerard and become his friend. He was a man with deep roots in religious traditions, and if I have acquired a little knowledge of those traditions, it has been largely through him. Being with him, and driving home through the Dorset lanes, I always felt I had touched something deeper, more real, and more serious, than I would otherwise have done. It was possibility that he opened to me – a sense of the depths in life (he would have said God), which are closed to our thought-world today.

31 OCTOBER
Worked on a lecture on Charlotte Perkins Gilman's utopian novel *Herland*. Late afternoon: M. has gone to an AA meeting in Caerphilly. A brave decision: she is more aware now that she needs help. That's the most hopeful sign.

Who doesn't need help, in one way or another? I owe my happiness to M. My dread is for myself as much as her when she turns away into shadowland. She's able now, sometimes, to talk about it, seeing herself when she succumbs as another person.

13 NOVEMBER
Frost melting & bright leaf colours in the sun. Hetty and Claire (Mieke's friends who have become my friends, too) have been staying with us over the weekend. They are good company, lively & affectionate, and it's especially good to see M. enjoying herself with them, laughing and talking in Dutch. We were both aware of the past yesterday, driving through country near Lampeter where she spent holidays with her first husband. We have, too, a common dream of a country cottage; on my part, though, I have some uneasiness – my life at Brynbeidog belongs to the past, and I have now, with M., a rich life, which I shouldn't try to fit into an old mould.

26 NOVEMBER
Yesterday, in pouring rain, we went to view houses at Wattsville and Pontywaun and later, after the rain had stopped, at Argoed near Blackwood. Earlier in the week we had come close to making an offer on an old farmhouse at Penygraig in the Rhondda, but the house was shut in, with estates behind, and without access by foot into the country.

Shopping in a supermarket at Ystrad Mynach, M. sent me to order lunch at the cafe while she remained at the check-out, but I came back prematurely, and found her taking a half bottle of vodka from an assistant who had fetched it at her request. Seeing me return, she asked the young man to take it back.

At the time we managed to make light of the incident. But afterwards it came back to me: Is this how we will be spending the rest of our lives?

Our years in Frome were the years in which my parents died. My mother lived with us for her final months. Mieke was marvellous with her, and with my father. She taught me how to grieve. She had such depth of emotional understanding. There is no doubt that she taught me how to live, to be open. This was the paradox, that I trusted her completely in things that really matter, at the same time that I knew she would lie about drink. Mieke experienced a lot of pain from physical conditions, and I could rarely be sure whether her illnesses were caused by these, or by alcohol, or the effects of drink mixed with painkillers. After my stroke, she was very good in helping with my recovery. As I became more mobile, however, drink took hold of her again. One motive I had, in applying for the job that would take me back to Wales, was the hope that the move would be good for Mieke. In a way, it was, for she had always loved Wales, the mountainous country that is so different from her native flatlands. But the change did not alter the pattern of drinking that would finally contribute to her death.

A new life began for us with the new millennium, when we moved to Wales. After a long search, we bought a house on the outskirts of the former mining village of Treharris, on a hillside below Treharris Park and above Quakers Yard and the Taff – Bargoed Valley. Mieke was not well here initially, and received hospital treatment in Bristol, after which she convalesced at home. For a few months in this period, alcohol played a smaller part in our lives. Thereafter, in the years left to her, it became again a major threat, and affected her more as she aged. About to begin on this part of our 'story', I hesitate, conscious of how much of Mieke, and of our life together, must escape me. The journal entries with which I am working is the selection of a selection. I have kept a diary for more than fifty years, and have published edited portions of it. It is part of my life as a writer, and records everything that touches me – weathers, excursions, natural observations, friends and family, books, ideas, religion, politics, wars, everything! Primarily, it is a poet's journal, concerned with poetry and poets, and in quest of meaning. During the period with which I am concerned in this book, I was working full-time in a university, and after retirement at the age of 68, I continued to write. Mieke took a keen interest in my books, both the poetry and the literary criticism, and was my first and best critic. I owe a huge amount to her perceptions and her encouragement. On focusing on her alcoholism, it is the depth of her person and the richness of our lives together that escape. I know that in this book I am not portraying Mieke as she was – 'known unto God', in a resonant phrase that rings true to me – but chasing a demon. There was much that was repetitive in this final phase of our life together in Wales, and with this understanding – that life escapes – I can only continue with more stringent selections from what I wrote at the time.

31 January 2001
Teaching starts again tomorrow. Am I ready? Not really. With my Utopia/Dystopia course in particular, I feel that I'm just keeping a step ahead of the students, as I did during my first year at Aberystwyth. M. has been ill from a virus, and I was mean to her in her weakness yesterday. Fear, frustration: I don't cope well with her illness while it lasts. I convince myself it's psychosomatic, but the fact is, when feeling well myself, I'm selfish, and impatient. There's no excuse.

4 February
M. was very taken by a large stone house in the Merthyr Road, Pontypridd. We both liked it and saw its advantages, but for me the lack of a garden was decisive. So, we argued; I lost my temper, we both got upset. Mieke feels acutely confined living in a house that isn't our own, without access to many of our things, which are in storage. Weak & depressed after long illness, she feels it more. She has no outlet, as I have my work in the university.

10 February
Last night, at the university, I gave a poetry reading for students on the creative writing MA. I concluded my reading with poems from *Arnolds Wood* which brought to my mind Old Schoolhouse and the surrounding area, from Les's Cotswolds to Salisbury Plain. I think of it all with deep affection, but, except for an occasional keen pang, can't say I miss it.

    Here we are balanced precariously on a future we certainly couldn't have foreseen when I went back to work a year ago. M. ill, her life a daily struggle with pain & debility. Myself (as far as work goes) energetic, but seized too often by a deadly selfishness as I blame her for being unwell. More harmony between us, but with this nastiness recurring, and, when I am honest, revealing to me a side of myself I'd rather not know. But through all, too, a hope in our life in Wales which we share.

24 February
A bad week. Some time on Sunday, after our walk, Mieke started drinking. Having found a bottle of vodka I allowed myself to be persuaded there was no more drink in the house. When I came in from work on Tuesday evening M. was on the point of collapse, no longer able to bear the pain she has been living with for so long. After a time of trying to comfort her, I realised that she was, also, drunk.

She is scared of the coming operation, but also welcomes it. Had she started drinking again because afraid? Or was it because she had to sabotage herself, and make herself ill again, at the first sign of returning health? It was this that made me mad. *This* is the thing I can't deal with, and can't stand. Not illness. I could almost say not alcoholism, except this perversity seems part of it in M.'s case. As she herself says, she has a long history of harming herself.

This is what Mieke's alcoholism amounts to: at worst, she makes life unliveable for herself, and for us. And for me at crises; for I actually feel better, and more energetic, than since before my stroke. At work, and last night, walking to the Chinese take-away in Machen, beside the Rhymney & on the pavement beside the main road – groups of boys playing on their bikes, as I used to do, and greeting me with a friendly word – above me the glorious stars and planets of a clear winter night – Venus burning bright, Jupiter & Saturn (I think), big stars whose names I don't know, scintillating. And I was taken out of myself, hearing the river, breathing the chill air.

27 February
Fires are burning across Britain: pyres of cattle, sheep, and pigs. Foot and mouth disease, carried by an airborne virus, is infecting thousands of animals and bringing the livestock industry to a halt. Where will it end?

How our lives turn around one another! In our dreams we were in foreign cities. M. saw me in an open café; I was dizzy and fell over. I was in an upstairs hotel room trying hopelessly to find my shoes and cram clothes & a pair of wellington boots into a suitcase. She was downstairs refusing to help; she had decided to leave me.

This morning we started again with a reading from *Twelve Steps and Twelve Traditions*. I was shaken to be reminded that cure is virtually dependant on AA. M.'s stubborn independence is the very thing that will destroy her if she doesn't break its hold.

3 March
This morning after our reading M. remembered, between the ages of 3 and 5, making sandcastles. She wasn't making them for their own sake, absorbed in the activity, but was thinking whether she was making them 'right', and whether they were 'beautiful' – both in the eyes of others.

It was a compact memory, rather than a memory of one specific occasion. This she sees as a representative form of behaviour, to which drinking is a defiant reaction, an assertion of independence – doing something for herself. She knows this isn't the whole truth, but as she reflected on the memory, it struck us both as being crucially important.

10 March
Our offer has been accepted on a house at Treharris, which we went to see on Thursday. It is on a hillside backed by woods, at the entrance to Treharris Park, and looks out at mountains to the south. It is a spacious house with two big living rooms downstairs and large windows, which take advantage of the wonderful views. If it had been nearer to Cardiff, we certainly wouldn't have been able to afford it. I'm so glad we've got to this point, for Mieke's sake, and for my own. I dislike being unsettled, with most of my books in storage. And I like settling in: the sense of a new beginning, the world around one newly strange.

18 March
Daffodils are out on the bank against Caerphilly castle – nature's yellow flags against grey battlements that have long since outlasted the purpose for which they were built, and only wear away.

Walking with M. in the recreation ground beside the estate, I remembered seeing Gerard and Mary Casey setting out for walks together, first thing in the morning, at Weymouth. All that depth of thought, the serious life well lived: would it be futile if death means the same non-being for all – Himmler and St Francis equally? Does it make sense to say the meaning of life inheres in life itself? Without a sense of connection (divine/ancestral), we are more atomized than people have ever been. And so, fearful of futility, the question presses in.

1 April
Delivered the final set of proof & index (both Mieke's work) of *Imagining Wales* to University of Wales Press.

Dandelions out on grass plots & at the base of stone walls.

Bumblebee on the river bank.

2 May

Mieke has been dulling her pain with drink in recent days. It's fear of the operation too. On occasion I've let myself go, under the influence of my fear of what alcohol does to her. But now, I'm ashamed; there's something horrible about my moral indignation. All that's required is love and understanding. The latter applies to myself too – as though *words of advice* offered any help or healing.

27 May

A long talk with a friend whose father was an alcoholic has left me with no sense of ultimate hope. I know he thinks the situation will continue, with periods of sobriety, but with M. always resorting again to drink. He knows how low 'rock bottom' can be, and that not every alcoholic reaches it, or is able to come back.

This isn't what I want to know, but it is what I fear. Something in M., and something in my friend's view of alcoholism, coincide to make me think nothing is ever going to change, until she dies. And what can I do, then, but offer what support I can, and brace myself?

But I revolt against hopelessness. I can't accept this picture of the future. I have accepted things that, once, I wouldn't have thought possible to live with, such as lies & deceit & secrecy. And these can be lived with, because love is more important, and goes deeper, and is the ground of a relationship.

My reasoning revolts me, but it is what I have to do; as long as I don't confuse it with an 'answer' for Mieke. For me, perhaps, it is whistling in the dark. For her, at least, it shows my concern; but any real change can only come about from within.

With actual human experience everything is so different from the verbal patterns one imposes on it. And maybe that is what we mean when we say that love is wordless.

28 May

On Rudry Common, open to walkers for the first time in months, but no one but ourselves about. Only a strong wind blowing cloud across the sky, waving the new bracken stalks which stand upright from the earth, fronds unfurling like tiny fingers. Tormentil, little yellow stars, among the short grass.

M. was able to walk a few yards, delighting in the open air & fresh wind.

7 JUNE
Cloud continents drifting across the sky, gulls visible against them and in blue spaces in-between. Already, after rain, the full-leaved deciduous trees are a darker green.

Mieke has been drinking again. It is hard for me to know what to say, because she is in pain, and because I know how little what I say matters.

This morning I did speak, however, in spite of having decided not to. I had felt angry and hopeless, because, last night, she wouldn't come downstairs to watch the second programme about Clouds House on TV. Last week she watched the first, and she asked me to call her down to see this one. But, in the event, I watched it alone.

And I remembered that time. What upset me, though, was Mieke's evasiveness. I realised again, too, that I am helping to protect her from the consequences of her drinking. Then there seemed nothing left to say. Nothing to do except listen, if she chose to speak to me. But she seldom really talks about her addiction, or expresses her feelings, as patients at Clouds are encouraged to do.

The more I experience of other people's lives, the less inclined I am to judge, or think I understand. In one way or another, we are driven, and although, for the most part, we want to be whole, and to live, it is hard, very hard, to come through life without damaging ourselves and other people.

I am most blind when most a reasoner over M.'s condition. In silence, feeling something of her confusion I understand more. Best are the times when she shows her feelings and I am with her.

8 JUNE
When they occur, the drinking crises are absolute, as if the world outside them no longer exists, or is a long way off, and I am alone in my anxiety with M., who scarcely communicates. Then, on another day, M. smiling, ordinarily busy & cheerful, it is the nightmare that no longer exists, and is hard to imagine. The difference is like that between dream and reality. The fear is always that the 'dream' will become the one thing that is real.

14 JUNE
In the evening I read from and talked about *Imagining Wales*, mainly to a

group of Professor Wynn Thomas's MA students, at the Dylan Thomas house, 5, Cwmdonkin Drive, in the Uplands area of Swansea. Arriving early, in heavy rain, we had the house to ourselves. I hadn't quite known what to expect, and found the house larger, roomier, than I had thought it would be. I suppose that, socially, Dylan came from much the same world as I did. It was strange being in what had once been his and his parents' home – empty, sparsely furnished, lived-in, a little worn with neglect, and with views of the sea from some windows. These, in particular, brought the boy & young poet to mind.

21 JUNE
Last night, after watching the fourth Clouds House programme, Mieke cried, and said she would like to go back in. She also referred to her 'secret', which she said she had been forbidden 'on pain of death' to reveal. We have been here before – almost – and I don't know what to make of it: whether she is referring to some childhood abuse, which she *can't* talk about, or intimating experiences that she *has* told me about, or whether…

I feel there is a weight inside me dragging me down. Being with Meic and Ruth Stephens and their grandchild was like experiencing another world, in which life is lived as it can be. But here, in spite of Mieke having said, with remorse, that she has had her last drink, I am sure she has been drinking again today. And now the bad days are merging into one another, drink & sleep, drink & sleep, always with the worry that she will not be able to come back.

24 JUNE
What Kay makes me aware of – I see it in myself; she doesn't point it out – is the irrelevance of self-pity. I may at times need to express anxiety, and anger, but in expressing my feelings, and talking about M.'s problem, I adjust. I see that it is *her* problem, and feeling sorry for myself is beside the point. Talking in this way makes me more aware of M., and of our love for one another. And it makes me more aware that this is the life I have chosen, and how good it is.

30 JUNE
At our new home, Dan-y-Lan, working in the room that is to be my study. I had intended to paint over the green wallpaper but found it necessary to strip it. The last time I did this was at Monks Road in Winchester twenty years ago – an experience that came back to me as I attacked this wallpaper,

almost mindlessly. As I looked up, absorbed in the automatic work, I was surprised by the view through the window, down over Quakers Yard and up, over wide, hilly country to the mountain above Pontypridd. At present we are strangers here, the house almost empty around us, and everything we see is strange.

4 JULY
We worked all day yesterday at Dan-y-Lan, as men from Pickford's delivered our belongings. By evening the house was full of furniture & boxes waiting to be unpacked, so that it's hard to see where everything is going to fit in.

At the end of the day we both felt ill with tiredness & the heat. Then, in the night, a storm broke, which is still circling round the hills, thunder crashing close by, lightning flashing or flickering, and rain falling heavily. The summer morning is like a winter evening, dark grey, only close not cold.

Unable to sleep, I talked to M., who was in pain after being on her feet most of the day. Exhausted & restless, I felt the full extent of my neediness, and how much I depend on her love & companionship.

I am always low at this time of year, she reminds me. She has been proof-reading my *Welsh Journal,* where (she tells me) the evidence is plain to see. It is the time of the weather I cope with least well – windless, sultry heat. This appears to correspond to nature's stasis – the plateau of the year, when most birds have fallen silent and fruit is forming inconspicuously among dark green leaves. It is time of the purples – vetch, buddleia, thistles, knapweed, white bramble flowers touched with purple, like juice of the fruit to come. There seems to me no freshness of growth, and days and nights are still and airless. If it were possible, I would creep into a cool corner and wait until the midsummer doldrums are past.

14 JULY
As I look out now, at heavy clouds moving over the hills and through columns of rain, I don't really know where we are. Years ago, I gave old Walter Haydn Davies a lift to Quakers Yard, where he was going to pay his respects to the Quakers in their burial ground. Now, I am vaguely aware of that part of the local history, and there is a Fox Street (named after George Fox) in Treharris, but I don't know concrete details, or what, if anything, the Quaker inheritance has left here. So, what I am seeing – houses, trees, hills, the configurations of the land – remain as enigmas to me, 'runes',

which I am less able to read than Alun Lewis could read the runes he saw from the mountain over Aberdare.

19 JULY
Day of Mieke's operation at Southmead Hospital, Bristol. No news until the afternoon, after she has been in the operating theatre for several hours. Her message: 'Tell him I am still alive'. When I visit, she is lying in bed festooned with tubes and wearing an oxygen mask, but is able to talk a little. She is 'the baby' in a ward with three women in their 80s/90s.

27 JULY
Heat wave. M. out of bed and walking about the ward. Some post-operative pain, but the pain that necessitated the operation has gone.

29 JULY
M. was allowed to come home today, arriving at lunchtime. In her pleasure at being back, she probably sat up too long, for afterwards, without morphine and unable to take painkillers, she experienced a lot of pain. This is the beginning of what will be a long period of convalescence.

Penny, a friend of a friend and a professional carer, is staying with us at present and working hard in the house. She had helped to look after a famous novelist towards the end of his life. Disabled by a stroke, he was, she said, an arrogant man, violently abusive. It seems terrible that anyone should end in that way, either changed by illness into something one was not, or out of control.

I hope to be always the better person that I want to be.

10 AUGUST
We waited anxiously all day yesterday for news of Elin who was in labour. At 1.10 this morning, after 24 hours, Ian Alexander was born.

11 AUGUST
Following M.'s first trip out into Treharris, with Penny, I found two half bottles of vodka, empty, in clothes drawers in our bedroom. She says she has no recollection of either buying or concealing or drinking them. Her body language told me she had been drinking; she was near comatose. I do believe she has no memory of buying or drinking the vodka – and this, perhaps, is more dangerous than if she had. It seems possible that, following the trauma of the operation and in her anxiety over Elin, she

could have acted automatically, blocking it out from consciousness.

What a day! Outside, misty rain was blowing round the house. Inside, I spoke a little about Mieke's drink problem to Penny, who urged acceptance.

How can one guard against automatic actions? At the time, it seemed like the ruin of all our plans for a new start. How helpless one can feel in face of certain things, and how easily the life one is building can fall into ruins.

7 SEPTEMBER

Yesterday, for the first time since her operation, M. completed a round of the supermarket with me. She then prepared a wonderful meal, which we shared with Anne Cluysenaar and her husband, Walt.

Afterwards, she was very tired, but she had been energetic and had enjoyed herself.

9 SEPTEMBER

M. commented on how still it was this morning when we drew the curtains. But on the moorland above Bedlinog the wind was blowing, and it became stronger, but not cold, as I climbed. Cloud & shadow brought out the contours – ridges & saddlebacks – of the blueish-grey Brecon Beacons. To the south we could see a vague outline of the English coast. It was exhilarating to breathe the air and see the spaces opening around us, and to smell again the moorland smell of sunwarmed grass & dried sheep's dung.

11 SEPTEMBER

After Elin rang to tell us what was happening, we sat transfixed in front of the television watching the same images as they were repeated: the World Trade Centre on fire, an airliner flying into the side of it, the building collapsing, Manhattan engulfed in a towering cloud of smoke, smoke pouring from the Pentagon – and feeling horror at the loss of life. It is the thought of people so terrified they jump to their deaths out of the burning building, of passengers in a plane flown to its destruction – the thought that horrifies, but cannot be held in the mind.

All over the affluent world people will be feeling more vulnerable after this day's work, and some will be celebrating a great success. There will be a strong urge in America to rush to revenge, an urge I fully understand, but the only sane choice is to look into causes, to understand the political situation that breeds such hatred.

What we see is loss of the life we worship and the personal agony that ensues. What the terrorists see is heroic, sacrificial death and a blow struck at a hated enemy. But the only hope, ultimately, is some kind of political compromise, and for that to occur there will have to be dialogue.

In the meantime, what we are likely to see is more carnage.

13 September
Yesterday morning, as I drew back the curtains and looked at the trees on the other side of the lane, I thought how lucky we were to be living here, far from terrorist atrocities. Afterwards, though, I thought of the forces that have driven through this landscape, the mines, the quarry on whose edge the trees I had been looking at stand. And I realised that nowhere is far from anywhere else on this globe, and we all live in the shadow of terror.

This morning was different. I felt no leap of happiness at the sight of the trees. The reason was two bottles of vodka which I found, by accident, in the airing cupboard. This is the pattern: a step towards health and she turns back. I talked, of course, angry and reasoning, and M., under the influence, answered, seeming to say CAN'T WON'T, hugging the miserable addiction to herself.

Later
Mieke, feeling shaky, was more remorseful than I have ever seen her. She said my words about taking refuge in illness had gone home. It was what she had always done when anything had been difficult.

As I was brooding on this, I came upon the passage in *Paradise Lost* Book VIII, in which Adam says:

> to know
> That which before us lies in daily life,
> Is the prime Wisdom; what is more, is fume,
> Or emptiness, or fond impertinence,
> And renders us in things that most concern
> Unpractised, unprepar'd, and still to seek.

It seemed apt to what was troubling us, and I shared it with M. I had stumbled on an instance of the concern that is central to the English literary (not just poetic) tradition, and simultaneously recognised that it belongs to a different moral & intellectual universe from ours. But still, *the words spoke to me,* reawakening my belief that true poetry addresses our 'daily life', and must somehow – however difficult – continue to do so.

26 SEPTEMBER
Deft concealment of a bottle under a bush in the garden this morning, but I saw it, and the danger was averted, for today. Mieke knows and does not know what she is doing at these times, her mind telling her one story, which isn't true. She thinks having a bottle in the house will keep her 'safe', and she needn't drink it. She suppresses the knowledge that it represents danger, and she will drink it.

  Slow suicide, is that what it is? Or an inability to *be* except on her own terms, which preclude admitting and confronting her weaknesses? It seems to me sometimes that she has to be perfect, or nothing, as though she avoids the middle ground of creative struggle. This can look like arrogance, but, surely, it is fear of failure.

  It is well enough for me to *reason*, but what M. needs is help.

3 OCTOBER
Mieke is feeling very sick today, after the doctor gave her medication to stop her drinking. If only it does! At least she felt desperate enough to seek help. It's the blindness of the addiction that I fear.

  I have turned my mind to other things, as I have to, in order to work, and survive, but it is difficult. Other people's concern helps me enormously, and I have gained support from recent phonecalls from Kay & Lee. They care for Mieke, but they know what her illness exacts of me. And, sometimes, that's what I need to share.

7 OCTOBER
Five o'clock on a wet Sunday afternoon here in Wales, trees blowing in the wind, rain streaming down our windows, we turn on the television and learn that allied assaults have begun on Taliban positions in Afghanistan. Impossible now for anyone, anywhere, to think of themselves as safe. But that has been the lesson of my lifetime: the direction from which the threat comes changes, but the threat remains much the same.

13 OCTOBER
Emily phoned to tell me she was very worried by something Mieke had told her. This turned out to be that I was worried because I thought I was dying.

Well! I see where this comes from. After this difficult summer and during the first weeks of teaching I have been feeling my age, and, yes, I do sometimes wonder whether I might die soon. All this I'd said to M. not long before she spoke to Emily. But what oppresses me most is this damned drinking, and the burden of M.'s self-sabotage, and drinking is the very thing that makes other people, including Emily, nervous of visiting her.

As for dying, I have felt afraid in recent months, and I no longer assume that I will live as long as my father and his father, or longer (or as long as) my brother Dave, who died at 65. But I feel too that I have work to do, and I enjoy life. Mere selfish fear, anxiety over self-loss, will occur, but if it becomes dominant, or a permanent inner corrosive, living itself becomes death-in-life. And that above all one has to avoid.

16 OCTOBER

This journal is now my life-line; in a way, it always was, but now, as Mieke's drinking affects her more, and the situation becomes more desperate, writing here is necessary to my very sanity. Last night, after two days of drinking, I saw her hunting for a bottle, rummaging in the kitchen & scullery, blind with need. In the morning she had lied to me, in order to go out and buy drink. But that's normal; nothing she says in this respect can be relied on. What worries me now is that she is deteriorating, her mind as well as her body, and no longer has any will to help herself.

It *is* a matter of life or death, more urgent now than when we first used these words, when M. went into Clouds House. In recent weeks she has been spiralling down. Sharing the problem with family and friends brings some relief, but I am the one who has to face it and whatever may come. I never forget, though, that if I am strong now, she helped me to find strength.

18 OCTOBER

Mother's death-day. Then, it was a clear starry night. Now, there's a hint of gold dust in sunlight in the valley.

An hour ago, I came in from work to despair. After two days of recovering from the last drinking bout, Mieke had been drinking again. Only this morning we talked, recognised the seriousness of the situation, made resolutions. I had gone to work feeling strained, come home with spirits raised – and walked into a wall.

When I think of the woman she has been, and is, when sober, I can't believe what is happening. Drunkenness sounds like some wild revelry, or stupor, but this is a gradual relentless poisoning. The shadow goes from her face, and all is well – we talk, discuss the 'problem', make plans, laugh – and then the shadow comes back, she retreats inside herself, sinks into silence. But where inside? Judging from face & body language, it is some kind of limbo, some grey no-place, some death-in-life.

I can't believe and I can't not believe.

There is a way back from here, but I can't make her find it. Just now, it looks as though all her hope has collapsed, all her desire for the new life we promised ourselves. Or if the desire is there, fear is stronger: this dull-eyed unkillable ingenious demon. In its effects it looks so stupid, so perverse; but every time it finds the means to win, and leaves us with fewer & fewer resources.

10 NOVEMBER

Elin & Aryan with their beautiful little boy, Ian, arrived in the evening. I know what Philip Larkin means when, in 'Afternoons', he says of the young mothers, 'Something is pushing them /To the side of their own lives'. Yet there are also very different things to say, and feelings to record, when one finds oneself with children & grandchildren. Mieke holding Ian is a wonderful sight to behold.

25 NOVEMBER

After five weeks, another bottle of vodka, a step back into the fog. Others alone *see* what the alcoholic is really doing; he or she is like a sleepwalker, who, in the sober light of day, may have little or no recollection of what they did in the night. M. says the last weeks have been difficult, but she has been alive (*that* is more difficult for her than for others, perhaps). I have told her she is complacent about her drinking: I believe she is, fundamentally, and I say it hoping to wake her up. Of course, I am afraid. Five weeks ago, I couldn't see how she could go on drinking and living. Then, when she achieved sobriety, I became complacent, accepting the life we were living together as normal: conscious and shared. She speaks now of another five weeks of sobriety. If only it may be so!

9 DECEMBER

M., suffering from a painful hip, has been diagnosed as having degenerative arthritis, which shocked and upset her. In consequence, she drank a lot, rapidly, and became hysterical.

Well, this has to be faced. It will be difficult for Mieke, who knows she is young to be afflicted by this condition, and who is still convalescing from the operation in July. I shall have to help her, overcoming feelings of impatience & intolerance, with which I initially respond to her illnesses, from the egoism of my own relative robustness, and the connection my mind makes between her alcoholism and *any* illness. The truth is, we are getting older, and we do need each other's support in ways that young healthy couples seldom contemplate.

16 December
Visitors exclaim at the attraction of our new home, the interior, the big windows looking out over the Taff-Bargoed valley, the position. The rooms are made more orderly now, and we feel at home, in spite of my twinges of nostalgia for the New Forest & the south coast. We are outsiders, in a way that most local people are not. What I want to know is where I am, and that's not as simple as it sounds. Settling for being unsettled is something I still haven't fully accepted.

Christmas Day
A mild, bright morning. Birds active in the woods: finches, long-tailed tits, a nuthatch – *twit twit twit twit*. Earlier we had seen a heron flying along the valley.

M. came with me a short way, up the steep lane and to a wooden bridge over a brook in the woods. Walking is difficult for her, but she is much happier now, feeling at home here. As she told me this morning, but I could see it. She feels less need for secrecy, which plays a large part in alcoholism. She draws me into the circle of life. Left to my own devices, I'd be a waster or a miserable recluse shut in with his books.

14 January 2002
Morning: a TV programme, based on Al Anon, about supporting an alcoholic partner. The struggles, the pain, the failure. It reminds me of something else, too, as the meetings at Trowbridge did: How the people telling their stories – many of them terrible – break through all our habitual babble & entertainments, and reveal something inspiring – a vulnerability, a love, a depth of humanity. God knows, one wouldn't wish this experience on anyone, but it opens people, and enables them to share. Alcoholics die of their illness, lives are ruined, families broken apart: *nothing* justifies alcoholism. But out of the experience can come, for

survivors, something profoundly worthwhile. Certainly, with M. & with my friends at Al Anon, I was sometimes granted an experience for which I'm deeply grateful.

11 MARCH
The problem of 'god-talk 'meets me almost everywhere. Each morning, before we get up, M. reads from a small book of daily meditations for women which her group at Clouds House gave her. Naturally, these are meant to solace and inspire those who are extremely fragile in their self-esteem. Often, though, they seem to offer false comfort with a soft-centred language of 'God' & 'destiny'. M. spoke this morning of what for her is evidently her most religious experience, when she feels part of things. This is the life-force, felt simultaneously in the solar plexus and outside her, in the universe. This is when she is least conscious of self, and 'in the flow'. Paradoxically, she then seems to me to be most herself, a woman with healing power.

Language of tension & the sickness unto death affect me much more. I think she simply doesn't need the God-idea, as it has been formulated by patriarchal cultures. It's not something I need either, but I can't let go of 'God', or the need to formulate a better – though always inadequate – idea of sacred power. For me, this is integral to human and personal identity, and is, paradoxically, about brokenness and the need for healing, not 'wholeness' in some self-pleasing New Age sense. The age preaches forms of completion that are dehumanising, and perhaps one can escape them, together with all the ways of self-gratification, only through having a sense of incompleteness. Not that this is a programme: one knows oneself broken. Need is the energy that drives one's life and work.

13 MARCH
Mieke had a kind of 'attack' today. When I came home in the afternoon, she was in bed recovering, her face blotchy red (she had drunk a little wine on top of taking Antibuse). She had suddenly been overcome with terror & grief at the conviction that nuclear weapons had been used in the Middle East and had sat in the hearth pouring ashes over her head and grieving, as we had seen women doing at Rachel's Tomb. Thinking about it afterwards, we can see that, as well as being due to abstinence from drink, this relates to her residual sense of Jewishness and strong feelings about the bloody conflict in Israel & the injustice to the Palestinians.

7 APRIL
Warm days, the birch-trees a greeny-yellow mist of leaves.

Talking with M. about my dream, in which I was crying and shouting out against the absoluteness of death, I could see that all philosophy, and perhaps all art & religion, does begin with death. This living being, now dead, this spirit, known and perhaps loved, that cannot be called back: *here* is where all our questions begin, just as it was for the first human beings. Thought strains to cross the divide, but it remains, leaving us on this side, seeing only that we can't see through, wondering whether there is 'another side', or only the absolute blank. Life too comes into question then, and quickens, brighter for the under-shadow, as we see a sunlit stream in shady woods.

11 APRIL
Started word-processing *Addiction: a love story* today. Divided the time between this, and reading and gardening, as I hope to be able to do for the time being.

15 APRIL
I woke up this morning to the fact that teaching begins again this week. I have been absorbed in 'Addiction', and in breaking my heart & back, as it sometimes seems, on our heavy, stony garden soil – in fact, feeling the better for it, and seeing the surroundings with a fresher eye, as I stop work, unbend and look around me.

1 MAY
Oak before the ash this year. How often I want to exclaim, 'Stay, thou art so fair', as the leaves and dusky bluebells appear. We can still see the quarry through the trees, but not for long. The brooks are flowing again, between ferny banks. The woods are filled with loud, melodious birdsong.

Home from college in the afternoon, I continue working on *Addiction*. There are things I am surprised to remember; sometimes I wonder that we survived. M. is in pain, but, for some months past, she has been strong in resolution, and enjoying life. In retrospect, I can see she was never really happy in Frome. But here she is happy, as if this were the home she has been seeking for years.

4 JUNE
Well, I'm not searching for Abercuawg, as R. S. Thomas did, but I do want

to hear the cuckoo. Once again, this year we've gone out into the country hoping to hear one, but so far without success. In the fields though, we found purple vetch, clumps of bright yellow trefoil, swifts & buzzards overhead.

16 JUNE
A green woodpecker was in the garden this morning, on its way between the wooded Taff-Bargoed valley and the quarry woods. We were lying in bed waiting for the start of the World Cup match between England and Nigeria, when I read a piece in *The Guardian*, in which the father of a Palestinian suicide bomber is reported as saying, 'To put it simply, we love martyrdom, they love life'.

How to understand that 'simple' truth? Here, and in the West generally, it's hard to realize the conflict, or our involvement in it, whether we want to be or not. For us, except when actually targeted (as in America in 9/11), it's like faint, discordant background music, a vague, disquieting feeling in the air, that calls our whole way of life into question.

But still – yes – I love life.

19 JUNE
M. lapsed last night – I had felt it coming for a while – and I over-reacted out of fear, and anger. This afternoon we talked it through with her counsellor, and afterwards, I felt almost elated.

I think of myself as 'open', but the truth is, I like to be in control, and am easily embarrassed by other people's strong emotions, and excessively anxious. None of this helps.

Late afternoon. I walked up the lane. Walking back down, a grey squirrel rippled in front of me. Two crows – *caw, caw* – on the topmost twigs of two tall firs, side by side; over them the blue bubble of the sky.

30 JUNE
Almost the end of June; a clouded day, rain on the wind. The brooks have almost dried up again. How quickly the spring & early summer months seem to have gone. Next month it will be a year since we moved in here, and M. went into hospital. Tomorrow she goes to Bristol again for an appointment with a specialist; her arthritis is painful all the time, crippling on some days. Yesterday, at her counsellor's suggestion – she said she would deny it if any official enquired – M. bought some hash, smoked it in the back yard, and was cheerful afterwards. I looked on amazed as she laughed at TV adverts, until she told me she was stoned!

Walking in the woods, I look back with gratitude to the time we have come through – the long wait for the operation, the operation itself, the period of physical insecurity, when I felt afraid to walk even a short way up the lane. Apart from the setback the other day, and some occasions when I felt insecure on the campus, this has been a good period. Good for both of us, in spite of M.'s pain.

8 JULY
M. flew to Amsterdam two days ago, where she's spending a few days with Elin, and will visit Bethan to see her before her baby is born. It's hard for her not to see her daughters for long periods of time, more so now she has a grandson and another grandchild on the way.

Alone in the house, I read a PhD. thesis on Welsh autobiographical writings, and creative writing scripts for the Certificate at Bristol University, and take notes on the ecocritical writings I read earlier. The nights bring loneliness.

Another welcome task has come my way: to write a short introduction to a new edition of *The Story of My Heart*. The thought of writing poems comes and goes. One thing I do know is that my confidence depends upon it. I was thinking the other day that we owe other people, especially those we are close to, confidence in ourselves. Not self-conceit or fall-out from our ambitions, but solidity, competence, being grounded in what we do and who we are. Lifelong, this has been difficult for me.

19 JULY
We returned yesterday from three days & nights on the campus of Exeter University, where we attended the 'Beyond Anthropocentrism' conference and I gave the keynote address. It had been organised by a group of young scholars whose enthusiasm was refreshing. The only sour note was struck by a professor's concluding remarks. The conference hadn't pleased him; he said that he still didn't know what ecocriticism was, and he missed any reference to Marx and Freud in the papers. He had a point – such conferences do have a 'soft' side. But clearly the subject was outside the terms of his discourse. He was, generally, graceless. Mieke was incensed, and told him in front of everybody that she had enjoyed the whole conference, except his contribution, and what he should have done was thank the postgraduates studying in his department, who had organised such a worthwhile event. Others in the audience agreed, and I was proud of her, at the same time as wishing I was somewhere else!

23 October

Mieke was able to come downstairs today, with difficulty. On Monday she was in such pain that we called the doctor. He could do nothing, only write a letter to the hospital stressing the urgency of the situation. Last night I was awake seeing nothing but a blank wall. M. talked to me lovingly & sensibly. How often this is necessary! I have a compulsion to turn difficulties into one complete obstacle. How would it be if it were my pain?

19 November

Having finished making my selection of Wilfred Owen for Gregynog Press, I walked in the woods late in the afternoon. A tiny piece of white down floated in front of me, making me wonder whether there is a God who cares for us. I am outside any community of belief. From the outside, I see the stories people tell one another. And what is the story I tell myself? Sometimes I seem to stand on a bleak bedrock of unbelief. At other times, pleasure in the falling down would suggest a world of mystery beyond it.

It is perhaps a year since I was seriously concerned about M.'s drinking. Nowadays, in spite of frequently being in considerable pain, she shows no desire for alcohol. But we must never become complacent.

I am aware of factors that have made a difference to her. But this morning she told me about another. Light. This house with its big windows, standing on a hillside, receives more light than any other we have lived in. From dawn until dark it is always in the light, and its open aspect, above the valley and looking across to further hills, gives us a wonderful sense of space.

9 December

Anne and Walt came to lunch yesterday. Mieke, in pain, worked heroically to prepare the meal, and is suffering in consequence today. But she knows it is better for her to do what she can, instead of giving in to the pain. There's nothing I can do to stop her anyway. Anne has been rereading my poetry from the beginning; she is a true reader. Could we go on without any? I am lucky to have a few.

Rowan Williams, in a television programme, speaks of God being behind all his self-questioning. I took him to mean that he refers everything to God. This, surely, is the only way, if self-questioning is not to occur in a hall of mirrors, where all is repetition or distortion. And if one does not believe in God? Still there has to be some larger Self, something against which one can see one's ego in all its littleness & deviousness.

11 December

Katrina, who stayed with us after she had been in Clouds House with Mieke, died in August. The news came this morning with her parents' Christmas card. She died of multiple organ failure, as did Christine, I believe, the woman, also in her forties, in the bed opposite me in hospital. 'Bloody alcohol', M. said.

28 December

M. says will-power had nothing to do with her stopping drinking. Nor was it the result of a decision. Her decision had been to enter Clouds House. Then – she used the metaphor of climbing stairs – it was like climbing to the top, and finding the last step very difficult. What has happened to her here is a complete mental & physical change, complex, with many layers. She related it to the light we enjoy in this house with its big windows, the space inside & out. I don't fully understand the causes, and perhaps she doesn't either; but the change is palpable.

2 January 2003

If I'd read *Long Day's Journey into Night* a year or more ago, I would probably have despaired. For O'Neill, the subject was obviously acutely painful, and dramatic – addiction & its effects weren't things he could take for granted, and he looked closely at the society that produced them. I find the drama painful for the same reasons I assume he did, but also because the play bespeaks an earnestness we seem to have lost. It's as if, now, unless it happens to us, we don't care enough when a person or a family disintegrates. I say we don't care as O'Neill did, perhaps because it's become so common, and perhaps because we're inclined to take addiction more lightly.

But that can only be if it doesn't come into our own homes. Here, in South Wales, one young person – usually a man – dies each week as a result of drug addiction.

15 January

In Bristol, staying with Philip and Zélie Gross. We came to Southmead hospital yesterday, at the appointed time. I have just heard that the operation has been carried out, and I hope to be able to speak with Mieke soon, and see her tomorrow.

17 January

Mieke was quite comfortable when I visited her yesterday, but was in pain today. Being lifted between beds for an x-ray had caused her almost to pass out. However, she was feeling a little better by lunchtime, and managed to sleep a bit. The main thing is that the operation was successful.

20 January

Joe picked me up yesterday morning and we went to see Mieke together before driving back to Dan-y-Lan. After a disturbed night I had an early morning dream in which Hayford had begun to collapse and I led the family away. Standing in the garden, I watched things falling out of the blue sky – possibly objects from space. This is a phenomenon I have observed in dreams before, which perhaps contain a memory of wartime. Waking, I felt tense, and became more agitated paying bills for Mieke, and – bastard – expressed my frustration to her over the phone. I am bleak here without her.

2 February

Early days yet, but M. has made some progress during the week, enough to reassure me that she did not leave hospital prematurely. More spring flowers on our lawn. Several more crocus flames in the park, and, nearby, a few impoverished-looking snowdrops, as though barely able to squeeze out a drop of snow. An eye of yellow in the daffodils.

The world has watched, and watched, the disintegration of the space shuttle in the sky over Texas. We have been able to imagine the instantaneous deaths countless times.

8 February

With M. continuing to make progress, life isn't difficult. Some discomfort remains, but she is continuing, little by little, to become more mobile. I know how it is: as she gets stronger, she will find it harder to remain patient. For me, convalescence was a lot easier, since it gave me time to write. I could have retired then. The prospect of retirement doesn't feel real to me yet. At times, when actually teaching, I don't feel older, until I catch sight of myself mirrored in a window. I was amused recently when, as I made way for a student on some stairs, he asked me if I was all right, and I told him I was, 'only slow'. 'Don't worry,' he said politely, 'we all come to it in the end'. I replied with a laugh, and went on my way thinking: *I'm not at the end yet.*

15 February

Mieke stepped over the threshold for the first time since her operation and walked up and down outside the house, delighting in the sun and open air, and taking pleasure in the flowers. Accompanying her watchfully, I saw the first dandelions, wide open on the roadside bank.

22 February

As I have learned from living with M., there are things one can only understand in loneliness. Wonderful as companionship is, one has to know one's spirit alone. And if one doesn't have that knowledge, or rejects it through sinking one's individuality in some mass movement, it's not only oneself, but humanity, that is betrayed.

8 March

According to William Boyd writing about journal-keeping in *The Guardian Review*, 'no true journal worthy of the name can be published while its author is alive'. Honesty, he claims, can only be guaranteed by posthumous publication: 'you have to be dead to escape the various charges of vanity, of special pleading, of creeping amour-propre'.

In my view, dishonesty begins in privacy, when a person keeping a journal deceives himself. I believe it's necessary to feel under scrutiny, not by a prospective reader but by one's 'higher power', which it would be futile to try to deceive. But since, inevitably, one imagines this, it's never possible to be absolutely certain of one's honesty.

I believe in expression, not confession. Expression of feelings, observations, intuitions, ideas, expression leading to self-discovery in the world one shares with others – recognition of one's human needs. Confession echoes only within the self. Expression – however personal – tries to reach below and beyond the ego.

8 April

M. saw the specialist in Bristol today. Another six months to wait for an operation on her left hip. She spoke with emotion of the long period of pain & waiting, when she hasn't been able to do any work; said it could make a person suicidal. We'll have to see whether the impression she made will bring the operation forward.

10 April

I became upset last night when M. told me Joe had said I was becoming like my father. I know what he means (which is why it hurt): my father in retreat from the world, excessively anxious. I've felt it often enough as a risk, known the nervous sickness. But of course, that wasn't all there was to him; he was humorous, sensitive, capable of sympathy, vigorous into old age. I could envy him the vigour he had when he was twenty years older than I am now!

The thing is – whatever the causes – I don't want to retreat. Drawing in, though, is inevitable. Twice today, writing to friends, I've used the expression 'in parentheses' to describe what our life is likely to be like in the months ahead, as M. waits for, and has, her operation. What I have to avoid is thinking myself into a state that means self-absorption, anxiety, the pride or vanity that dwells on failure, absence of creativity. My dad was often a delightful man – artist, gardener, singer, completely absorbed in what he was doing, or, with 'that smile of his', (as my brother Tony called it) talking with an originality that couldn't be imitated. It would be a great mistake for me to think that what I received from him was, mainly, harm.

13 APRIL

In my dream a poet had decided to commit suicide. The point seemed to be (as I discussed it with M. on waking) the suicidal tendency, as I see it, in 'confessional' verse. This led us to talk about healing poetry, and John Barnie's view that 'perhaps this is impossible in our times'. It would be presumptuous for any poet to think of him or herself as a healing poet. Prone to periodic depressions and a recurrent sense of failure, I have found healing through Mieke, and in learning to look away from myself. She surprised me – no surprise could have been more welcome – by saying that this direction in my thinking & writing confirmed something she was unable to articulate, and has helped to save her in the years of her sickness. It has helped her to look out, literally, at the wild life in the space surrounding us, and to escape from despondency at her condition, which would otherwise imprison her inside herself.

15 APRIL

Twenty years ago today, at the Poetry Festival reception in Cambridge, M. and I met for the first time. I remember walking there with Glen Cavaliero, who fell in with George Steiner – and I couldn't think of anything to say to him, or he to me. Later M. told me I was 'the most miserable looking man' at the reception, which I can well believe. The attraction between us was immediate, and really, from that moment, I've never felt alone.

27 April
At Buckland Hall for the last morning of the annual Vaughan colloquium. A car journey of some 45 minutes, but what differences within the distances covered. All one work this Wales, Roland Mathias wrote; which is true. Wales is a land strongly marked by human labour over long periods of time, and sometimes one can feel the mountains have looked down on it impassively, though they too have been marked by the work of human hands. Marked but, here, not spoiled, their grandeur undiminished.

It wasn't certain that M. would be able to come. It had to be her decision; but she was determined. She's been shut in, with little company, for too long. And she was received with such love, and was, among friends, in her element.

14 June
Early start, M. driving, for Credenhill, where, in the church, I gave the opening talk of the Traherne Festival. Immediately after my talk an elderly woman approached me, and thanked me, with emotion, for what I had said about Edward Thomas. She was the daughter of Julian, Edward's younger brother.

After lunch, on what had turned out to be another hot day, we drove home, but stopped first at Kilpeck, and then at Abbey Dore in the Golden Valley. The admixture of paganism & Christianity has been strong in the Marches, as we see in the work of the Hereford sculptors at Kilpeck, in that wonderful gallery of mages, which must once have spoken to men & women, admonishing and encouraging them, as they cannot speak to us. It's the work that I think of, always, the work and the worship, embodied in the buildings, and connecting them to the fields among which they are situated. Abbey Dore, in its valley, struck me as being a ghost, with most of the colour gone from its walls, together with the life of the Cistercians. Bereft of its function, the deteriorating building haunts our world with a remnant of its former function.

21 June
After the reading in Winchester Cathedral, which I shared with nine other poets, I asked Mieke what she thought of the cathedral. She spoke of its 'threatening silence' and compared it to Wells Cathedral, which says, 'Come in and be safe', while Winchester says, 'Come in and obey'. She referred to its 'masculinity', and said, 'its presence is its power'. That accords with my impression too; but, standing under the west window

looking down the nave, I was struck by the immense grandeur of the contained space but also, simultaneously, by the grace imparted to it by the tall slender columns. At the same time, I was uneasily aware of the irrelevance of such aesthetic judgements, and conscious of my unsteady tread on the uneven paving stones. At night a thunderstorm broke, and I lay in bed in our hotel room watching lightning illuminating the bulk of the cathedral.

26 JULY
Yesterday ended with M. drinking. I had felt this coming after tension during Elin's visit. M. feels Elin criticises her. It seems to me that what she is seeing is guilt at the past, which she converts into anger, while perhaps knowing at some level what she is doing. All very complicated, as we humans tend to be. Even loving family relationships can be so painful. I don't see how they could *not* be. I don't value them less.

12 AUGUST
This is weather in which I feel desperately mortal. Walking with M. in Caerphilly – two sticks & one stick – among the crowd of able-bodied people of all ages, I *saw* us tottering along, and wondered how at our ages we had come to seem so old. 'Wrong question', M. would have said, rightly, as she does to any hypothetical question that temps me to self-pity. And in truth, while loathing the oppressive weather outside – more so these days when it smells of human-created pollution – I have enjoyed writing in the shade of my room.

26 AUGUST
A late summer morning, cool and still. Rosebay-willow-herb seeds almost ready to take to the air, a few already airborne.

Mieke is struggling within herself at the uncertain prospect that she will be crippled. I'm not always the help I should be, when I focus on myself. In fact, we are both having to come to terms with being older and less physically able.

27 SEPTEMBER
Towards the end of the long vacation, which I've used mainly for work. A good feeling not to be too far behind myself. With the poems, I've written more this summer than I expected to.

'One day at a time,' M. wisely says, with regard to our health & mobility. True (and a lesson I have to relearn daily), but it's a pleasure to record that she has been experiencing less pain, and in consequence has been able to be more active, recently.

25 JANUARY 2004
It annoys M. when I talk about myself in public as though I think myself a failure, and it puts a strain on her when I do it in private. I tell her this is how I am, and my thinking flows from it. I talk about original sin. But I know too that it is a form of egotism – the phrase *negative narcissism*, which I came upon recently, sums it up well.

FROM THIS MOMENT: how often I have said that to myself, meaning, I will not repeat these faults, but live from now by the best I am capable of. Everything points to the necessity: the people whose lives one affects, one's sense of purpose, the world outside the window – here, now, the Taff-Bargoed valley on a Sunday morning filled with smoky light. What I see looking out is magnificent indifference – a world that is not me or these thoughts, but whose reality I have to recognise. When I first looked, there was a magpie on the top of the fir-tree across the road. Somehow just the sheer fact of it took me out of myself, made me aware of this moment, now: the need to begin.

29 FEBRUARY
I have become less certain of some things since I first lived in Wales, and certainty seems to go on declining as I grow older, but the thing is to live and work creatively with unknowing – by definition, a hard thing to know how to do!

Yet if I can do it, that's because I owe an enormous amount to the stability of my marriage, of the love M. and I have for one another. This is a great gift, and if I ever forget it, out of sheer security, I'm completely self-deceived. If I'm able sometimes to venture out, unknowing, that's because *our* place is where I start from, and to which I come back.

28 MARCH
Yesterday's class, on Kerouac's *On the Road*, was definitely the last for this academic year. Afterwards a student, a young man, came into my office and talked with such openness and enthusiasm that I was reminded how much this job has given me over the years.

M. has felt she is 'burning up inside' and at the same time not in her skin since receiving steroid injections. This has led to drinking in recent days. She's in pain, and she suffers from not being able to see her grandchildren more often, and her friend Elly is seriously ill.

4 May
Wind rising in the night – nearing full moon – cats howling inside & outside the house. M. very tired after being active while Elin & Ian were with us.

Earlier she listened sympathetically while I complained – fool – about my general sense of deterioration. I'd like to turn my age around and be 36 again – but was there ever a time I didn't complain? Now, the subject is health, age – in the sense that I formed my expectations on the examples of my father and grandfather, whose lives were very different from mine. I feel acutely my lack of potency in all respects; the effort it costs me simply to walk around. I won't be again the man I was physically, robust, careless of health. But I still have my mind, my spirit.

'You have your work', M. says. I know too how much I owe to her, and the support she needs – the support we need of each other.

It was always my ambition to write the poetry of each stage of life, including – as I hoped – old age. It's a nice question, of course, whether I was ever that kind of poet, e.g., writing a young man's verse, etc. Not perhaps obviously, as a form of self-expression, but by implication, yes, I think I have. In any case, somewhere to go on from.

25 June
Back and forth to the hospital in Merthyr, where Mieke was admitted two days ago. She had been feeling very tired for some time; we suspected anaemia, and eventually I persuaded her to see the doctor who arranged for a blood test. The important thing is, she is now where she needs to be. The doctor & consultant have impressed us, and M. says the atmosphere on the ward is caring. It makes such a difference. The young Indian doctor who first examined her was especially gentle & considerate – he & the nurse even likened me to Sean Connery, a piece of flattery that made us all laugh, and therefore no doubt had the desired effect. Yes, it makes such a difference! We have both been used to being treated like body parts. It's kindness and efficiency one wants – it makes for good medicine, too.

9 August
Towards evening, Marla died. This was the little kitten Megan Arnold found up a tree. Later they discovered a litter of kittens drowned in a local stream, and assumed she had escaped. For a period when I lived at Buckland Dinham, she was my only companion, sleeping on my bed, and running away mischievously, with tail up, when she got outdoors. At Old Schoolhouse she had her only litter of kittens, when she was still very young. Mieke helped her with the difficult births, and sat with her now for a while, wrapped up in a silk scarf. She'll lie on a table in the yard overnight, and I'll bury her in the morning.

31 August
In the dream I had given up my professorship, doubtful whether I had done the right thing, and gone to work with a team of people on the land. I was disabled, but not incapable, and worked clearing brambles, nettles, grass with an older man and others, with whom I discussed serious questions. Would I fit in? Was this what I really wanted? I would have to give up writing criticism, but could write poetry when free from work. M. wasn't in the dream, but seemed to be behind the chance I had been offered.

Responding to *Arnolds Wood*, Fiona Owen spoke of language 'alive to the deeper river that runs through our lives'. That's the truth I want of poetry. Is one dependent on others to know whether one has achieved it? On one or two maybe. And is that enough? When it occurs, it feels like everything.

26 November
Mieke is recovering her equilibrium after a crisis brought on by drinking. I had been keeping an eye on a box of wine bottles which she had ordered to have in the house over Christmas. The box appeared to be intact until, finding an empty bottle in the house, I discovered a hole in the bottom of the box! Emotions come back from the bad days: fear, anger, a sense of helplessness. A distance opens up between us – in drink, she is unreachable.

Easter Monday 2005
First purple violets under firs. There seem to be no thrushes in the park this spring. Usually the place rings with their song.

"'Nowadays', declared a writer in 1603, 'very few exceed the age of sixty-three, because that year is fatal and climacterical'" (Keith Thomas, *Religion and the Decline of Magic)*

There were times when I wondered whether I would survive my 'grand climacteric'. While the mind can leap, the body creeps and totters; and after a while there's a temptation for the mind too to imitate a snail, and confine itself to the body's limits.

8 MAY
Mieke, on the eve of her birthday, had a terrible night. Pain in her arthritic bones, but her whole system, body, mind & spirit, in turmoil. I dressed again and lay on the bed wondering whether to call an ambulance. As she became a little calmer, I read her a story, Sarah Orne Jewett's 'A White Heron', and this and my voice had a soothing effect. Later she went to sleep, and I, too, slept.

It's hard to tell how critical these episodes are. There's something here she's experienced periodically lifelong. But now the arthritic pains are crippling, and she worries acutely about the children. Her birthday is another cause. She says they bring back to her that she was 'unwanted'. And of course, she worries about *our* condition, my health as well as hers, our greater difficulties in day to day living, and the uncertain prospect.

11 MAY
Good food, good friends: a meal to celebrate Mieke's birthday with Norman and Deborah at the Riverside Chinese restaurant. Afterwards we walked in the space outside the Millennium Centre under the splendid façade inscribed with Gwyneth Lewis's poem. (I see that J.C., *TLS* Commentary, says: 'We can't see how this is a poem at all'. 'We', presumably, have no sense of concrete poetry.) We had the space to ourselves. Gulls flying above the neon lights were a ghostly orange.

29 AUGUST
'Summer is over,' M. said, as we looked out of the window this morning. A season in between: nuts & berries ripening, a few yellow leaves falling from birches, leaves turning golden-brown on horse-chestnuts. Three jays flying across the hillside, silently.

Walking down the lane the idea came to me of a study of poetry and power: the power of poetry, and its opposition/relation to other powers. This springs from my thinking about poetry and the sacred, but indicates a further step. It also has a bearing on the poetry I want to write.

But first things first!

14 October

Joe visited and stayed overnight with us during the week. He is gaunt and looks ill. He will die if he doesn't beat his addiction – again. There was a fearful row on the evening of his arrival. M. had been drinking, and out of concern for him and in the mistaken belief that I'm not awake to the situation, shouted, instead of listening. I find both their addictions impossible to deal with – one can't deal with another person's addiction; it can only be endured, or not.

17 October

Message from Joe: he and his new partner will be attending the Drugs Help Centre this afternoon. With other travellers, they're squatting a former industrial works yard & buildings in Brockley.

Mieke walked a little way into the woods with me on a damp morning. A pleasure, and an effort, but she's more mobile following her hip replacement operation than for some years.

Sometimes I wonder whether I shall ever write poetry again. I feel that a shift has occurred, due partly to external conditions – the political & ecological crises of the new millennium – and partly to the erosion of my idea of returning to home ground. Yet I know, too, that focus is the issue. A poet often doesn't know what he has to say before he says it. Saying doesn't inhere in message or moral, but in animate language, in the whole poetic process. When the time comes, I believe that I will surprise myself.

17 November

Mieke spent part of the morning in a prison cell at Aberdare after having an accident in the car in Treharris. She wasn't badly hurt and no one else was involved, but she was tested for alcohol and found to be over the limit. The young policeman who dealt with the incident was very decent.

There have been recurrent bouts of drinking recently, but the problem has rarely been absent for any length of time since I first became aware of it, in the year M. went into Clouds House. Overconfidence is part of it – the assurance that she's in control; but now she's deeply shaken, and faces the probability of public exposure and the loss of her license. This could work for the better. This could be 'rock bottom'.

18 November

Stiff frost overnight followed by a most beautiful, cloudless day. Worked towards a lecture on Emily Dickinson and took a walk in the park in mid-afternoon, the brief twilight already beginning to flare. Frost remained on dark, turned soil. Mossed bark on the big oaks & beeches was beautifully dry to the touch.

M. quiet & remorseful, still shaken by what she has done. We began to talk in the morning, and, of course, she said Never again. What's ever clearer to me is that she needs a life outside the house, where she can use her gifts. The falling out on the part of her closest friend living nearby in the summer has left her dangerously isolated, as it has upset me, too. We must break out of this isolation.

16 DECEMBER

Mieke contrived to buy a bottle of whisky at the supermarket when I wasn't looking. Later, in a state, she told the doctor she was suicidal (the only way to get his attention) and he referred her immediately to the Psychiatric Assessment Centre at St Tydfil's hospital in Merthyr. I drove her over there the same day, and she spent time with the team, a young doctor & his assistant. She came away feeling more secure and better able to cope. Since then, she's been sleeping better too – an irregular pattern of sleep being part of the problem.

29 DECEMBER

I want to think about why I keep a journal with a view to writing a short preface to 'Upstate: A North American Journal', which is now ready to submit for publication.

Julian Green, in the first entry in his *Diary 1928–1957,* writes: 'This diary... will help me, I think to see more clearly into myself'. That wasn't what made me want to start a journal when I was a student. Rather, it was a sense of wonder. Later in his diary, Green speaks of obeying 'the incomprehensible desire to bring the past to a standstill that makes one keep a diary'.

That's more like it: to capture the moment, which one knows is impossible. Seeing, of course, has been a large part of my aim. Seeing nature, appreciating and, as far as possible, understanding what I see. Knowing myself in relation to the life around me. Knowing the people through love

Knowing, in this sense, and knowing the limits of knowing, isn't separable from thinking. So, I use my journal to think with. I found in Richard Jefferies' journal and essays the determination I so admire: to think to the end. I'd say this is a characteristic of every poet who has negative capability, because there is no end; the writer is always in doubts & uncertainties.

I keep a journal for pleasure, too. I love the form and the pleasures of the form, in, for example, Dorothy Wordsworth, Coleridge, Kilvert, Thoreau. I love the detail of their seeing/sensing: the sensation of life.

And, of course, a journal is selective. I aim to be truthful, but know I am living in the dark; there must be things about myself I don't know. One reveals oneself in the totality of a journal, in what one chooses to see and value, and also in what one doesn't see. All I know to do is to keep my eye on the object, whether sensation or feeling or thought. *Self*-consciousness in any other sense is not what I seek

13 FEBRUARY 2006

On Saturday night I came downstairs to find Mieke sitting on the sofa acting like a person in a trance. After I had helped her up, with difficulty, she fell and cut her hip. Later, when she talked about the episode, she had no memory of it, and no memory of drinking. On Sunday, at a meal with friends, she was herself, beautiful, intelligent, charming and we both enjoyed ourselves. It's the contrast that baffles me, the ugliness of M. stupefied, out of control, scaring me at the time, and scaring herself afterwards at not remembering, and the person I know her to be.

11 APRIL

A change to cloud & rain after several bright, warm days during which Mieke's old friend, Hetty, from Tilburg, stayed with us. One morning Hetty talked to me about death & dying. She believes absolutely in the survival of consciousness – in her professional work she helps the dying, and she has experienced what sounds like a kind of out of body state. She sees 'things' also – auras, and misty figures of the dead. She spoke of seeing the latter in the woods above the house – peaceful forms in what she felt was a happy state. I'm not sure what I feel about all this, but it chimed in my mind with what the woman at Llangwyryfon said about the presence of past generations in that area. I'm not the least 'psychic', but a solid materialist when it comes to what I actually sense, but this idea of the continuing presence of the dead accords with what I've always felt, though I'd be hard put to explain what I mean by 'presence'.

Easter Sunday

From the moorland above Gelligaer, a view of the Brecon Beacons partly veiled by cloud. Lambs with their mothers on the moor.

We went in hope of hearing a skylark, and did. As soon as I stopped the engine and we got out of the car, we heard several larks, high up, out of sight, their notes falling on us like a thin refreshing musical rain.

This helped to clear my head of a shouting evangelist I was unlucky to catch on TV performing to a large enthusiastic audience.

2 May

The Cut of the Light has arrived. Two boxes of books, their arrival coinciding with the beginning of the summer marking.

A handsome volume. Stephen Stuart-Smith has done me proud – again. He's a good friend to me & my work.

40 years of my poetry in print. How do I feel about the work? Don't really know, except never satisfied. I can rarely see my own poetry except as something to go on from. It's desirable to avoid false modesty; but that's not what this is. Knowing that one hasn't 'arrived' – and never will – is partly why one ventures.

8 May

M.'s 60th birthday. In the evening Elin took us with Ian to a pub near Bedwas where we had a meal. This wasn't up to much, but M. had a good day.

Ian is a bright affectionate little boy. And I am a tetchy old man, irritated, as my father was, by children playing loudly around me.

I know how lucky I am with M. Constancy in love was the one thing I always sought. I suppose that was the form my romanticism took, even in days when drawn to any attractive woman. Oh well, still drawn, but now I know what constancy means.

27 July

M. was on a bender recently. These recur, and isolate us within ourselves, or she's oblivious, and I can only look on, and wait for the episode to pass. I feel powerless and afraid, and my weakness makes me ashamed. Once the cloud lifts, we're together as we have been from the first.

20 August

A wonderful party organised by Mieke and Bethan to celebrate our birthdays (65 & 60) this year, and our 20th wedding anniversary (in October). Joe arrived on Saturday, looking much better than last time, thank God! Maddy came with Chloe & Holly, and Bryan had a marvellous time with them, playing and falling in love. Many friends, including Lee & Kate, joined us outside and inside the house. Towards evening, Jim played and sang to us, circled round him in the yard. He sang with all the old zest, and more than a little of the beauty, that I remember from nearly 50 years ago. It was a glorious day, although, afterwards, M. was annoyed with me because I had persuaded Bethan and Ard to take away all the drink that was left over.

6 October

Continuing wind & rain. Now, the sound of the brook is loud enough to be heard in the house. Flashes of light on water & wet leaves as clouds cover and uncover the sun. Not the great fall yet, but flurries of leaves on the wind.

End of my first full teaching week. Yesterday, walking in rain the short distance from car to class, weighed down by the Norton Shakespeare, I wondered whether I would make it. After the class, I came home exhausted.

Classes are larger this year, and I teach by generating energy/enthusiasm; it's the only way I know. I would like to get through this year, which should be my last full year of teaching. And be able afterwards to continue working on poems, completing the prose books, starting new work.

21 October

Forty years since the black mountain came down on the school at Aberfan. Vincent Kane observed that the children who died would have grown up to have different occupations, except one – none would have been a coal miner.

22 December

Mieke fell heavily last night. I heard the noise downstairs, and found her sitting on the edge of the shower unable to get up. She didn't seem to be hurt, only in an alcoholic daze. I had thought her ill during the day – as she was, but I still don't always know the difference.

She seems to have given up, lost her old spirit. What happened to the idea of herself as a healer, which was more than an idea? 'It isn't about *you*', she'll say, at times when I speak despairingly. Isn't it? Obviously, I'm affected. But I wonder, too, whether I've failed her, and whether she'd be better off without me.

She is a different person – even looks different – under the influence. How can that be? It's this, though, that has enabled me to go on: the fact that the M. I love is *not* the one who makes herself almost a *thing*, spiritless, corpse-like, but sometimes, when questioned or criticised, cruelly abusive.

Part of the problem is boredom, isolation. I have my work in the university and my writing, But the roots of the problem were apparent in Frome, where she refused to make herself known, so that she could obtain work.

I know the problem isn't me, unless it's my inability to force what might be a healing crisis, by walking out. Anyone close to her would be part of the problem, if only by becoming part of the life she finds difficult from day to day. As a disabled man, without the passion I once had to take her out of herself…

At times like last night I fear the future. Yet when M. talks and I hear hope in her voice and see it in her face, I can forget the nightmare of only hours before.

1 JANUARY 2007

We saw in the New Year with Jim & Liz, enjoying a splendid meal which Mieke had prepared (a brace of pheasants) and drinking wine & champagne. (The thing with M., as we agree, is to make drinking a shared, convivial activity, instead of secret. It has worked over the Christmas period.)

For us, the great event of the year was the party in August, a joyous occasion, in the company of friends & family. For me, the publication of *The Cut of the Light*, marking forty years of poetry. Intellectually, I have gained mainly from immersing myself in 'nature' writing – J. A. Baker, Darwin, Rachel Carson and contemporary British and American poets. Helped by my thinking and reading, I feel the beginning of a new way.

14 JANUARY

M. made herself very ill towards the end of the week. Over the past two days she's been fragile, vulnerable, and I've felt drained, but we've fought the demons together. Today, I had to prepare Scott Fitzgerald's 'An Alcoholic Case' for a class next week…

Nothing scares me more than the thought of losing her. What we feel she must regain is her sense of herself as a healer, which is her essential self. Without it, she becomes bored, empty, and prey to self-hatred. The compulsion is terrible. May she find strength – be given strength.

2 FEBRUARY
I received what at first was a nasty shock last week with an official invitation to deliver my inaugural professorial lecture in December. Mieke was delighted and encouraged me to accept. In fact, I've also got quite excited by the idea. This will also be valedictory, of course, and I must say something about the ground I have tried to cover. But I want also to point forwards – in any case, it's never arrival I have to speak of.

11 MARCH
This has been a critical period with M. drinking, followed by remorse and the most serious, heartfelt talks we have ever had. Ah, talks! But I think we both see how critical the situation is, harming her, but also threatening our life together. My own struggle now is greater than it was twelve years ago in Frome, when M.'s problem first surfaced. I didn't then feel the temptation to give up, which comes with dwindling energy. But all is changed now: if there's to be a future for us, we'll have to make it.

I want to go through this. I want to go on. And our life together has always been *us*, however self-centred I am, however secretive M. is. I've known in recent months that I could tip over into a life of sloth, not because I want to, but because my energy is low. In these circumstances, M.'s addiction drags me down – fear of the hurt she does herself, always, but also the sheer lifelessness, when she is under the influence, and the repetition, and the lack of trust.

She is her own worst victim. And I want to cry out against my obsession with her obsession, because I know that none of this is her true self, and how much she gives me.

26 MARCH
I dream every night, but usually forget it all when I wake. Mieke says one can learn to remember one's dreams. I'd like to; for there's this sense of another life within one's mind, a life with its own creative principle. This is dreams' importance: the fact that their language of image and story is soluble, transformative, so that reality isn't only a hard given we have to accept. Dreams are a form of poetry which practically every mind makes

beyond or perhaps at the margin of consciousness. Without that margin, we may perish of our fixed ideas, the images we are sold.

EASTER
In this beautiful weather the woods are lyrical with blackbirds' songs. Sun's reflections blinding in the brook. First bluebell half-opened among daffodils and vibrant grass blades. Stooping to what I think is a pussy willow flower, a small fluffy yellow thing, I find it's a dead nestling.

Anxiety is affecting my mind, corrupting me, making me silly and, sometimes, cruel. One morning I pick up a glass of Lucozade and find it mixed with whisky. At first M. is genuinely baffled. 'Where did that come from?' I'm constantly alert for tell-tale signs, and find it difficult to think about anything else.

8 MAY
Mieke's birthday. In the morning we learnt that Elly had died at 6 a.m. Her voice on the phone rings in my head; I had spoken to her only days ago. She was one of Mieke's closest friends, utterly loyal. I too was very fond of her. M.'s reaction was to think of her – that she died without pain – and her family. One good woman thinking of another.

28 MAY
Spiritless Whitsun. We're both unwell, suffering from a virus that began more than a month ago. M. is worse, with a cough that leaves her feeling drained. I drag myself round indoors – read – watch TV – sleep – drive into the university to hand in marks. Older, one is less resilient: it's one of the things one has to learn, however many times one has seen other people grow older.

14 JULY
Nightmare start to a journey down the Neath valley to visit Jim & Liz at Tonna. M. had been drinking in the night and now refused to stop the car and let me drive. I shouldn't have let her start, but hadn't realized she was still under the influence. After a few hazardous miles, I did persuade her to stop, and took over. But I was aware during the whole visit that she was still in a state that makes her unsteady and artificial, so that I was ill at ease, and couldn't do justice to the fish curry Jim had made.

4 AUGUST
While we were shopping together in Morrisons, M. bought a bottle of whisky without me noticing. Drank most of it in the night together with some other drinks (meant to be shared) and was under the influence during our friend's visit. It poisons our life together. I really don't think I can go on with this if it continues. It's a compulsion, which the secrecy is part of. I fear less for her health now than for all her most important relationships; for a life with meaning.

When she is herself again, I feel nothing but death can ever separate us.

5 AUGUST
With M. on the moorland above Bedlinog, Beacons a hazy blue-green to the north. Here we found a strong fresh warm breeze. Purple thistles and the warm smell of moorland vegetation and shorn sheep. A solitary raven was flying round overhead, and, a few yards from the car, I found what might have been a dead one. But it could have been a crow – it had deteriorated too much to tell.

Today we spoke positively of the future, planning to move into a smaller house on the coast. If I live, this will become necessary within a year or two of my retirement. I long to be near the sea, to smell it and see it and be by it, now I can no longer walk far. When M. is well, when she is herself, such things seem possible.

18 OCTOBER
Mother died fifteen years ago on a cold clear starlit night. A believer might speak of being born into death, and fantasise about being young or old in that 'other world', because the living can only think in terms of life and time. Eternity teases us out of thought, Keats says. Did Hardy invent the word 'existlessness'? It's strange to think there are words for things we can't think.

31 OCTOBER
I have set in motion the process that may enable me to continue working beyond my scheduled retirement date. Is this wise? Financially, the choice is between this and living on a small pension. It's the involvement I want, the contact.

I sometimes think, sardonically, that, as the poet, I should be the one drinking and self-harming. That would be a conventional sad story. But what M. does to herself is no joke. It's a terrible thing I'm witnessing in a person who gives so much, and has so much to give, yet somehow lacks self-belief. This is part of the story, but what the underlying causes are, neither of us knows.

20 December
Already nine days since my inaugural professorial lecture, which was a wonderful occasion with many friends in attendance. Afterwards I was presented with a handsome volume of poems and essays in my honour which Chris Meredith and Jane Aaron had edited and John Coch had published, and for which Lee had provided the cover illustration. Colin Edwards and Richard Kerridge from Bath Spa presented me with a framed photograph, and Ceri Thomas with one of his engravings. It was all a marvellous honouring, conducted with great warmth.

Afterwards I felt dazed and a little empty. M. was as happy as I've ever seen her, and tremendously pleased and proud. She had kept the secret of the *festschrift* almost until the end, and only partially revealed it when I began to panic and spoke of cancelling the lecture.

In the days following, she lapsed, perhaps partly because of the earlier tension. After triumph, disaster. In consequence there's been a strangeness about this period, an intellectual vacuum, filled with Christmas shopping! As far as my work is concerned, I feel the lecture marks a boundary, drawing a line round what I have sought to do, and pointing beyond.

6 January 2008
M. determined not to drink after a period over Christmas & the New Year when, heartbreakingly, she made herself ill. Tomorrow I go into the university for the first class of my last term of teaching. May I be able to get around and do the work!

28 February
Last lecture in full-time employment: on Metaphysical poetry to a first-year class. Afterwards a young man came up to ask me to repeat something I had said. From his notes, it looked as though he had been trying to follow me word for word. His interest cheered me. It's reward enough.

6 March
M. in crisis, drinking.

My last seminar, on Raymond Carver's 'Are These Actual Miles?' A small, silent class, so I talked for an hour. Home in the afternoon, I felt washed out.

Talked at M. Not much of a start to 'the first day of the rest of my life'.

Sometimes I feel she knows me through & through and I don't know her at all. I've always been a fool as far as women are concerned. But, between us, from the beginning, everything has been different. Yet she can't trust herself, and while I would trust her with my life, it's impossible to be confident in her from day to day. I can't see us going on like this until the end of our lives. Or without each other.

A crisis rarely lasts long – a day, two or three days – and when it is over, and M. comes back to herself, I realise how fortunate I am, and how easy life is for me most of the time. Alone during a crisis, I have a sense of what real loneliness must be like for those who have no one – loneliness that has not been chosen. In a way, I'm too simple to understand alcoholism. Nothing in my family or personal history prepared me for this. Even my experience of depression is different – something that passes, like a life-killing shadow, that moves on to reveal an essentially stable, sunny landscape.

23 March

67 today. As old men & women over the ages have known, life is short. But to each, perhaps, as to me now, it comes as a surprise to realize how the years have fled. It's almost as if I could reach out and touch the young man I was, or look inside and find him. We each live in face of the door that can never be opened again. And time that remains, for me, is to live with, and work with, grateful that, although slower, mentally as well as physically, I still have my wits about me.

13 April

Can she stop? If she doesn't, what will become of us?

There have been times when, if I were able-bodied, or if I'd anywhere to go, I might have walked away. But the truth is, we're bound to one another, not against our wills, but because we want to be. What's most telling, perhaps, is that during a period of sobriety, *when she is herself*, I forget the time before, which has almost driven me mad with desperation.

The bad times bring out things about myself that I loathe and feel ashamed of: weaknesses, moralising, cruel words. This helps me to know myself, as constantly living in the warmth of our happiness would not. So, I could be grateful, if she didn't harm herself!

24 May
'All is good' were the only words Mieke's mother, who didn't speak English, spoke to me. Which was true then, and is true now. I realise how the litany of complaint will sound to anyone who ever reads it. But the truth is, I wouldn't have – or have had – any other life. The waste is terrible, the risk frightening, but the bad times are like a nightmare in our waking lives, which we share in love & harmony.

6 June
My last meeting in college two days ago, when my mind went back over similar meetings, at Bath, at Groningen, at Aberystwyth over the years.
    So that's it, I thought, remembering walking down to my first class, through the woods from Dan-y-coed, with shining morning face & new leather briefcase, to my room in Old College, Aberystwyth. How little I knew then about how to teach, and little enough about the texts I was teaching. Was it worth it? For some students, some of the time. For me, a lot of the time, with difficult periods. But it would be foolish to attempt a summing up, and perhaps dangerous, when feeling unwell, as I do now. I feel strange thinking of that young man walking down through the woods, the sea showing through trees, about to begin.

8 July
Joe rang this morning, from a ward in Brighton Hospital, with his son Harry crying – they sounded like happy noises – in his arms. I remembered the day of Joe's birth, also in Sussex in July. That too was near the sea, but I looked from an upper window on rain pouring down and standing in pools on a flat roof. Now, my son with his son was commanding a view of the Downs and looking out over the pier at the sea. Different again from my entry into the world during an air raid. How will it be for Harry, I wonder, with two sisters to spoil him, and in a world different from his father's as well as mine?

17 July.
M. is recovering with bruised ribs after backing the car across the lane and into a wall. She had no knowledge that she had been drinking in the night. The unconsciousness, and what it might have led to, shocked both of us. As it was, the car was wrecked, probably beyond repair. She is determined now to go back to AA.

13 SEPTEMBER
This demon, I say, this thing, and it's like that, for this isn't her, this isn't Mieke. Bethan speaks of Jekyll and Hyde. And this comes close; this is what I've seen, which is completely different from all my previous experience. I thought I knew something of the demonic ways of the mind from my own experiences of depression & anxiety. But, compared to this, I knew *nothing*.

When she's possessed by this thing, it poisons life at root. But for me, there's something about it like the weather. Mieke being herself, smiling, calls back the sun, as if it had never been away!

21 SEPTEMBER
What I know now – talk with my old friend, Noah, confirmed this – is that if Mieke's self-harm and danger to others continues, I shall have to seek outside help, and may have to get her hospitalized. It may be the only way of saving her health and her sanity. Noah's understanding helped a great deal, and I was able to talk freely and express my feelings to him. But what helped most was something Joe said on the phone: 'She's not a bad person. You must realise, it's a disease'. I have realised. But also, angry & desperate & sorry for myself, forgotten. And I've talked, talked at Mieke, *moralized*. All to no effect, except for the damage it does me. Now, I have to hold fast to the knowledge.

4 DECEMBER
A visit from David & Maryke Tress, who brought me David's painting *Green Winter Spring (Celandine)* which M. has given me as a retirement present. It is a work with the feeling of spring: a little yellow among the early green, nesh (a word I first heard from Kim Taplin), meaning weak, sensitive to cold, vulnerable life in its first freshness. A quickening that both delights and hurts, as returning life does.

7 DECEMBER
We are at the end now of a bad period of M.'s drinking, which, for me, cast a shadow over visits from friends. Shyness, I know, is part of the deep trouble she has of being herself with other people, that I do and do not understand. It's a terrible condition, and we both know, in cold, sober light, where it will lead. I talk, of course, and when we talk together, there's hope. But sometimes it seems all I can do is watch, and take measures to prevent her from doing herself more harm. The compulsion for M. is the

secrecy. In a different way, I too live secretively, since there are few people, apart from M. herself, with whom I can share what preoccupies me. And even to speak of it to myself offers little help, because of mere repetition.

3 JANUARY 2009
My lost Christmas this year. On the evening of the 23rd (I think) the pain in my right leg was so acute I could no longer stand. M. called an ambulance, which took me to Prince Charles Hospital in Merthyr Tydfil. Diagnosis: sciatica. Undramatic, but causing sharp spasmodic pain when my leg jack-knifes leaving me helpless. I think it was probably the evening of Boxing Day, when Joe was sitting on my bed talking with me, that Mieke, who had been drinking, fell over downstairs, bruising her face and breaking her nose.

Through the window, I've watched blackbirds & tits pecking at the last apples on the tree, until the fruit fell or was consumed. On nights which have been still & frosty, I've heard owls. Awake, I've wrestled with Rowan Williams's *Wrestling with Angels*.

20 JANUARY
In the watches of the night, I am afraid. The pain has diminished, but recurs. I make slow progress, followed by none, or a step back. I think of the stroke and its aftermath, of being more disabled. And in the dark, in memory, time shuts up like a telescope – boyhood, first marriage, early fatherhood, the years teaching, all gone. Strength of mind remains, but physical weakness doesn't affect the body alone.

27 JANUARY
Mist in the valley today, but less in my mind than there's been at times during the past month.

There are, no doubt, different reasons for believing in God, and for disbelieving. Belief, for me, has always related to the need to believe in an all-seeing, all-caring 'mind', a power far beyond anything we can conceive, immediate always & to everyone & thing – its most poetic expression, care for the fall of a sparrow. It's against this idea that I see all human knowing. What I scorn is most thinking *about* God – thinking which inevitably measures 'him' in human terms – and thinking that is confident about 'his' non-existence. I don't hide in mystery. I do find mystery whenever my thought delves into being. The only wisdom is like St Thomas's: to know that all one's mental efforts are straw.

19 February
Early morning: an idea for a piece on my father's paintings. Then I slept, and dreamed of swimming, fearlessly, buoyed up by the depth of water below me, in the sea between the mainland and the Isle of Wight.

Most days now I can get to my desk for an hour or so. But I'm usually on half-days out of bed, and walk about the house with difficulty.

St David's Day
In the park, walking on earth again, while M. waited for me with the car by the bandstand. Only a short way over uneven ground, which felt a little like shifting sand under my unsteady tread. For encouragement, what I must remember are the nightmare steps from the ambulance to the house, and weeks of near immobility.

Daffodil spikes, with a little yellow beginning to show. How assertive they appear, thrusting from bare earth.

No one can live in a state of constant amazement, but nothing is more startling than to wake up to the fact of being alive.

9 April
Working on my paper, 'The Poetry of Touch', for the Vaughan Colloquium. Dandelions almost everywhere, common & breathtakingly beautiful. White pear blossom, which washes the eyes. Small red fists of blossom on the crab-apple trees.

In the shrubbery outside the house, a sherry bottle half to three-quarters full. M. says it must have been there for a month, that she's been free of drink for this period. I want to believe her, but there's always this shadow, this corrosive suspicion. I rarely deal with it wisely, becoming childish in my nagging, and joking nervously when I should be silent.

30 April
Speaking to me on the phone, Elizabeth Bewick (who will be 90 tomorrow) said how her limited ability to get out and about affected her poetry. The same is true for me. It's not just the life of sensation I miss – seeing & feeling things, *touching* them – but the experience of walking, which generates thoughts & images. In the absence of physical movement, how the mind stagnates!

It is different for the hermit in his cell, his movements restricted almost as much as the toad under a stone. He is focused on God. Poetry is mostly quite different. More self – ish, more experimental, a hit-or-miss seeking among words. Poets have rarely been saints, and are mostly pretty gross livers, in love with sensation, if not drunkards or sexual predators. I've weaknesses enough, but simplicity has been my pleasure, just nosing about in the open air.

8 May
Mieke's birthday. New resolution after drinking following Elin's visit. More ineffective speeches from me. On good days – and there are many good days – it's hard to believe in the disaster I predict.

10 May
In the early hours, Mieke is incoherent, and would fall getting out of bed if I didn't help her. How serious is this? Should I call an ambulance? I listen, praying she will sleep. She does, as the first birds wake.

When able, I've been making a selection of Les Arnold's poems for a magazine based in Bradford-on-Avon. My mind goes back, of course, but the poems are immediate, dancing with life. Outside, another day of big, beautiful clouds coming over from the west. Once more I wonder at the young oakleaves, unable to find words for their colour, or texture, or shapes, but simply loving them.

18 May
'It's a day for dreaming,' M. said, as she looked out on the garden in wind and rain. The landscape of my early morning dream was 'outside Frome'. Why hadn't we come out here to live, in this village of old, stone houses? Outside the village, under tall trees, I was waiting impatiently for M. Then I was driving through the woods, on a narrow gravel track. Deep in the forest, in some old farm buildings, M. was visiting clients with a child suffering from Alzheimer's. There was something vaguely threatening about the whole situation, and, with the light beginning to fade, I was anxious to get away, back on to the road. After a delay, which heightened my impatience, we drove back through the woods, passing through a scary mist, which seemed more than natural.

1 June
There's no doubt drinking will kill M. if she doesn't find the *passion* to stop. I know how much she feels for others, and that in feeling she seems to have no defence. But in this there's the demonic perversity. Last night, I talked her down from a panic attack. So, I can help, to a degree. But I can't

arrest the demonic impulse. Only she can save herself. But does she have the passion?

In going back to Martin Buber in my reading, I notice the emphasis upon 'man' in 'between man and man'. This might be described as generic. But it strikes me that Buber's thinking is exclusively male-oriented, as perhaps from its emotional roots in Hasidism, or indeed, in Judaism of the prophets. What I miss in this is any sense of woman as other, with a view of reality that differs from the male's, and a different capacity for emotion and its expression. Even in M. when she is harming herself, I know this difference, which includes an emotional generosity. I don't say men are incapable of that, but there are differences which are not gender-constructs: differences which have to do with giving and self-transcendence.

10 JUNE

Keeping a journal, as I do, could be an extreme form of the Ife of monologue. I have feared this might be so. In the main, however, I am aware of a sort of double consciousness, implicit in my way of seeing and thinking, which springs from my sense of language as dialogical. Where this originated, I'm not sure. But, from early on, I've been convinced that no one can write a poem for himself alone, since language is a shared medium – in a sense, the element in which we live and know ourselves, through relating to others. In thinking, I am usually responding to other minds, other voices. I am defined by the range of things of which I write, each of which constitutes a meeting, whether with a person, a cloud, or a blade of grass.

None of this means I don't know the hell of self-enclosure. Meetings matter more because I do know it. The journal, in fact, is a means by which I struggle to climb out of it. I write, too, under judgement. It would be foolish and hypocritical for me to say 'in the eyes of God', because I know nothing about God. But I remember Gerard Casey saying, 'God sees us just as we are', and I have a constant sense of the gap between my expression and the reality I seek to express. I trust words most when they spring from the 'between', the meeting, whether with person or thing.

30 JUNE

I was recently moved to tell my friend Stephen Batty about M.'s drinking problem, and to ask him to pray for us. I believe in prayer; I have always believed in prayer. Is this just superstition, since I'm not sure whether God exists? It may be so, yet for the person who prays with complete honesty, knowing how little he really sees of himself, there is an opening of heart & mind.

20 July
Joe's birthday: 37 today. We talk on the phone and I tell him about the thunderstorm in which he was born, blue light flashing off metallic surgical instruments – as I remember, though I may have embellished that. The weather continues stormy here and now, too, with humid days of cloud and heavy rain.

After a good week M. has been harming herself. Is all alcoholism self-harm? It has that effect, certainly. I've known drinkers who are loud and celebratory, but for M. it means misery. I remember the old man at Al Anon who spoke of having married two women when he married his wife. I knew no such thing, and it was years before I discovered that I had. I pride myself on my observation, but it seems to take me years to know anything. In this case the illness was hidden, perhaps even from Mieke herself, until we returned from America.

Now, I am a spy in our own house.

24 July
On the moors above Bedlinog in rain, Welsh rain. Not much to see except purple thistles, and dark cloud & grey cloud & rain. Driving on, we saw sheep huddled against stone walls, and ponies standing together, a picture of dejection. Then a cormorant flew over – it might have been a bird from the Ark. I wondered if the day seemed as dismal to these creatures as it did to us.
Not wholly dismal, because M. is talking to me about her addiction, and because we were out together enjoying what there was to be seen, including the rain.

1 August
Since M. had been drinking the night before, I had to drive us to Andover yesterday, and did so the long way, on roads that I found almost as frightening as the M4.

On a wet afternoon, at St Mary's church, Andover, we attended the blessing of Emily & Steve's wedding. This was a moment I had dreaded, in case I stumbled, but in fact it was a wonderful experience leading my beautiful daughter down the aisle. The service was memorable, with well-chosen hymns, and I stood to read my 'Emily' poem, written when she was a little girl, which made some people cry, as it nearly did me, too. The other big responsibility that I'd worried about – would I strike the right note? – making the speech at the wedding reception, also went well. With M. fit to drive, we made the return journey on the motorway in half the time it had taken me to drive to Andover.

5 AUGUST
Mother's birthday. Fine at last, sun & a light breeze, butterflies fluttering round one another.

Emily is like Mother in certain respects, as I said in my speech before the toast: resolute, determined, with emotional reticence. There's some physical resemblance, too.

Each life distinct, yet we know so little about the deep connections that make us.

What has made me a poet is awareness of how much cannot be spoken, or described, or known. Silence comes before our first cry, and returns after our last breath. Silence haunts the words I speak or write. But as a poet I need words – words shadowed by silence.

10 AUGUST
After several fine days, some light rain, blackberries ripe in the hedge, M. is in bed recovering after a bad bout of drinking. I found one bottle but she managed to get others, as she always will when compelled to. 'Recovery' is always temporary. The wisdom I hear from experts is that things are likely to get worse before they get better. The signs that they will get better aren't good.

There's little help available to us here. But when there has been help Mieke has sabotaged it. She doesn't want to die, I'm sure of that. But something in her – the illness – wills her not to live.

This time, I was beyond words. I've spoken all the words I could, tried every approach. All I can do is be by in case of need.

2 SEPTEMBER
In the early hours of the morning, attempting to get out of bed, Mieke fell heavily, and it was some time before I was able to help her up. She swore she hadn't been drinking. I have just found an empty whisky bottle, and caught her about to open another one.

M. feels 'horrible'. Again, she says, 'it has to stop'. It's monstrous, demonic, this thing we're up against.

21 September

It's not quite 10 in the morning. After several days of nightmare Mieke is in bed barely conscious. I thought I'd found the last bottle yesterday, apparently not. This began on Thursday with what she called a 'blip'. There had been ten perfect days, free of alcohol, when she had been resolute, and her true bright self. Gradually things got worse until, this weekend, there have been long periods when she has been completely shut in on herself, silent. In the bright days I'd made two arrangements, which had to be cancelled.

Having written the above I stood up to go to the toilet and fell on the floor, shitting myself as I struggled to get up. This was twenty minutes ago, since when I managed to stand and get myself to the bathroom where I cleaned myself up. No use asking for Mieke's help as I lay on the floor. Before, I was thinking all I could do was watch, and, if she gets worse, call a doctor or an ambulance. This is still the plan, if I can stay on my feet.

I'd searched thoroughly – the house, the garden, the car – but I can never be sure, though this time, with the evidence of empty bottles, I was.

All the words have been spoken – anger, compassion, analysis, advice, recrimination. This is our life, not a life I can walk away from. In many ways it has been a good one, and still is, at times.

It's now 10.45. Outside, in low sky, the fir-tree is full of pockets of darkness, branches moving only slightly. It's a relief to look out, steadying myself. But there's no one here, outside officialdom, I can call on.

30 September

Returning from taking her brother, Johan, to Cardiff airport, Mieke stopped at the little shop in Quakers Yard, bought a half bottle of whisky and drank half of it, sitting in the car outside the shop.

Why had she done it? 'Loss'. She felt such a sense of loss when Johan left, and at the family she had left behind in the Netherlands. Next day, another half bottle.

Frightened, I raged at her for what she had done, for the criminal danger. Later, I realized the futility of this, and felt compassion for what she does without wanting to do it, without willing it. Anger and compassion. The addiction is such a cunning adversary, using any strong emotion, sadness or happiness or simply boredom, equally.

18 October

Mieke is recovering after three days of drinking, and a day yesterday when she lay in bed scarcely moving. Once again, we've talked, or I have talked. New resolution.

Kay rang, fortuitously, when I was at my lowest. She said: write it in your journal. I said, yes, I do. But this isn't what I want. It isn't what I want for Mieke, who is so much more than this. It isn't what I want for myself, this repetition of wretchedness, this shadow that threatens to take over everything. There is so much more – but when it becomes hard to think, to see, to live... This doesn't help.

26 November

Dramatic light in the afternoon as November days darken. Sunlight squeezed between cloud, or bright behind a cloud veil, low over hills to the west.

Thirteen days since a crisis, M. has harmed herself again. She won't talk about it. She says she doesn't know what to say. I talk, of course. But her silence conspires with the addiction.

With my poem, 'Self-portrait with falling leaves', it was as if inspiration came with the actual wind blowing down leaves off trees. Now, I feel flat again, tired, disinclined to put in the work, without which inspiration simply blows itself out.

2 January 2010

There was snow on the ground when we woke this morning, less than on the days before Christmas, but more than a smattering. Last year was difficult, due mainly to M.'s drinking. I allowed my disability to get the better of me, becoming housebound, and doing little work before November.

Drink fills an emptiness. It's little good me saying 'this isn't really you, you are a wonderfully warm, intelligent person with so much to give'. I do of course say such things, which are true. And they have an immediate effect. But no resolution lasts. How unlearn the habit of a lifetime? A way of being, or being unable to be, for herself, alone. I see a tragedy unfolding, and there's nothing I can do to stop it.

5 January

Another night of fear when I went to bed in my clothes. M. very unstable. Early afternoon now, white sun over western hills, ground & roofs mottled with snow, which fell quite heavily this morning. Twigs & branches shining where snow has melted.

How quickly the dark comes on. While I've been writing the sun has sunk behind the highest hill in the west. Where the light pulses up, a great wing of cloud is passing over. Dark is gathering among houses & trees in the valley, bringing out where snow lies, beginning to cover it in shadow. And as the sun goes, suddenly the cold increases.

30 January
Yesterday I found 4 empty half bottles of whisky and one half full. All drunk with more calculation than usual, to conceal the effects. Today the madness seems to have run its course and M. is feeling ill and remorseful.

How powerless we are.

29 March
Twice in recent days I've caught Mieke bringing bottles of whisky into the house, and have disposed of them. What is love? I feel the obsession takes over her whole being leaving no room for anything else. It sucks her down into an inner place she can't escape from, and no one can reach.

Writing the above, I looked up and saw the first blackthorn flowers, not yet fully open, on the tree across the road. Magpies have been busy in the fir-tree above it, where they seem to live all year round.

8 April
A bad night followed by a bad day, which isn't over yet. I was awake until about 6 listening to Mieke sleeping, noisily, after taking 2 sleeping pills. Whether anything else, I don't know. But this morning she was out early, returning with a bottle of whisky, which I persuaded her to throw away. Later she brought in more and has been drinking it. I could walk out if there was anywhere to go. Could I? Could I leave her? – as effectively she leaves me when like this.

Probably not. So, does that mean I have to watch her killing herself? If not that, then betraying everything we live for. Seeing her become this other person – this negation – is very hard. And frightening. This recurring fear, for her, for myself, is the worst.

And outside today the sun has shone, the air been sweet, buds are pricking into leaf on our garden trees, and indoors it's been hard to live.

11 April
Mieke is feeling fragile, but returning to life after days of withdrawal & obsession, shut off from the world and from me. Today, one beer to steady herself. New resolution.

When she was safely in bed, I was able to work, drawing up a plan for my essay, 'Marches of the spirit'. A rich terrain, with a complexity I'll scarcely be able to do more than point to.

It's our shared life that returns when M. comes back from the no-place she's been in.

23 April
At dinner on the first evening of the Usk Valley Vaughan Colloquium at the Castle Hotel in Brecon, Mieke became faint and weak, and collapsed at the table. Anne Cluysenaar and I helped her upstairs to the bedroom, where, after sleeping, she felt better. This collapse was the result of a period of not eating and the after-effects of drink & depression, and then of emotion at meeting friends, and an outgoing that masks frailty.

I gave my talk not long after we had taken M. upstairs. It wasn't easy, but it went well, and I was pleased to see and talk with Chris Meredith, who came in for the occasion.

5 May
Stepping out of the car on another damp morning, a whiff of bluebell-scented air.

Beside ourselves at the chair-based aerobics class at Aberfan Community Centre were three elderly ladies and the instructor. I was the least able of the group.

14 May
How on edge Joe is; he lives on the edge, agitated unless he takes his Valium, and full of self-criticism, but quick to anger if anyone criticises him! But at last I managed to say something which I think he heard: 'Let yourself be loved. You are a very lovable human being.' I reminded him of all the happy faces of children & friends in the photographs he had shown me – happiness in which he shared a large part.

Joe showed Mieke his photographs from the Gambia, where he hopes to return and help to set up computers in a school. There was a momentary flare-up when she tried to advise on his medication, but it passed, and they settled down lovingly together.

22 May
Suspicion confirmed, alas. Mieke has been drinking heavily. It was her illness that took me in. She was using it as a screen, as I should have

known. Now, she's feeling dreadful, and full of remorse. 'This *must* stop. Never again.' I tried not to talk this time. It does no good. I only repeat myself, and probably the only effect is to pacify me, which isn't the point. There are moments when I feel that I must get away. But I know that I can't, that we're bound to one another. A tragic effect of the addiction is that it infantilizes our relationship. I find myself treating M like a child I can't trust out of my sight, and I become childish. But with M., *because of her*, I am most fully myself. Inevitably, the habit poisons both of us. And I rage, rage, with a reasoning that simply misses the point. I hear myself warning, explaining, planning avoidance, and in full flow, or in the silence between words, catch a sense of something in M. I can't reach, which she alone could control. But how? I feel the strength of this thing, which at times we personify, calling it demon, devil.

> Alcohol is a vampire.
> It drinks the blood of the drinker,
> and consumes the flesh of those who love them, and those they love.
> Is love stronger than death?

23 May

Mieke 'feeling good', she says, 'back to normal'. So, we get out of the house late on a hot morning and go shopping. Other people are out in their summer undress. I discard my old man's cardigan for the first time since last year. Sky flawless blue. Some smoke from distant fires. A heady smell from blossoming may thick in the hedges.

Talking in bed this morning, I remembered things friends have said to me in later years that have made deep impressions. Anne: that I have never accepted being a stranger. Kay: that I expect to be happy, while others accept unhappiness as the normal condition, and are surprised and grateful when they are happy. Since Anne said that, I have realized its retrospective, and current, truth. As for expecting to be happy, yes, I have been guilty of that. It came from a happy and privileged upbringing, and perhaps also from a disposition to find pleasure in life itself.

'Souls communicate, but always imperfectly. They are always more or less at cross-purposes and cross-meanings. It is well to remember this…' (R R. Marett)

12 June

Mieke is recovering today, feeling extremely fragile. She had bought lager, calling it 'weak' (it was in fact the strongest), and she had refused to let me go out with her, denying that she would buy drink. I thought her complacent, which made me angry, and for a day or two I met silence with silence. But when it comes to seeing her suffering, I can only feel for her and give what support I can.

One good talk with Elin, who loves her mother, but says she is struggling to learn from her what to avoid in herself. Apparently, she has been talking with Bethan about coming to my aid *when* M. becomes impossible for me. The concern helps me, but as long as I'm alive and capable, I can't imagine letting go.

Cold anger passes, and M., in her suffering, comes back – to herself, to me, to our life together. This time, at a desperate moment, she said she would kill herself. She might, with the drink, but not, I'm sure, in the way she meant.

Here we are then, together again, on a sunny early summer afternoon, with white clouds drifting over in a blue sky. If only Mieke can remember how she feels now, and what has led to it – the secrecy, the first drink.

It's strange how one can find loneliness most *in* relationship. Is that true? Someone who is quite alone might mock the idea. And rightly, for I'm a man blessed in love & friendship. What I mean, though, is the experience of not knowing another, of knowing and not knowing, in intimacy, of meeting, as it were, a wall... Without otherness, surely, there can be no love, only admiring oneself in reflections. But when there's that in the other which is absolute, which shuts us out, and perhaps shuts them in? No; there's something no one can share, some inner 'place', which a believer would call a soul. Is that it? The place turned to God, which only God can know? But this isn't what I come up against in M., or she in herself. This is an illness, some demon within which wishes her harm. Or call it, as we have, a frustrated creativity, a need without an outlet, turned back on itself... And then she is unable to communicate, forced back on the silence she's unable to break, and I'm unable to enter.

No doubt I'm aware of this because of all she has let me share, knowing me as no one else does, allowing me to be known. I feel she has read me through and through, that nothing is hidden, either of what I know of myself, or of what I don't know, but reveal. To her, I'm completely transparent, or as see-through as any person can be to another. But where we can't meet is just here, in this deadly silence.

14 June
'Just an old man,' M. says lovingly, when I say the sight of me naked must be depressing. And she simply sees what I am, which helps me to see too. And, seeing, to recognise that the time is coming – the time that can be any moment – when there'll be no time left for work, or anything else.

18 July
A colder, grey day, the sky featureless and everything still. But when I look closely, I see movement: smoke-thin cloud moving across whitish-grey cloud, branches swaying or trembling.

It is Sunday afternoon and M. has gone back to bed, at the end of another bad period which began with intensive dope-smoking – supposedly medicinal but which, when available, she consumes addictively – and continuing, or coinciding, with beer. Now she is chastened after talking with Elin on the phone. Yesterday Elin said to me: 'Mieke is scared of living'. M. admits to finding 'safety' in being ill. This is the sickness I find hardest to bear. I've felt angry, but now only feel sad. It's a relief to me that now, after these days away, she's coming back.

29 August
This morning I drove up onto the mountain above Bedlinog and sat in the car in the rain. Since coming home from her visit to the Netherlands, Mieke's been as bad with her drink obsession as I've ever seen her. Later, I went out again intending to book into a hotel, but came back. I've poured away 6 or more whisky bottles, so perhaps she hasn't drunk so much. But her mind is dark with the obsession and life around her is extremely difficult. I've spoken several times to Elin who's offered to come over. But I don't want that; she has responsibilities at home. I'll hold on if I can.

30 August
'It's over,' M. says. I want more, not this 'over for the time being'. Life has been disrupted, people have been badly hurt. It isn't enough for M. to work over things in her own mind. The problem's too deep for that. And she won't face it.

It's a perfect day: small white clouds in a blue sky, sun hot, a few distant windows ablaze with light, butterflies intent on the white buddleia, fluttering past outside the window. M. was up early and is now in bed, where she's been much of the time since she returned. When I think of all that's happened, I feel weary, past anger, beyond compassion. If only she showed real remorse, with intention to do all in her power to resist this evil thing. God forgive me, but I felt this morning when she said 'It's over', she was almost complacent.

Yesterday, I spoke to Emily, who gave me her understanding, and reproached me – justly – for not speaking to her before. Joe sent me a wise word: 'Mieke doesn't want to do it. How bad she must feel.' He understands the futility of blame, which I'd given way to. Even as he spoke, I felt my feeling change. In these bad days, I've felt the love of friends, and of my son and daughter and stepdaughters. Their support has sustained me.

9 September
Yesterday evening, after secret drinking, M. was crying bitterly, her whole body wracked with grief. I felt the emotional storm, and the desire it expressed to stop her self-harm, could only do good, unlike denial.

Still shaken, she was calm today, when I drove her up onto the mountain. No rain, but sun and masses of cloud round the horizon, where we could see the Beacons to the north, and, south, a gleam of the Severn Sea. It was warm in the sun and the air smelt sweet, like healing.

How good life is when M. is well. She gives me the companionship I always longed for.

26 September
M. ill after drinking on top of antibiotics. At first, I didn't realise, the pain from her gum infection seemed sufficient cause. A familiar story. But she must *know* where this will lead. Or perhaps not, periodic oblivion being an end in itself. And I make it possible, by always being here, and giving comfort when she comes back. And if I were not?

Christmas Day
Christmas alone together this year, but not by intention. It was too dangerous for friends to visit us because of the snow. Phone calls from or to children & grandchildren. Joe rang from the Gambia, in the sun and eating fish straight out of the sea. At night, with the curtains drawn, I saw a light at the top of the hill in the quarry woods. Intrigued, wondering what it was, I looked at it from time to time, as it grew. A white light, which, as it came clear, I suddenly realized was the moon!

28 December
When I finished Paul Mariani's biography of William Carlos Williams, I

wept. Why? Because, for all Williams's faults, the book bears out the truth set down on the penultimate page: 'he was above all a lover, a lover of people, a lover of his world, a lover of his craft'. It is love that reaches out, seeking connections that take us out of ourselves and enlarge our sense of being. Near death, at the end of their long life together, Williams admitted that he did not really know his wife, to whom he owed so much. It may be generally true that a man doesn't really know the woman he loves. I think it is true for me. But in this loving without really knowing – this mystery charged with desire – is the driving force of the poem – towards the woman, and towards the world.

4 JANUARY 2011

Despite resolutions, the year has begun badly with M. drinking. Looking out of the window now, at a closed – in day with rain dripping from our broken gutter, I feel as dismal as the weather, at how Mieke's addiction confines us. Earlier, I saw a squirrel leap from the oak tree to the fir on the other side of the road – a prodigious jump. How I wish I had just a little of that vigour, or a good supply of the exhilaration – come & gone – which the leap gave me.

31 JANUARY

Awake in the night, I'm overcome by a feeling of complete vulnerability, because of M.'s illness and our isolation. At such times one knows oneself. All other thought seems childish self-delusion. So much for the 'exploratory' self!

During the days I've completed my introduction to a new edition of Lawrence's *Look! We Have Come Through!* for Shearsman. I finally found this more alienating than inspiring. Lawrence's problem with mother-love, and his antagonism towards child-bearing, as distinct from the conjunction of two individuals, aren't feelings with which I can sympathise. It's his blazing creative energy that I find inspiring.

13 FEBRUARY

Mieke woke in a panic in the early hours of the morning. Had she been drinking? She didn't think so, but wasn't sure. I'd suspected during the day, but wasn't sure either. She was very shaky for an hour or so while I tried to calm her.

I didn't think she would drink, ill as she's been for several weeks. I was mistaken, and must now become alert again.

Jeremy Hooker

20 February
After a bad night when she hardly slept, M. was still able to ⟨prepare a⟩ meal for Anne & Walt: a *musselfest,* which Walt especially relishes. La⟨ter⟩, going to a shop in the village, I found it difficult to walk the few yards from the car.

    Now that, in 'Saltgrass Lane', I've got the fact of disability, and to a degree the experience, into a poem, I don't feel it's something I want to dwell on. I needed to acknowledge it. To dwell on it, though, could be a narrowing, even a turn to the sort of 'confession' I find limiting in modern verse.

3 March
A bright day following frost in the night. Mieke is feeling very weak. She has eaten little for days. Earlier I persuaded her to take Complan. Now, in late afternoon, she is lying in bed. Outside, sun approaching the hills, a smoky mist veiling the valley. M. asked me to be with her – a sure sign that she's feeling very ill – and I sat on the bed, cheering her as best I could. She seems a little better now, but her condition is very worrying.

7 March
M. very low. She says she has been surviving, not living. Yesterday she was drinking. Afterwards she talked to me. She has been ill for some time but this was the second day of black depression. Hoping to sleep, she'd taken the rest of the sleeping pills, which had no effect. As she talks of suffering in the past, she talks of it passively, as victim. I listened, I talked, I think we understood each other. Then, on a bright morning in early March – season I love – I sat at my desk in the sun trying to rewrite a poem. There's nothing else I can do. If Mieke lives, it will be because she wants to. I can only do what I can.

25 March
Outside, another warm spring day, blackthorn in full flower, dandelions & cowslips around the garden, forsythia & magnolia in neighbouring gardens. Inside, our nightmare continues. M. had bought drink before my birthday, was drinking yesterday, and last night was very sick. I'm afraid I gave her a terrible tongue-lashing. Anger, yes; anger & fear; but as always the urge to find the words to help her to stop it. Knowing that words can't; but urged, talking against hopelessness.

With M. there is such a depth of negativity, something in her childhood that has shaped her whole life. Can that be true? And if it is, can she change now?

In my distress, I have talked of suicide. Unthinkable for me. Except at very lonely times, when it becomes imaginable. I have talked too of going into a home. It's all *talk* – talk that brings some temporary emotional relief, which I fear is all I achieve, for myself, by lashing Mieke with words.

10 April

After several days recovering, M. was drinking again yesterday, and had a bad night in consequence. Lying in bed this morning, I talked. Outside the pear tree was covered in blossom, flowers & fine green leaves moved slightly in a breeze. Only Mieke can get off the particular train she is on; no one else, it seems, can help her down.

Age is like a slow drowning: the past comes back before the inner eye. I can see the boy I was, quite clearly, but at a great distance. The good years with M. are closer, but seem almost to belong to another life. But surely, we are still the same people? So much has been waste in these later years – hope followed by near-despair, and a narrowing of the mind; waste of M.'s gift for living, my thought moving desperately in a tight circle. And I hold onto words for my very life.

And still hope springs, etc. In spite of all, I can't believe she won't find somewhere in herself the ability to live – M. who in good years has been life itself to me.

6 June

Mieke went to bed early. Sometime later, getting out of bed, she fell heavily. Once back in bed, she slept deeply. Waking up after more than an hour, she obviously had no recollection of the fall. She is still drinking periodically. But does she know she is? This blanking out is frightening. I remain alert, but I can't watch her every move.

Fear has dominated so much of my life. She, more than anyone, taught me to deal with it. Ironically, it is she who makes me fearful now. At the same time, I'm more afraid of the possibility of a life without her.

13 July

All day watching by Mieke who was in great pain, scarcely able to move. Drink inflames her condition, making her bones ache. This has been occasioned by anxiety over Elin and her premature baby. Not that M.

needs occasions; but anxiety makes her more determined to drink. While she was still sober (as I thought) I asked her what she would do if I couldn't take any more, and left. 'Kill myself,' she said.

But this wasn't Mieke speaking. This was the blind 'self' that takes over; 'the drink speaking', as people commonly say.

This not remembering is partly what allows the cycle to continue. If she *knew* what the outcome of drinking was, it would help her to resist more. So, I have to tell her; but telling isn't experiencing.

One can't *make* another live.

If the will is weak, there seems something *wilful* about the drive. Where does this come from? I've exhausted myself with questions, with useless advice. All I can do is watch, and help her not to fall.

14 September
Mieke slipped out this morning while I was still in bed and came back with a bottle of whisky. She pleaded with me not to throw it down the sink and I left some, which she mixed with milk and drank, saying it was the last. Two days ago, she fell and was unable to get up. At first she asked me to leave her, saying she would be able to get up after resting. But she couldn't, and at last I called an ambulance, and she was taken into hospital. In the evening, she returned in a taxi, having walked out ... Drink makes her pain from fibromyalgia worse. This morning, she talked, blaming her action on boredom. She simply isn't using her talents – but she sabotages herself, finding reasons not to. It isn't me she's bored with, she insists, and I know it's true. But how difficult she finds being – she who impresses others as being itself! I suppose I would find it difficult if I didn't have something to *do*. Even writing this, Mieke, I believe, safe, cloud mass moving over slowly, sun mellow. But what are we tending to?

23 September
Liz Insole remarked acutely, after I'd mentioned my childhood animism, which I've never outgrown, that it must be uncomfortable living in my skin. It struck me as being one of the truest things anyone's said about me! Last night, though, it was Mieke who was uncomfortable, waking in panic from a nightmare. But she didn't have drink to quell it. And that's the hope – if she can go through such unrest, and remember, and avoid bringing it on again.

3 October
Sitting outdoors on a sunny morning, a breeze turning to strong gusts, oak trees creaking as leaves are shaken down, floating, spiralling, blown erratically sideways, like butterflies. Leaves blown in through the open door lift my heart which is heavy with anxiety.

Nothing equals talking with a friend. Friendship, as William Blake said, is man's home. But sometimes talk won't do, and silent prayer is all.

4 October
'I need you more than I need whisky.'

18 October
A life can be described, as Paul Tillich described his, as standing 'between alternative possibilities of existence'. Much that I have written over the years might be seen in this light. What, though, are the possibilities when one comes to the last boundary?

26 October
Talking to Joe & Kay, I realize that I've never really accepted that Mieke has an illness. I'm too much the talker, the reasoner, as if I could persuade her not to be ill. Alcoholism *is* difficult to understand: perhaps only a few professionals or exceptionally wise ones really understand it. It seems wilful, a moral failing, and the deceptions it involves – the lying – feel like a betrayal. For the alcoholic, it's more like demonic possession: a periodic invasive force, which they don't choose, and can't deny. It quietens my mind to know this – anger falls away, anything except caring for Mieke seems pointless.

Joe is a great support to me with M. because he understands her condition better than most people.

27 October
Our 25th wedding anniversary. Silver, but we are both white-haired now! Not extinguished!

Zachary Leader, reviewing Alfred Kazin's *Journals* in the *TLS*, says that Kazin, in writing, feels 'you have paid back something of your debt to the Creation, to look at things more sharply, attentively, and above all more lovingly, with the senses and coordinates aroused by the act of writing'. This appeals to me immensely. The emphasis must fall on *something*. As I read back in my journals, preparing to make a selection from my first years with Mieke, it's the value of the living moment and all it contains that delights me. Sometimes a poor record, but with gratitude for being showing through. That above all is what I hope to convey as a writer.

23 NOVEMBER
'What have I done, Jerry, what have I done?' M. feeling very ill. She knows we'll have to get her into a clinic if she continues to drink. Joe thinks that it will be necessary. He thinks me over-optimistic.

Now Mieke is sober, and suffering, but her dear self, the 'other' Mieke, so careless of everything but drink, is hard to believe in. I suppose this is why I go on believing she can beat the addiction. Believe, or still hope.

It's impossible to understand why anyone should make themselves so ill. Alcoholics go on drinking, perhaps, in order not to feel the consequences of stopping. But M. does stop, and does suffer the consequences. Calling it 'binge' drinking doesn't explain anything.

Not understanding is, really, what I've understood: that the compulsion is beyond reason. And alcoholism, though a common condition, with various social contributing factors, is also individual in each case. It blots out the person but is also, somehow, very personal – an infection in the self that is very hard to reach. So, I feel that when Mieke can talk, or cry, *from there*, she does herself most good.

8 DECEMBER
Earlier, in Dowlais, I waited in the car for M. while she had her session with the cognitive behavioural therapist. Mist filled the valley shutting out the view of Merthyr & the hills. Blasts of wind shook the car, and rocked one dark, flame-shaped fir-tree in the foreground.

Last week I was unable to go with M., and on the way back she bought drink. This resulted in three bad days. Recovering, she said, truly, 'I'm killing myself'. I've arranged with Joe to seek family support.

What I've realized only slowly, and partially, is that my 'place' is the poem. Not that words alone are real – far from it. But that writing, in poems, in this journal, is how I discover who and where I am. Home once suggested to me not changelessness, but life as a river, always changing, always the same. But if one doesn't belong to oneself, if one is a stranger and knows the world as strange, the metaphor doesn't hold.

So much in my lifetime, in Britain and throughout the world, has changed. We live in change. I'm aware of sharing a sense of life with ancestors. Whatever else changes, there are threads that bind us. Yet in our time of rapid change I know that in all times the human experience is to lose the world.

14 December
Excitement is reported among scientists at CERN, because they have glimpsed the Higgs boson. Apparently, the subatomic particle may be a 'ripple' in the invisible energy field by virtue of which we and all things exist. So much is speculation, as the scientists acknowledge. But why the nickname, 'the God particle'?

Is it assumed that if we discover the 'building blocks' of the universe we will know 'the mind of God'? But surely, if God exists, we will know him, not as a construct only, or in the ways of subatomic particles, but through our 'make', our human depths.

20 December
Drove with Joe to Drugaid in Merthyr, where we met our family support worker, and talked with her about the situation with Mieke. This was something I should have done some time ago. How it will help we can't know. But it was good for us to share our anxieties with a professional supporter.

M. has been down for several days with a bad cold. Also, as I've just discovered, a bottle of whisky, hidden in a clothes' drawer near the bed. I shouted and left her alone with it. So much for wisdom.

New Year's Eve
The happiest New Year I can remember, with M. & Joe, Jim & Liz. Jim played his mandolin and sang, Joe played music cassettes and made mulled wine, and a spirit of companionship and great good cheer prevailed.

6 January 2012
The year has begun badly with Mieke's drinking out of control. Sometime after Christmas, in a spirit of independence, she stopped taking certain crucial medications, and started to drink more. She has been driven, and very ill.

Late in the afternoon, when Joe was out, she came downstairs and told me she was suicidal. Talking a little, she found some relief, and I felt the immediate crisis was over. She *is* resilient; if only, as she recovers from this episode, she remembers.

16 January
Last night I dreamt alarmingly of isolation, which became, as I interpreted it to M., a personal history. Will I never be free of feeling myself to be a failure? Only when working, perhaps. But what for anyone constitutes success? Isn't falling short what being human means, if we have a sense of possibility?

30 January
At 7 yesterday morning I called an ambulance to take Mieke into hospital. I had been aware for some time that she was breathing badly and uneasy in her sleep, and when she slipped out of bed onto the floor, I realised she was only semi-conscious. Joe was in Cardiff but he joined me at the hospital in Llantrisant. Mieke regained full consciousness during the morning. She hadn't suffered a stroke, as I feared, but was 8 times over the alcohol limit. This, together with painkillers and a newly prescribed sleeping pill, had caused loss of consciousness. At midday the doctor released her and we all came home.
    On this occasion, I really did believe she was going to die.

1 February
I talked freely, and listened to my support worker's advice. But I fear I will only be repeating myself.
    Joe rang, a cheerful voice, from the train. Holly's 10th birthday had gone well and he had just cycled from Waterloo to Liverpool Street, enjoying London sights from the cycle path.
    Now, in the afternoon, I sit at my desk enjoying the sun's warmth, like the bullfinch in the blackthorn across the road. My ulcerated leg troubles me. I joke about being a one-legged man, like Jim. Not much of a joke. I put off tasks, continuing instead with making a selection from my 1980s journal, meeting myself again as I was. Not always a pleasant experience, but when I look away from myself and the writing comes alive, it please me.

22 February
A wet morning in late February. We've stuttered forward this month, with alcohol scares & anxieties, and visits to the Leg Ulcer clinic. So far so good.
    After a difficult day yesterday, I spoke to Mieke of my despair. But it's a passing emotion with me, not a fixed state. Our life together is a good one, punctuated by some bad and some desperate times. I think I always

expected too much tranquillity, even – as Kay said – happiness as the norm. But life isn't like that, unless one is insulated, living in a bubble.

23 February
With our old friends, Hans & Agnes, who is now a representative in the Dutch parliament. When we were alone together, Agnes spoke to me about Mieke's intense privacy, relating it to her Jewishness and the fact that Jewish women in Holland were always on alert, ready to pack a bag and move at a moment's notice. I confess that I'd never thought before of the influence on M. of historical trauma, and especially of the war experience of her parents and their generation, which would have been felt strongly in her childhood. Fortunately, I found and removed a large bottle of whisky before Hans & Agnes arrived. M. naturally resented my intrusion, but if I hadn't removed the drink she wouldn't have got through the day.

Dydd Dewi Sant
Joe winkled me out of my chair and, as the sun was setting, drove us up the lane past the church onto the mountain, where we got out near the radio mast. Above us, cloud & vapour trails in blue sky, below, in light mist, Aberfan, a gap where Pantglas school had been, and the rows of children's graves. We stood in a fresh breeze by a large stone, which might have been part of a cromlech, its surface beautifully patterned and coloured with lichen, like an abstract painting. Two larks ascended, twittering, singing to one another, as they rose high. I walked back across uneven ground to open a gate for Joe to drive out of the field, feeling more alive than I have for days.

10 March
Back from her visit to the Netherlands, Mieke has been drinking. She was shocked when we pointed out she was proposing to do something – ring friends – she had forgotten doing two days ago. Wiping out memory has been going on for some time, and is getting worse. She was shocked; hope lies in her realization.

Awake at 4 this morning, panicking, she asked me for beer, which I gave her.
Looking out as I was writing, I saw white tufts on the blackthorn across the road, the lightest feathering. Recent nights have been cold with a big moon, but the warming air of these days is a springing air.

15 March
Finished typing and printed a selection from my 'European' journal. Now, while M. reads it and helps to make a publishable shape, I'll continue reading Geoffrey Hill & R. S. Thomas for my Usk Valley talk next month.

23 March
Seventy-one today. Sat outside on a perfect March morning: blue haze in the valley beyond flowering blackthorn and the fir-tree with magpies coming and going. Looked with Joe at a book of old photographs of Merthyr which he'd bought for me. How crowded the world that has gone from South Wales. How much of the industrial age has been dismantled and grassed over. It is hard here to realize where we are – to imagine what has been, and what is.

26 March
At I this morning I got up and got dressed and went back to bed in my clothes, since I knew Mieke was suffering the effects of drinking. I had suspected drink and was tense during the outing for my birthday. The day after, I caught M. with an almost empty sherry bottle. 'Caught' is the humiliating word for both of us, as I constantly watch and search, playing sleuth in our home.

Nothing new; only a deadly repetition. I don't know whether either of us will survive this. But I do what I can, and go on with my work, as well as I'm able. The sun still shines and flowers come up in dry March weather.

It is M. negating herself that hurts. I look out and see new life asserting itself, and indoors she makes life difficult for herself. I feel crushed. As we struggle on, time passes, I am afraid, and a feeling of terrible waste weighs on my heart. I turn to my journal for release, and repeat myself, and feel the dead hand of repetition in what I write.

12 April
It is the inner voice, the voice or voices in the head, that become the lyric poem: voices of self and 'other'. Here also is the voice of prayer, which addresses Christ or the Wholly Other, the voices that seek an opening beyond all self-enclosure.

In my case the journal became an outlet, a form of self-colloquy. It has helped me as a poet to find my voice, and it may also have hindered me, releasing pressures. I would say now that my model for a poet's journal would be Mary Casey's, where the voice in the prose and the voice in the poems are the same, with varying intensities, and the prose has more discursive expression.

In Mary's case it was a voice without a public. She may at times have drawn in her intimates, but she was always talking with herself, with Mary. Would it have been possible to that degree – would it have been necessary – if she had been published? I doubt it. Nor perhaps would my journal have evolved as it has if I had had a stronger or more consistent sense of a public.

6 May

I was woken around midnight by M. wailing loudly and Joe trying to rouse her. He called an ambulance, and we went on trying to calm her, and to get her to tell us where she was in pain. The only words she was able to speak as she continued to wail were: 'I am sick', and 'I need help'. I asked her to squeeze my hand but she was unable to respond. She was quieter when the paramedics arrived, and able to say that she didn't want to go into hospital. They made tests, and found that she wasn't in physical pain, but her agitation was due to alcohol. In the morning, she had no memory of what had happened in the night.

For two days she'd been distant; I'd taken away one bottle and had suspected drinking, but had no proof. Lonely and depressed, I'd rung Elin, who spoke to Mieke next day, urging her to go into rehab. I think this may now happen. Joe thought the wailing manipulative. Her support worker called it a psychotic episode. All we have are words for something deep within which is destroying M., and will kill her if she isn't able, with help, to deal with it.

7 May

Having persuaded M. to go out with us in the rain, Joe drove us over the high moors and down to Deri. On the edge of the park, a cluster of cowslips, and as we walked up the stony path to the waterfall, we heard the cuckoo from or near the woods. Standing by the pond, flint-grey and pitted all over with circles made by raindrops, I could see that for M. too this was an enchanted place. I know that I'm an essentially simple man who enjoys simple pleasures, and M., when she shares things like this, is truly happy.

11 May
A friend drew my attention to the opening words of Louise Glück's *Proofs and Theories*: 'The fundamental experience of the writer is helplessness'. M. says I should use my experience of her addiction in my poems. I questioned whether I should, not wanting to. But this has become such a large part of my life that if I'm to speak as myself, from the depths, I don't see how I can avoid it. Impersonality could stifle me. Looking back over the period since my stroke, I feel it has.

16 May
Is the belief that each person has a soul which God cares for only a monkish fable? The world of the senses is wonderful, but it is our horizon. Beyond, all is speculation. God cannot be thought. To think Him is to realize ourselves, the reach of our minds and senses, our limited being. Even our own past is a ghost. I watch myself slipping away, a boy, a young man. Like Alun Lewis, I ask what survives of all the beloved. It's plain enough that we're natural beings. If inclined to forget, age reminds us; we feel our aching flesh, we know our bony skeletons. What should we be but clay, and dust?

Words seem to offer more. But what are words but breath? They may tell who we were when dead, but they cannot make us live again. If there is spirit that survives, it must be more than breath – that something Other. The monk says it is close, closer than breath; that we do not know ourselves; that our true existence is with God, and only God is real. So, we are present dreams, past ghosts. Words break on words, like wave on wave. We are lost in our sea of language.

1 June
M. is depressed. For the first time after visiting the Netherlands she's not glad to be back, finding herself burdened here. Wales hasn't meant to her what we hoped when we came here to live. She admits this is largely her own fault, for not making contacts. But boredom and depression are facts: there's no point in arguing over causes. I feel bullied by her moods and sometimes let anger show, which makes things worse. Talking to our social worker yesterday, I felt myself beginning to sound sorry for myself, which is sickening, and worse than pointless.

3 June
Today was a miserable day, when I saw Mieke coming in with a bottle

of whisky, took it away and poured it down the toilet. I have remained watchful and on edge all day. She went out alone, early. I've just found another bottle, half empty, and poured it away. Will it do any good?

I feel that she no longer loves me, and only wants to drink. I know the former isn't true, but the addiction – desire for oblivion? – takes over everything, and there's nothing that can't be sacrificed. So, it seems. Love alone isn't enough. One can't *give* a cure. Only the addict can find a way.

5 JUNE
Awake in the night with M., who was panicking. I gave her the beer I'd kept back for such an occasion. In the morning she pleaded to go out. I went instead, and bought her more beer. Better – less harmful – than whisky. Seeing her like this is horrible: the driven look, the obsession with getting drink, the subterfuges. I feel acutely the failure of sharing. At times like this the only relationship we have is one in which I watch, and talk *at* her. Which is no good. But nothing I can do is any good. One day, perhaps, my words will be of use to someone else. But now…

Fool, look outside. Grey sky, the fir-tree shivering in a light wind, rain fine as spider-silk, and drops on the window or sliding down the glass. What a different world it was when I was with Lee at Moor Farm recently, or with him in the church at Little Witchingham, the Passion alive in fragments of red ochre on the walls, fading, but with vines as quick as grasses climbing to the windows. Fading, as the story does not fade, as long as we can recognise ourselves in the figures, the soldiers with scourges or holding the ladder against the cross.

6 JUNE
Thank God, M.'s obsession is over, for now. This morning she said to me: 'It's like seeing with one eye and hearing with one ear – being cut off'. I'd seen the blind look on her face, as, looking out the bedroom window earlier in the week, I'd unexpectedly caught her crossing the yard with a bottle of whisky in her hand. Her eyes were wide open but it was like something in Brueghel when the blind leading one another fall into a ditch. All these days she's been locked into a deathly half-life. What a difference when she recovers! Even the weather seems to know it, as great clouds march over, like tottering giants, and in-between there are glimpses of blue.

7 JUNE
June has begun with rain and strong winds. An ill wind has blown in a

letter from Enitharmon offering me a large number of my books (more than 500 copies of *The Cut of the Light*) at discount prices. 'Old stock', the letter says. The probability is that most will be pulped.

28 JUNE
A terrible day, when I sat on the edge of the bed or the window seat, watching, in case I needed to call a doctor, and uncertain whether I should. At lunchtime I managed to spoon-feed Mieke soup. Afterwards she slept, and in the evening was more herself. Earlier, she'd been barely coherent.

This was the result of drinking earlier in the week, which greatly increased her rheumatic pains, affected her mind and blanked out part of her memory. I have to admit that, watching her, I felt anger and disgust as well as fear.

Addiction? Yes, this is an addiction. Yet when she comes to, I come back from it, back to the loving companionship in which we live.

21 JULY
In Dorset, at Studland, we indulged ourselves with a night at the Manor House Hotel, its beautiful lawn and gardens stretching down to the cliffs. Bournemouth across the bay, and below the hotel, Old Harry, and far across the water, a glimmer of West Wight, the other end of the broken chalk bridge. A sea garden, in which we sat out on a warm, still afternoon – summer having finally returned – enjoying the sea air and light.

27 JULY
In mid-week, after visiting her support worker, Mieke came home with whisky, as I realized later. Sheer self-sabotage, as she later admitted. Sickened and angry, I spent the day on watch. But when she returns to herself, restored, the feelings pass. It's almost as if I've accepted that this is part of our life together. Or, because our life is together, I've no choice. Anger this time was heightened by disappointment. I really had believed.

One day, my dear, you may read this book, when I am gone. It will hurt you, but I want you to know that the life with you was the life I wanted.

15 AUGUST
It's taken me years to recognise how insecure M. is, probably because she's helped me to deal with my own insecurity. Fortunately, I've been able to conceal the fact that she's been drinking while Bethan & family have

been with us. In the night, in cold anger, I turned on her. At last, I see that she doesn't want to stop drinking. So, it appears to me. Yesterday she was crippled with arthritis, in pain, moving around with difficulty, and asking me to help her upstairs. This happens every week or so, when she drinks. There's a painful underlying physical condition, but it is manageable – she is more mobile than I am – until she drinks. And this has been going on for some seventeen years, as a way of life. What the deep causes are – the fear – I don't know. But she doesn't want to make the effort to help her helpers. So, I rage. And what good does that do? But if she could see a core of truth in what I see? For in some ways I know more than she does, since I have to tell her when she's been drinking. She does not see herself. Do any of us? Not completely. But there's a blindness that may be fatal.

Today, too, I know that in my writing – my poetry – I am horrendously blocked. I've wanted not to know, and have thrown myself into research, which is supposed to provide me with material. But the truth is I've lost my way. The stroke contributed, and especially decreasing mobility, as, simply, inability to walk up through the woods, to feel the sun, and rain, and wind. In movement and sensation to start thought, to quicken the mind.

17 AUGUST
Rain, stronger winds, mist in the valley. A day like autumn, except autumn is often sunny and warm.

I felt ashamed of what I wrote the other day. I was harsh with M. out of my anxiety. And I gave in again to the demon of failure.

The truth is I need to research, and am afraid of becoming bookish. Like many poets with a feeling for nature, I owed a lot to walking, looking around me, experiencing a skin-to-skin contact with the world. More housebound now, I'm thrown back on reading, which is necessary, but can result in sapless writing.

The demon tells me that I've lost my way. Any poet is prone to feel that in a longer than usual gap between poems. What's happening, rather, is a shift. As I come to explore more where we now live, I've much to learn, some of it from books.

But I have to venture – research is one thing, and striking out on a blank page another.

24 AUGUST
On another damp, misty morning, leaves trembling in a breeze, I sent the

text of *Openings: A European Journal* to Tony Frazer at Shearsman. M. had read this closely twice, and helped me to make a shape of the original material. The whole process of typing and revision seems to have taken a long time. There was a lot to exclude, mainly passages that might be hurtful to others, and boring repetitions. At times it hurt me to remember my active life, but, mostly, I recalled the quick of it with pleasure.

26 August
Morning in the window. Patches of shadow pulsing on glass as breeze stirs leaves in the quarry woods and garden trees. 'A dying light,' M. says. 'A warmer colour yet a colder atmosphere.' Ancient sunlight, I think. And, later: There's a lot to be said for window-views. Witness David Jones and his beloved Bonnard.

6 September
Catching M. coming in with drink this morning I lost my temper, shouted, shook my fist in her face. She thought I was going to hit her, and was frightened. I don't think I could, but I wasn't sorry she was afraid. How often she frightens me and everyone who loves her. My reaction was born of fear, with our lives out of control, and going where?

It's hard to see a way forward. M. driven is another person than the one I met and married. As she was this morning, only drink matters to her. But this isn't *her*; this is a woman with no life of her own, with nothing but a craving for oblivion. This is a woman who frightens me.

And she spoke accusingly, saying that I'd frightened her. As if she didn't really know what all this was about. As if it were all right to tell lies, assuring me that she *absolutely* wasn't going to buy drink. Not this once only, but countless times. As if it were acceptable to make herself ill, and feel better, and make herself ill again… If only I could feel she wanted to stop.

Look out, I tell myself. There's a world out there, if for me now a narrow one. But narrowness is in the mind, a failure of imagination. One can't make another person live, and can only help them if they can use the help one offers.

Evening: M. told me how scared she was by my reaction this morning. I said I hoped the scare might do her good, and read her what I had written above, and other recent passages. She said how bad she felt. Then secretly filled a glass with vodka, and after drinking a little went to bed.

Back at my desk, I look out of the window. A lovely mellow light lies across the valley, on trees and roofs of Quakers Yard, on the silver-grey walls of a quarry and the hills beyond. I feel alone, not knowing what to do for the best, whether there is anything I can do. I don't want to be the kind of man who reacts violently, as I did this morning. I don't want to be what I've become, complaining in the pages of this journal. It's terrible to see what M, with her gift of life and healing, becomes. There's a death of the spirit, as well as the body. It seems the light knows nothing of this, the gentle evening light, the indifferent light.

7 SEPTEMBER

M. was very agitated last night. Finally, I got her to sleep by telling her a fairy story. This morning, she said: 'Life is such a struggle'.

After midday now the sky is perfect blue, cloudless I would say, until I look closely and see one thin, faint wisp. The leaves on trees across the road are still. After getting up briefly, Mieke has gone back to bed. I can talk to her now, but won't talk at her. The reason for my threat of violence yesterday morning was that it was my only way of stopping her from going out immediately to buy more drink, after I'd taken the first lot away. My other choice might have been to call the police. If I hadn't stopped her, I'm fairly sure she would have ended up in hospital. As it was, it was a close-run thing.

I don't need to justify myself. But I do need to keep a record. It also helps me to write, makes me feel less locked-in, alone. I feel sometimes as a child does, that I would like to be somebody's child, with a grown-up to turn to, to ask to take responsibility. But this is what I have to do. Mieke has given herself into my keeping; she says she couldn't live without me. The question is, whether she can live *with* me.

The sun falls in a yellow pool on my wooden desk top, shines on book covers and envelopes. I love the warmth in my face, the valley rising to hills beyond the trees. This isn't my beloved Wiltshire downland, which I would see from the window of Old Schoolhouse in Frome, and looked at longingly from the hospital window. But this too has become dear to me, and more mysterious, with a history I'm coming to know. And, yes, I shall always be a stranger here. But I also feel that its only in recognising ourselves as strangers that we're able to know anything.

8 SEPTEMBER

We have survived, so far we have survived, but drink takes its toll of body, mind, and spirit, and, with aging, becomes more dangerous. Last night, with M. back from the edge, how I talked, so reasonably, so persuasively! But what good are my words, or any words? Only M., if she would really speak, from the depth of her wound …But my fear is that she has grown an extra skin, a defence of denial, against the admission of vulnerability that would help her.

15 September
Another day spent mainly in the bedroom watching by M. The drive came on her again two days ago. At first, I was unaware. When she came round, I spoke more pointless words. Mostly, I felt lonely.

Of course, I risk making an idol of not knowing. It isn't that one knows nothing. To claim that would be to justify absolute quietism, with no views on politics or anything else, no values. There are things one has to know, such as the holiness of the heart's affections. Not knowing, as I understand it, is an antidote to knowingness, worldly assumptions, intellectual certainties, arrogance. Its ground is a sense of being which we are part of, but did not make. This results in religious scepticism, which may have originated with the ancient Hebrews. But I wonder. How do we explain prehistoric standing stones? Weren't they raised to a power beyond, something Man can only point to? And the stone circle: a beginning of concept, an image to enclose the mystery, a trap like R. S. Thomas's stone church? Everything we raise to the unknown god, we must also remove. Completeness of thought – knowing – is walking round and round inside a circle of words. Once I dreaded emptiness; now I see the need of it.

26 September
Some difficult times here with M. getting vodka past me. I dread the prospect of another autumn & winter like last year, alone. She said reading my *Diary of a Stroke* made her angry with herself at the drinking episodes. It hasn't stopped her.

2 October
Last week was difficult, and on Friday I threw away a bottle and a half of vodka, M. having drunk the other half while sitting in the car. I wonder about disposing of drink, contrary to Al Anon wisdom. But if I hadn't, over this past year alone, would M. have survived? Or would she have reached rock bottom, and stopped? Futile questioning. I *can't* see her harm herself and stand by.

Jane Aaron has contacted me to ask whether I agree to her and Wynn Thomas proposing me for election to Fellowship of the Learned Society of Wales. Of course, I'm honoured, and agree. But this idea of being 'learned' sits oddly with me. The only thing I've ever known is the struggle to begin, and dissatisfaction with anything completed.

7 OCTOBER
First frost overnight, followed by another bright morning.
    M. is feeling unwell, but her face is open, vulnerable, not closed as it is when the obsession is on her. Yesterday she came down on beer from vodka, which is poison to her. I'm at peace, and can write, when I know she's not in danger.

14 OCTOBER
The sun in my eyes is dazzling. Over the hills a dark mass of cloud is rolling up. I love the bright edges of clouds, and the shapes changing even as the mass slowly moves on.
    I woke late to the brightness after a night of almost no sleep, when M. was panicking. This began when I went with her to Merthyr and stayed in the car while she shopped in the Coop. Late in the day I realized she'd used the opportunity to get a bottle of whisky past me.
    Remorseful today, M. is her dear self. At times like this she sees the pattern, knows how it begins, and resolves 'not to go there again'. This is the second time in a fortnight. This time, the fail-safe we agreed on, me accompanying her when she went out in the car, didn't work, because she sabotaged it.
    On nights like last night, trying to calm M. and get her to sleep, I tell her about my early life. Stories she's heard many times before, but it's my voice that soothes her.
    Now, I'm in shadow. Cloud overhead like a bunched fist, light from the hidden sun at the edge. Cloud fraying. And all across the heavens, as the sun is released, dazzling me, and then is partially covered again, magnificent icebergs and ruined castles of cloud.

18 OCTOBER
Twenty years today since my mother died. From her, I learnt to love poetry, and poetry sustained her to the end of her life. In her last years she kept a notebook for quotations, poems, prayers, reflections on silence. Reading it is like entering into her mind, in the part of herself that was always free.

27 October
Leaves on the air on a bright day, as we drove to Abergavenny, where I'd arranged, secretly, to celebrate our wedding anniversary at The Angel. I'd bestirred myself to this after feeling, in mid-week, a burden to myself and others. Why did I let myself go? It was the feeling of age and disability, a literal heaviness that weighed upon my spirit. But now, surprising M. with pleasure of the excursion, all was good again.

5 November
For the second night M. was agitated, saying she felt 'weird', and close to hysteria. I thought she was going to wail, as she did before, but fortunately she became quiet and went to sleep, only to wake up in the early hours and become agitated again. I slept at last, and managed to stop her going out this morning, when she would certainly have bought drink. This mental distress isn't only about alcohol, but drink is what will send her over the edge.

8 November
Lonely, lonely. M. almost as bad as I've seen her in recent days. Alcoholism is solipsism, a life of monologue. Thank God for my work and friends, and the company of cats.

10 November
M. is feeling and looking a lot better after a good night's sleep. She was so ill in recent days that I was close to contacting Elin & Bethan & her brother, Johan. Joe coming over on Thursday evening helped me a lot and I was supported by knowing that Kay is coming later today. But if I had contacted M.'s daughters and brother, what could I have said? That she was ill; but unless terminal, that would have alarmed them unnecessarily. The truth is, I was close to feeling that I couldn't cope. I needed help.

But, again, M. has recovered. She has survived this bout. But it was a close call: even if her body could survive, her mind was in chaos.

I have always believed it possible to begin again. For as long as life lasts: ever the new day. But it is impossible to make this true for another, and help them, by argument or entreaty, to live. Wisdom and common-sense fail. Love is not enough. There are some things we can only do for ourselves, or with God's help, if we believe.

19 November
Sometimes I wonder, as old men do, where it's all gone, all the time, all the days and years of teaching. Occasionally I dream of university, of the different departments, subtly transformed. And I'm applying for a job, or just starting, not finishing. And always there's time, and I'm younger. It's strange to think that I'm one of the last survivors of the original department at Aberystwyth. Others will be walking the corridors and occupying our former rooms. And so it goes on, but with more theoretical intellectualism. When I started, I knew almost nothing. When I finished, brilliant, younger colleagues were living in a different mental universe. I'm only glad that I helped some students to become better readers.

20 November
Dad's birthday. I wonder if it was such a dismal day as this when he was born, at the beginning of the last century. Weather with a smile would have been more fitting. Racked with bad nerves though he was, I doubt that any man who lived as long, had a happier life. In his marriage, in his painting, and in his gardening, he found complete fulfilment. Well, if anyone could, he did. Human beings aren't made for completeness. At best, we're always works in progress, with troubled spirits pushing us on.

23 November
I came down from reading at my desk to find M. sitting on the sofa, almost unconscious. This, after a good fortnight. She had been due to attend a course preparing support-workers for alcoholics. At first, this had seemed a good opportunity, something that, in using her gift to help others, would also help her. But on the two days that she attended, she bought whisky on the way home. Now, she realizes the course isn't for her. Being around talk of drink brings on the urge to drink.

Despite the periodic self-harm, our normal shared life is happy. This would be difficult for anyone with no equivalent experience to understand. On bad days, I don't understand it myself. Life is now this, now that. Under all, a warmth of being together, a recognition and acceptance of each other.

7 December
It's terrible how addiction draws Mieke into the shadows, into herself, into a kind of no-place. Not her true self, but a negation of her being. How I talked last night trying to reach her! But I can't find her in that darkness when she retreats from life.

8 December

At 3.30 in the morning I had to give M. a beer. Half of the night I kept my clothes on in bed, in case of emergency. She's been in free fall over several days. Finding an empty bottle beside the bed, I was disgusted, and angry, and shouted: 'I'll divorce you'. Anger springs from fear. I have to look after her, and she frustrates my efforts.

18 December

A good period with M. Why don't I write more about the good periods? I think, because I don't want to see them as periods, times within closed brackets, outside which drinking will begin again. It is literally true that I live in hope.

It is an afternoon of beautiful, mild light, the sun shining white between upper branches of the fir-tree, which is darker against the valley. M., still in bed, is coherent, and safe now, and, knowing that, I can sit here at peace. I record because I must. I am a writing animal. But I no longer want to analyse why M. does what she does. I don't understand. She doesn't understand. I hope it will stop. But whatever happens, it has to be lived with.

21 December

So far today the world hasn't ended, as the Mayans predicted. But our little world has come close to ending in recent days, with M. drinking whisky and dosing herself with Lorazepam. Of course, someone's world ends every day, every second; countless worlds end all the time. 'What do we believe to live with?' George Oppen asked. What can we believe when someone we love seems bent on self-negation? Years ago, walking in the woods near Shearwater, M. spoke to me of her inner emptiness, which she could live with only by turning towards others, through her gifts as a healer. I chose not to believe, or couldn't believe, perhaps because what I called my own experience of emptiness was temporary, and far less extreme. Now, I wonder. And perhaps what she experiences is common, and my boundless optimism is rare. Many people struggle daily with despair; and many lose the struggle. I'm lucky in that I find life constantly interesting, and am carried on a surge of energy – 'the pleasure which there is in life itself'. So perhaps I'm not best equipped to understand what M suffers; and all my talk is only finally self-referential. That's the question: whether any word can cross the boundary between person and person, and actually help another to live. I rage at her demon, I plead with it, I pray to some power beyond us, to God, to some mothering ancestral spirit... But if she cannot break through within herself...

13 JANUARY 2013
When Joe arrived at 4, a few flakes of snow had begun to fall. M. has made herself very ill, having taken the opportunity of my absorption in writing to buy and drink alcohol. It was touch and go whether she would need to be hospitalized. If this continues our co-dependency (as Joe sees it) can only lead to disaster.

> Don't tell me the devil doesn't exist.
> I know it does; it's compulsion.
> It's a mystery to you, beloved,
> and a mystery to me.
> Who understands it?
>
> It takes you to a place
> you can't escape from,
> where no one can reach you.
>
> It's stronger than love.
> It's a living death stronger than life itself.
>
> What would it say if it could speak to us,
> this thing without horns or cloven hoof,
> this dreary obsessive sprite
> that drives you to destruction?
>
> It speaks only with a kind of silence,
> shutting your mouth, turning
> round and round in the mind,
> saying without speaking the one word –
>   Compulsion.

25 JANUARY
Sun on snow yesterday, but snow is falling again today and the sky is low and uniformly grey over the valley. I wrote four 'God's Houses' poems, all of them duds. Not complete failures, perhaps, but, as M. helped me to see, repetitions of things I have done before. With this realization came a sense that I may have moved on in the new poems.

27 January
M. has been under compulsion for two days. When she could talk about it, she said that it leaves no space in her mind for anything else. I can see that. She also said she's glad when I find a bottle and dispose of it. In the night, watching by M., my mind filled with words, as it has on other nights recently, and I composed 'Boldre Church revisited'. I don't know yet whether the recent poems succeed: the ink has to dry, and I'm waiting for M. to be able to read them. Succeed or not, something has been released in me.

When writing, as I have this month, my mind's like a magnet. Consciously and subconsciously, it attracts images and ideas, and seems to be an active field. That's why words seem to come from nowhere, because the mental field is activated, and not just attracting bits & pieces, but ordering and re-ordering them. I seem to have tapped into a 'ground'.

30 January
Last night I had a scare. I was enjoying myself with Joe, and, laughing at one of my own jokes, seemed to pass out. I was aware of struggling to come back and of Joe talking to me, urging me to breathe. He'd called 999, and a paramedic arrived and did various tests. I was myself again, but felt shaky. Struggling back was the scariest experience I've ever had, much worse than the stroke.

I might have died laughing.

1 February
After pacing about unable to sleep for most of the night, M. is now in bed and getting some sleep. It's what's in her mind – the compulsion – that won't let her rest. How she hurts other people. Joe on the phone to Elin in recent days, both of them crying.

2 February
M. got out of the house without me knowing this morning. She had another car key, which I didn't know about. Soon after, she walked back, having got the car wedged against a wall just up the road, and unable to start it again. I called the AA. Joe, on the train back from Southampton, called the police. Two officers arrived and talked kindly to M. They will inform Social Services.

I was desperate, which is why I rang Joe. He spoke to Elin, who told me she wanted to come over this week – she's wretched at the thought of my loneliness. I dissuaded her. Now, mid-afternoon on a sunny day, things have settled down. M. is in bed, having drunk some Guinness that I kept back for such an occasion. I'm at my desk, calmer.

3 February

Last night, in an attempt to calm M., as my voice can do, I ran over our time together, from the beginning, recalling Groningen and any of the places we have visited. This works for me too, bringing back a sense of the fullness of our life together, as an antidote to the tight, dangerous little corner we inhabit during these crises.

M. has started using the word 'dangerous' after her Drug Aid worker told me what I already knew, that it's dangerous for an alcoholic to stop drinking abruptly. The word's subsequently become a sort of mantra for M., which she uses to persuade me to get more drink for her. With M. calmer, and definitely back in this world, I'm feeling optimistic again. I *know* she doesn't want to be what drink makes her; that it's something in her that makes her drink, but not her true self.

Oddly, even during this crisis – at least, during periods of less intensity – the poems have gone on working at the back of my mind.

4 February

Talking to M., I realize how much I love life – it's what I wish her – and delight in simple things. Just looking out the window and seeing sunlight gleaming on bare blackthorn branches across the road... We are what we desire.

21 February

A social worker came in yesterday to discuss our needs with us. This involved filling in a questionnaire. When asked about my religion, I found myself havering, and answered 'marginal Christian'. But I wonder what on earth that is. If I'd been listening to myself, I might have heard a cock crowing.

Whatever I am, my *make* must work in my poetry.

22 February

'I'm so stupid,' M. says. 'I'm so stupid.' She was too ill to talk with her support worker, but denied drinking. In the middle of the night, she admitted to me that she had. First, she has to realize it, and admit it to herself. Strenuous denial is refusal to acknowledge, which, for a time, is certainty:

'I have *not* been drinking'. Clever devil: This is part of the psychological mechanism that enables M. to drink in spite of her determination not to.

> Clever devil,
> whose art is denial,
> who says you do not do
>   what you do,
> who persuades.
> Devil that does not appear,
> and cannot be accounted for,
> that enters the mind and empties it
> of all but itself,
> a visitor today
> that leaves you comatose,
> a visitor that intends to return.
> We too have plans
> and clever words to work with –
> not clever enough.

5 March

Our sorry story continues. When her support worker came to see her yesterday, Mieke cried, saying how sorry she was to hurt me. I was surprised, since she seldom expresses this emotion to me. God help me, but I thought it might be a performance, a form of manipulation. In the night she was drinking again. Now, after 12, on a beautiful sunny early spring day, M. is in bed asleep. My head feels cold. What I see is morally corrupt behaviour – all the lying, all the subterfuges, the induced incapacity. I feel I could leave, make another life for myself. It seems that everything I've tried to do for M. has failed. Worse, that my protection enables the way she is living. At the same time, I know that I won't leave. I regret writing this complaint, but if I don't try to tell the truth there's no point in keeping a record.

> Devil whose cleverness
> depends upon lies.
> Father of lies, to which
> we ascribe a character
> a personality.

But what self has it
except our self – deception,
the space we make
    for a lie?
And what is that
but our absence,
vacant for a visitant?

It is a lie to speak of
the devil's cleverness.
It fathers nothing.
    The nothingness
we make in ourselves
becomes its harbour.

How should I know?

9 MARCH

Restless all night, M. went out early buying drink, while I was still asleep. What will it do to her if she does read this journal? Could she bear to? I thought once it might do good, showing her how drink affects her – which, coming to, she doesn't really know. But now I'm not sure.

But to let her go on not knowing, isn't that to infantilize her? But how can I get M. to address what she won't face? Realization, or partial realization, seems always to send her back to drink. She, though, has helped me to face reality in my own life.

You, who have showed me
the truth, brought me lovingly
to know what is real,
can you bear knowledge
of what the devil does to you?

Can you see
what I see – the thing
that possesses you?
Can you bear
to look, to see
the damage, the waste?

I am afraid
of what you don't know,
    afraid
of what you might see.

10 MARCH

The day began with Joe shouting at M. because she had searched his travelling bag in the night hoping to find drink. Could this be rock bottom? I don't see how we can go on like this.

The thing
that possesses you
relaxes its hold.

Abandoned,
you feel wrecked.

For a time
good days return.

I watch for signs,
never quite free
of the grip.

23 MARCH

Woke to snow on the ground on my 72nd birthday. In bitter cold, Joe drove me onto the moors above Bedlinog, where I was thrilled to glimpse two lapwings as they tumbled in the sky and disappeared over a stone wall. I've always loved these birds, which used to be common in downland, but are now rare everywhere. While Joe got frozen taking photographs of the snowy landscape, I sat in the car looking out at the bleak prospect of pale-wheat-colour bristly grass standing out of the snow. Long barrow shapes of snow-covered slagheaps loomed out of the gloom.

2 APRIL

Easter this year was a wash out with M. in bed most of the time. She recently started drinking port, on the grounds that it wasn't whisky. For a few days this seemed to be working, then the slide – port & wine & beer & two bottles of champagne, bought to share with me! I shouted – to no purpose. It is again a fine morning, but cold outside. M. is still in bed, on what I hope is a day of recovery.

> What deters a demon?
> Certainly not Easter.
>
> Lambs buried
> with their mothers
> in snowdrifts are born to die.
>
> You too in a drift of sheets.
>
> Farmers stumble
> waist-deep through snow
> searching for the living.
>
> And you, in the tomb
> of our bed, still breathe.
>
> Such emptiness fills our days.
>
> I prod, I probe, I shout.
>
> Silently
> the demon embraces you.
> You sleep,
> folded in his cold arms.

At midday, I took Mieke out to buy beer and to the Taff Bargoed Park, just down the road. Cold wind off the water and a pair of Canada geese with the lake to themselves. How hard to visualize what this must have been like when collieries occupied the site. An old resident speaks warmly of the sense of community, which was like one family. She also says: 'there wasn't a blade of grass you could touch. If there was a daisy it was dirty'. Now, the dilapidated villages, Trelewis and Treharris, their economies destroyed when the pits were closed, sit on the edge of a pleasant piece of Welsh landscape.

9 April
M. has finally driven herself to a standstill, which means she is ill, but open. What a relief when she turns to me, looking for comfort and support, and admitting what she has been doing. It's lying to herself that makes deception and drinking possible. Driven, with a false confidence that results in manipulation and bullying, she is unreachable. Her will is so strong when she drinks: everything sacrificed to the one compulsion. Now, in her face, it is as if a window has opened. How, though, help her to keep it open?

> A blind journey.
> And this is where it ends,
> at a wall.
>
> Then you look at me,
> eyes open
> and I know the demon
>   has left you
> in the wreck.
>
> Stay open, dear eyes.
> See what brings you to this,
> the demon that drives.
>
> When it comes back –
> it will come back –
> refuse to be driven.
>
> Be yourself,
> not the thing this thing
> drives you to.

12 April
My ulcers on both legs are very bad. 'Absolutely atrocious', the practice nurse at the surgery said. She was nonplussed, consulted other nurses and a doctor and bandaged my legs. The pain was less afterwards, but I felt leaden. One positive point: both she and the doctor agreed that it wasn't really serious. M. had been worrying that I might lose my legs; a fear I'd also had.

Feeling in the country is ever more divided since Margaret Thatcher's death. Now, it's about her legacy, with her heirs swooning with admiration, and her opponents savage with anger. Joe played us the whole of Glenda Jackson's speech in parliament, which spoke for many of us who remember a kinder, less materialistic England. Like Jackson, I'm a child of the 40s. Thatcher's 'children' find it difficult to imagine a world without her, or any world not driven by monetarism.

15 April

Thirty years ago today since M. and I first met. Afterwards she cried and cried, knowing her life had been changed for ever. She felt it was destiny. What relief I felt walking through Cambridge streets at dawn. Light and warmth came back into life with that meeting. Despite all difficult times, this remains my element.

16 April

Openness to the end is what I want. It means acknowledging one's end, and hoping one's work survives, and generates a living interest, as work of the dead has done for me. In one sense, a dead poet is more 'alive', as readers find new things in his or her work. This can't be consciously aimed at. But it's one reason why poetry matters: it voices some truth for the living in every generation.

18 April

Strong wind banging around the house at night. A chastened look about things this morning, puffy clouds crossing mild blue sky, trees shivering in breeze.

M., who has been drinking whisky again, finds it so difficult to *live*. I don't mean she wants to die; I feel sure she doesn't. I mean that for her life is obstructed, as if illness in childhood has never been thrown off. In her stubbornness when under the influence she becomes a child again. All of us remain children within; at best, there's a happy connection. Never trust the man (or woman) in whom there's no sign of the child they were. But for some the connection is negative, a retardation, or a habit learnt to deal with mental or physical illness. With M. I always think, how can someone so intelligent... Then I lose patience, usually concealing it. But I'm furious with frustration. Such waste of life, M.'s life, my life, when I'm itching to live... I'll never understand.

Slowly the poison…
Some potion
the wicked fairy
gave, that you must take,
a toxin that curdles blood.

Look, look out:
    clouds
are driving over from the west,
grey-bellied, lit edges
white as angel wings.

Spring has come alive
with this wind.
Trees shake,
dandelions
splash the verge
with common gold.

Look, only look,
    see
life outside
and all around,
    release
in yourself an answer.

How can I help with words?

Some old story
of witch and angel,
a tale of a demon,
how does it help?

Look, my dear,
only look out.

Look at the clouds.

20 April
Horrendous: Mieke's word for recent days. Whisky days. I thought it was over, but last night, when I was asleep, she found a half empty bottle I'd hidden ready to dispose of. How happy she was: 'It sparkled'.

Few periods have been as bad as this. With bandaged legs that prevent me from wearing shoes I can't get out of the house. When Joe came yesterday, he raged to me: 'I hate her'. It isn't M. we hate but the monster she becomes, denying life and making life almost impossible for others. As I sat with her yesterday afternoon, she was like a sick child, but a dangerous one, at risk of struggling up and falling. Once or twice she's managed to say, 'I want it to stop' and shown herself eager for rehab. But will this hold when she sobers? Joe sees me as a hopeless optimist, easily taken in.

Outside new life is asserting itself. The sun is warm. Buds are pricking up on apple & plum trees. A bullfinch has come to the blackthorn. When free to sit at my desk, I've made some progress with an essay. Does understanding come when one puts things into words?

> 'It sparkled,' you say.
> Yes, it sparkled –
>   in your glazed eyes
> it was gold.
>
> A holy relic,
> an object consuming all light,
>   something
> that excludes the world.
>
> An object sparkling
> in a worldless vacuum,
>   how it burned
> with a deathly flame.

4 May
Days and nights of nightmare, M. dangerously incoherent with whisky. In the early hours I poured the contents of a bottle down the toilet. Joe gives me hope. At first he raged at me and at himself, then settled to being companionable and helpful, cooking, and removing my leg bandages (a nasty experience) and taking me to the surgery for new bandages to be

put on. This morning, I've given M. beer. Outside, under clouds bringing showers, the perfect green is burgeoning, with leaves that are the equivalent of light and air. I only wish M., who gave life back to me, could see and feel the quickening.

7 MAY

In *Autobiography in the Seventeenth Century*, Paul Delany observes that "an autobiography, since it is almost invariably written to be read by someone else, cannot be a piece of pure and disinterested self-expression. Rather, it is a 'performance'". I don't think this is true of my journal, in which talking about myself I forget about myself. Is that possible? Yes, because I aim always to tell the truth. As much as possible, I want to deal with the subjective objectively. It's a question of writing as well as I can – not face in mirror, but eye on object. If I 'perform', it must be when I'm pleased with myself for saying something well. I'm aware, though, of a judgement of truth that's not aesthetic, and has no interest in a writer's vanity.

15 MAY

Snow on the Brecon Beacons, which we saw from Prince Charles Hospital, where Joe took me for a check-up with the kidney specialist. Cheerful nurses, and lively conversations with fellow patients. This is South Wales!

Earlier, I'd given M. a tongue-lashing for drinking herself stupid in recent days, when, in pain, I most needed her help. No good for either of us. I can't change anything with my words.

>   You are my woman
>   with a sunflower.
>
>   Remember
>   summer dawn
>   on the roof garden,
>   a heron flying over
>   which the sun caught
>   bringing news of reeds & rhines –
>   the country – your country –
>   a broken mirror for the sky.
>
>   Remember
>   bending your face

to the sunflower
which lifts to you,
open, shining.

Think of this on driven days.
    See the flower
with the sun in its face,
open in your eyes.

19 May

White clouds, blossom on crabapple trees, a few white butterflies. Oak leaves unfolding damply.

    M. fearful at the prospect of rehab is drinking more. She does not see that she will bring on hospitalization, or worse. Or she does see, but can't stop. We have been able to talk a little, but she finds my truth-telling 'harsh'. It's not what I say, it's what she's doing, the reality we're living, that's harsh.

No, dying
is not an art.

Dying is devil's work.

It takes your life
in exchange for nothing.

Now, now
is the time –
oak leaves unfolding,
bluebells in the wood
you would love to see.

But in your eyes
there is darkness –
desire
that takes you in,
and draws you away.

Hearing about my poem, which she hasn't read (any more than she's read about her drinking in this journal), Mieke calls it her gift to me. This, the poem I don't want to write; which I write because I must express myself; because this is how I try to survive. I find myself wanting to say things that will hurt her, and sometimes do. Not to hurt, but to shock, to penetrate the shell she's living in. And nothing works; occasionally she'll speak about being hurt, and go on drinking.

I see the woman inside the shell, hear her voice, as if we were both in the same world, sharing our concern for one another. Her gift? Yes, I felt once she had given me back my life. And now that seems like another woman. What kind of gift is negating life? What kind of gift is seeking oblivion in a bottle?

> This is not a poem
> I wanted to write.
> It was your life
> I desired to celebrate.
>
> I would not willingly
> invoke a demon.
> It came. I had no choice.

21 May

My legs ache, bound up like an Egyptian mummy. At times the pain is sharp, but mostly they just ache. It seems strange to me that the early months have passed. I always want them to stay. This is the moment when we touch life; religious people would call it eternity. I only know it as the quick – a living being aware of life, as perhaps only a human being can be. But I don't know – the thrush I heard at dawn was pouring out a pure music of feeling.

4 June

Terrible days. M. drinking whisky. I try to talk her down from panics in the night, only for her to contrive to get more drink the following day. At the same time, I'm in pain with leg ulcers, and now blisters on my hands, and itching almost everywhere. This morning, I lost it, and shouted: *'I want you dead!'* This is what we've come to. If it weren't for Joe and his support life would be impossible, unendurable.

I still don't believe Mieke wants to die. It's as if there's something in her that doesn't want her to be, and seeks oblivion. She *knows* I don't want her dead. It's her negative self that stands in the way of M. herself. This is what I rage at. We've come so far on what now seems like a steady slide. And I feel she *could* have used her will to get off. I speak such ugly words to her, to M., my beloved; words that until recently I couldn't have thought myself capable of. It's life that rages in me, desire to live, faced with a deadly enemy. How can she not *live*? Alcohol shuts out everything but itself. To someone under its influence nothing else matters. Even when it causes panic and despair, it remains the one object of desire.

20 June
A grey day of weeping mist, heavy and still, the dark green oppressive, a muted bird voice at dawn. The day turned darker when Joe discovered five empty whisky bottles hidden in the kitchen. Naturally upset, he blamed me for the optimism that blinds me. M. spent the night mostly awake, desperate for a drink. 'I'm an *alcoholic!*' When she speaks like that, I feel we may come through.

Later, Joe spoke with care and decision to M., saying he would ration her drink – wine – for the present, if she could keep off the poisonous whisky she buys secretly. The thing is to get her through the period before rehab, and since she's unlikely to be able to stop drinking completely, this is the way. M. listened and agreed. I felt proud.

1 July
The nurse at the Leg Clinic commented that I looked pale and not so well. M. had a bottle of whisky in bed; turned away from me, she was drinking, as I finally realized. Of course, I shouted, spoke ugly words. We are in the middle of another bad episode.

> That freshness
> deep down things.
>
> On surfaces:
> leaf oozing life,
> song liquid
> in throat of thrush.

Jeremy Hooker

>Each distinct face
>of small wild flower –
>herb Robert, buttercup,
>dandelion seed flying
>under sunlit cloud –
>
>naming things you do not see
>I am afraid to stop.
>
>And you, my darling,
>complicit with the demon
>that wants the whole world dead –
>ashes in a bottle…

(*From notes in my pocketbook, written at Prince Charles Hospital during a wait of nearly 2 hours to see a dermatologist.*)

Sometimes I don't seem to realize how *ill* M. is. Addressing a *problem* suggests a solution. But an illness, like cancer, can't be cured in that way. I felt recently that we're living in parallel universes. It's the old sense that, for all our intimacy, I can't reach her. Words mean nothing when she'll swear black is white. And I am a man who lives by words, and words betray me. I'll talk myself to something like a resolution, and M. will assent, but all the time her mind – the drive of her being – is elsewhere, in the other world of compulsion.

>Words fail
>in face of fact.
>
>Your face closed
>to the world, turned
>on a desolate landscape.
>
>Some no-place
>birdless, flowerless
>poetry cannot reach.

4 JULY
This morning, M. realizes how ill she is. I took her out to buy white wine.

The number of empty strong lager tins revealed when we put out the rubbish shocked me. Elsewhere in the house, empty whisky bottles. I've no idea how she got all this drink past me. Somehow yesterday I managed to write a review while keeping watch on M. restless in bed. I felt ill this morning and lay on the bed with a book. These days, I'm barely holding on.

8 July
M. left for rehab at Brynawel at 10 this morning and has just rung to tell me she has arrived. She went cheerful and resolute after several sober days. The decision to go and the spirit in which she has gone are hopeful signs. We take nothing for granted.

Mieke spent 8 weeks of the very hot summer in Brynawel, and initially she seemed to benefit from the rehab treatment she received. We were both desperate at the time of her admission, and I stayed awake the night after she had gone in, dreading that every engine noise was a taxi bringing her home. When Joe and I talked after her admission we were like shell-shocked survivors, and a visit to her, with support workers, at Brynawel, was a disaster, since we had misunderstood the reason for the meeting, and became very agitated when she showed no sign of recognising the harm her addiction had caused us and others. In the main, though, she looked and sounded better in Brynawel, and she said that she found the behavioural cognitive therapy of this rehab centre much more helpful than the 12 Steps of Clouds House. She acquired a reputation for serenity among her fellow inmates, in whom she took a friendly and caring interest. This was admirably characteristic, but also worrying, since it meant that she was continuing to be the therapist, instead of the alcoholic in need of help. After 8 weeks of what should have been a 10-week course she insisted on coming home, and within a week she was drinking again. The roller-coaster of our life together continued until the end. With 'Compulsion', I had found a way of personal survival by responding to the crises with poems – informal, rapidly written, simple expressions of emotions, which urged Mieke, and encouraged myself, to look out from the horror possessing us. She had in this period help from an exceptionally good support worker. At the time, she responded to these talks positively, but, when he had left, turned to the whisky she had concealed in another room. On one occasion, when the whole family was present, the police rang following a complaint that she had been seen drinking in the driving seat of our car outside a shop. With her agreement, we acquired our own breathalyser. But nothing worked to save her from the addiction.

27 September
At Brynawel the other day M. was breathalysed and sent home in a taxi. There was a horrible scene when Joe came in, and M. asked him to take her back to Brynawel so she could collect the car. He shouted violently, calling her 'a mad fucking bitch' and stormed out. Some hours later, when I was sitting alone downstairs, he came back. Since then, there's been an uneasy peace in the house. It astonishes me how little M. understands the effect her drinking has on those closest to her.

28 September
I walk in my mind with my brother David now because I feel lost, unable to deal with Mieke's madness.
    Our good friends Jim and Liz have come over in response to our distress. They're being very kind and supportive.
Mieke has talked and cried. In the night she was drinking again. This morning she's talked to me about being very damaged from childhood, and mentally ill. She says she's committing 'slow suicide'.
    I hear in her a huge self-pity, and her behaviour kills my sympathy. This Mieke is utterly self-centred. She claims to have understood herself from the stay at Brynawel. What she hasn't wanted to know is that, whatever her problems, drink makes them worse. She is ill. But I can't feel for her as she is.

3 October
For M., the horror of these days & nights may have been lying in wait for her a lifetime. There's a photo of her as a baby with wide-staring eyes and such a scared, desolate expression. And perhaps that's always been there, even behind the face of the woman holding a sunflower. I don't think any lover could have helped her more than I've tried to. But the pain and the madness have always been beyond me, and beyond her capacity to self-heal.

11 October
Dipping into my journals written years ago, I see how I return again & again to the same few ideas and the same perceptions. And, often, it feels like a discovery: that I am saying something for the first time. It seems there are certain things given to me to work out – things arising in my time and from my situation. What matters is seeing them afresh.

22 October
A good visit from Bethan and her family. Bethan is strong and stable and happy in her family life. One afternoon we had a long talk about Mieke's addiction and my life in relation to it. She herself suffered from it when she was a girl and especially at the time M.'s first marriage ended. She said her mother's problem is that she's very intelligent. Yes. She's smarter than anyone who tries to help her. Stubborn, too. Intelligence and stubbornness misdirected are a person's worst enemy. If only she could turn them against the compulsion.

1 November
Mieke is in hospital. After a bad night, I called an ambulance at 6 in the morning. She was then sitting on the sofa downstairs, barely conscious. Earlier I'd found an empty bottle of the usual.

I spoke to Elin this morning. We both said the same thing – she was crying – that we want this to be over, and for Mieke to be at peace. We don't really mean that we want her dead. It's a small, but disturbing part of this whole bloody process, which makes people think the unthinkable. For a split-second last night, seeing her in a disgusting state, I could have hit her over the head with the empty whisky bottle. It might be easier to deal with *if she cried for help*. But it seems to be what she does voluntarily, and denies. Each time she finds a way of not accepting help, with an appearance of casualness, even arrogance.

14 November
I had to call paramedics again last night. Mieke had fallen on the floor. She wasn't hurt but couldn't get up. Early in the day, I'd found a large empty whisky bottle. I shouted. She went out and bought more. I found the bottle but she begged me not to throw it away. I left about half, knowing that if I got rid of it she'd only get more. It wasn't the right thing to do, but what is?

> Dreary demon,
> I know what you are.
>
> How you shut out the light
> of sun and moon.
> How your monologue
> silences every voice.

I know you: vampire.
What do you know?

Take this leaf
that drifts across my view.

Do you see it?
Do you know
the valley trees
yellow and reddish brown
under a clouded sky?

What is this leaf to you?
This wanderer
between earth and sky.
This messenger
of life that will come.

17 November

When I was 11 or 12 years of age, wretched with depression, walking about on Pennington or Wainsford Common, or in the New Forest, I felt the words I was speaking in my mind were listened to. Had I known George Herbert's poems then, I might have believed the answering words spoken in them were not his own. This early experience may have precipitated my later longing for some breach in the human world, which has become in my lifetime ever more claustrophobic.

I think the profoundest thought from ancient times was always reaching out. Our times differ from all previous times, because it is commonly assumed there's nowhere to reach to, beyond the human sphere. And much that constitutes our public world is merely banal. We find it harder to imagine anything beyond the human. Even nature is commonly translated into human terms, its many voices unheard. It becomes harder and harder to imagine that we're not alone with ourselves on Earth, and in a universe crowded with our projections. The brain is a great mystery, which neuroscientists are exploring, but it is also the ultimate trap, shutting us in with ourselves.

Without a world beyond, it is hard to breathe in this one.

4 December
An owl was calling in the quarry woods last night. In my dream I was asking a former colleague whether I should come back to teach, and to tell me frankly whether he thought I was capable of doing so. The episode was extraordinarily vivid.

Later I realized that I've had similar dreams. With my conscious mind, I think I'm done with teaching. But more than forty years as a teacher aren't easily dispensed with.

8 December
Afternoon & evening with Jim & Liz, who brought food which she and Mieke cooked. Jim got out his mandolin and sang some of the songs I remember from our early years – Hank Williams, Slim Whitman, etc. The voice, the music and the occasion made me want to cry, just as my father did when he heard me reading my poems or lectures. What an emotional lot we are! Joe said we all looked 10 years younger, enjoying ourselves together.

31 December
It's been an unsteady year for us – isn't it always! – with good short stretches and bad ones. Rehab offered hope, and provided ten sober weeks, but was counter-productive: *not the way for M.*, who in those circumstances becomes a mother-figure for others, but doesn't address her own addiction. There is no answer, unless she finds the strength to resist in herself, or in some higher power.

The year has been good creatively for me, with poems, some critical writings, revision (on-going) to 'Art of Seeing', and final touches to my *European Journal*.

4 January 2014
Four days into the new year and M. is drinking whisky. When she came round, I spoke to her harshly, meaning to help. But it isn't my words that can make a difference. Feeling dispirited, I spent the day in bed – so much for that resolution! Yesterday, M. had shown a wonderful acute intelligence in arranging the new sections of my poems for me. I owe so much to her insight. She is herself so quick-seeing, and so loving. Yet this true self is one she seems incapable of living with permanently.

15 January
My friend Stephen Batty is a responsive reader, and a thinker who sees connections. There's nothing more heartening for a poet than to find his poetry living in another person's mind. Stephen also makes me feel that my work belongs to a tradition I revere, that it contributes to a current of live thought. The time has long gone when I believed any of us could have our meaning alone.

25 January
I don't want to risk a curse, but I have to say the past two weeks have been Mieke's best period, and therefore mine, for many years. New medication has helped, but she has shown a strong spirit and a real interest in things. This afternoon she was all confidence when she went out by herself for the first time during the fortnight. We'll see what the outcome is.

5 February
Rain, rain, slender apple & plum trees whipping in the wind. A solitary daffodil out at the front. 'Brave', M. says. First copy of *Openings* with Dad's painting, *Red House*, which Joe photographed, on the cover. It would have meant so much to my father if he could have seen the book, with his image. None of us can know what anyone in the future will make of our work, if anyone does. I vaguely remember Dad doing the painting of the house near Boldre. Life in the mind teases with such reality, which can't be brought back or returned to – moments in the stream of time.

12 February
Christian Wiman, in *My Bright Abyss*, quotes Auden's description of poetry as *'the clear expression of mixed feelings'.* I like that! He also quotes Augustine: *'From bad choices an urge arises; and the urge yielded to, becomes a compulsion; and the compulsion, unresisted, becomes a slavery'.* This too resonates in my mind.

18 February
I feel *Ancestral Lines* is almost finished now, requiring only a little revision (mostly suggestions Chris Meredith kindly made). The lesson I've learnt is about the depth of a source, or ground: that work *releases* the poem, drawing up material which shaping develops further. But first one has to make a mark, or perhaps scribble a few lines. If successful, it is then as if a spirit comes awake in the words. In this case, more of my life, and the lives

of family and ancestors, emerged, and became an animating principle. I couldn't have foreseen the work that has come into being, and could only see where it might be going as it evolved.

27 February
Openings: A European Journal is out. This is Mieke's book. Without her, my life would have been very different. Her love sustained me then, and still does – as I know when she is truly herself.

23 March
Here's a birthday I won't forget. Mieke was out of it through drink, and Joe is in hospital in Cardiff. He may have been mugged and/or under the influence of drugs & drink. I haven't been able to get much information so far, except to learn that he's reasonably comfortable.

Someone once said John Cowper Powys had a tormented early life in order to enjoy a serene old age. In early life I was surrounded by people I could trust. At 73, I'm swept up in the chaos of those closest to me.

The cats brought us a rat they'd killed, and left it at the top of the stairs: a gift which summed up my 73rd birthday.

> A yellow butterfly –
> a brimstone –
> but nothing here
> that speaks of the wrath of God
> raining down hellfire
> that turns cities to ash.
>
> So why do you, once more,
> shut out the whole world
> springing in bud and wing
> and let the demon in?
>
> This yellow one,
> frailer than a leaf,
> wanders along the wood edge
> looking for a mate.
>
> Finding each other,
> they soar, higher and higher,

out of human sight,
and at last tumble down
into last year's leaves
and unite to continue their kind.

Little else moves
In the garden and among the trees.
The day, it seems, is a quiet surface.
But what we don't see
we begin to feel –
in bud and wing
lighter than a leaf,
not wrath, but energy:
a wave gathering
in least plant and smallest creature,
a force to blast out any demon
that seeks to possess your heart and mind.

All round us it begins –
yellow butterfly on blue flower,
alive in white fire,
the power of the March sun.

5 APRIL
M. was out at 6 this morning when she thought I was asleep. Now, in the early evening, having drunk a half bottle of whisky, she's in bed, half-sleeping and feeling ill. I crave normality. Joe has learnt, more or less, to accept Mieke as she is. I always hope, and am deceived.

Blackbirds are singing under the dull, polluted sky. Here's a music only a nuclear winter will stop, or the end of life on Earth. How can a person not hear it in their heart?

What Mieke's support worker said, hesitantly, with due respect, made sense. It's not organic compulsion that drives her to drink, but the way she was treated as a child, and her subsequent response and thinking. She is trapped in an idea. We are all creatures of ideas, as I know well.

GOOD FRIDAY
M. in bed feeling ill and Joe away for the weekend, I worked on my paper on Rowan Williams for Brecon. Paul Evans, in his *Guardian* Nature Diary,

which I admire, recently described a 5,000-year-old yew tree, saying it had witnessed the beginning of Christianity, and its end. At least, that seemed to be the implication of his words. Of course, there's no sense of this in Rowan Williams, or in the faithful minority representing this once Christian country. To them, the idea would be absurd. Not to me, intent on understanding a world which I know I'm not part of.

8 May
Mieke's birthday: 68 today. A good day, M. relaxed and cheerful. In the evening we went out for a meal with friends.

When we first knew each other, M. would say she didn't expect to live beyond 40. I'd try to argue her out of this, as false romanticism. But it was more than that: she does periodically find living difficult. And despite self-harm, and the hurt it does others, she is life itself to me. With her, I've learnt about actual love, not the romantic dream. Not that we're dead to romance!

10 May
After her support worker was here talking good sense, I found Mieke with a large bottle of whisky. She'd drunk more than half of it, with the excuse that she was drinking only a little at a time, instead of 'glugging' it, as she usually does. In the morning she'd seen her psychiatrist: a session that usually results in drinking, though meant to have an opposite effect.

12 May
Elsewhere cuckoos will be calling. How dumb the landscape I look out on, a surface of cloud-shadowed hills, scar of a quarry, houses among green trees. Nothing above ground to indicate the tragic history, no sign of the generations of labour. And what honours them now in a society in which we hear daily of celebrities convicted of sexual misconduct or tax evasion, and of cuts to care provision? Resolutely we look forward, with money signs in our eyes.

Somewhere along the way in Britain, thought stopped, or stopped getting through to the opinion-formers & disposers of power. The consequences are all round us, in hopeless lives, and a world wearing out under the pressure of our depredations and folly.

How hard it is to hope!

Yet I do hope. It's something I simply can't help, and without it I might die. As I write this, a magpie leaves the fir-tree, and, with a looping flight, like a green woodpecker, seems to fall through the air down into the valley. And at once rain begins again, streaks smearing my window, through which I can see a cloud mass, which has come up without me noticing it. And this is hope, or a manifestation of hope: life in its countless ways going on outside the mind, unaffected by my thought or mood; always, this *quickness*.

16 May

In an early morning nightmare M. was hitting me on the head quite hard and saying over & over again: 'I hate you, I hate you'. I woke her with some difficulty, when she told me we'd been at Frome and I'd held her legs in a vice causing acute pain.

Dawn is all bird conversations now, many voices that also sing to one another throughout the day. At night, a big white moon.

18 May

A terrible night with M. 'smashed', as she said. Barely coherent and dangerously unstable. Two days before, in Merthyr, she'd had an appointment with her support worker and the psychiatrist who's Head of the Substance Abuse unit. This should have been helpful, but was a trigger. In the morning I 'battered' her verbally – her word – and she went for a drive and came back with a litre bottle of whisky. She begged me not to dispose of it, but I did, and, much later, she thanked me. Now, remorseful, she's said she won't drink any more. I feel exhausted.

Desperation made me furious last night and I threatened to hit her. But I wouldn't. All I can do at such times is stay awake and see she doesn't fall.

23 May

In an early morning dream I was talking sceptically to Rowan Williams about his conviction that we hear 'the voice of God' in the Bible. This is the doubt I always come to. To my mind, William Blake's idea of the creative imagination, in spite of his invocation of Jesus, *internalises* all religious phenomena. And that's where I hover, uneasily. Matthew Arnold's confidence in poetry is alien to me. I have no faith in human powers, including powers of the mind. I believe in humility as a necessity; and in prayer. But to what? To whom? Poetry, to me, is not mastery, but searching.

9 June
The artists I most admire don't tell us what we already know, reproducing the advertised world, or versifying opinions. They hammer against the wall of received ideas, or simply ignore it. They dream of making something with meaning, ultimately lifework that forms an imaginative home for others, too, not a final home, but a place in which to regain faith and energy before moving on, always making... For what are we when we cease being makers and passively accept the world as given, the world of money & comforts & entertainment – secure enough, maybe, but spiritually dead?

23 June
On another pleasant morning, solace in tiny wild strawberries & two young trees, a graceful, slender rowan and a cherry with small red fruit, in our front garden. It was a terrible night, with no sleep for Mieke, and none for me, until well after dawn. She was dreadfully agitated, and unable to stay in bed for more than about three minutes. It was like madness. I'd intercepted one half bottle of whisky in the morning, and later found three empty ones, including one in the bed. Panic follows drinking, as night the day. I don't know what to say: she might survive, as some drinkers do, but I couldn't live through another night like this.

> You were awake
> under the devil's wing.
> It was in you, beating
> in your head,
> casting out reason,
> drying up the source of speech.
>
> All night, like a black moth
> it beat at the light behind your eyes,
> dimming it,
> a bulb madly swinging
>   dusted with death.

2 July
Another bottle under a pillow in the bed, another sleepless night. In anger this morning, I told her that if Joe left as a result of her drinking, I'd go with him. But how could I? I'll see this through to the bitter end, for one of us, or both.

It's a relief to look out – the sky heavy, leafy branches moving in a breeze. Looking out is what I urge Mieke to do. But her face is closed, she's shut up inside herself, barricaded in. This is the wall I hammer at with my words, the wall only she can break down from the inside. Sleepless, I remember good times with M., and the days when I was a boy. If she could *live,* we could enjoy good days together now.

> Summer morning,
> and a light breeze moves
>   among the leaves
> and each leaf seems to say:
> 'Life is possible'.
>
> Of course, we know leaves
>   say nothing.
> We see them simply being,
> together with wild strawberries,
> and tiny cherries on a young tree,
> and the slender, graceful mountain ash.
>
> And it is I who want to say to you,
> after the terrible night:
> Look at the leaves,
> feel the swelling of the fruit,
> taste on your tongue
> a juice that is not death.

24 JULY

Two friendly reviews of *Openings* in *The Powys Newsletter*. A characteristically thoughtful piece by Charles Lock and an appreciation of my 'prose poetry' by Kate Kavanagh, who finds me 'a good companion', which is what I would like to be.

    A year on from M.'s time in rehab, with the same sapping heat. These days she smokes spliffs, which Joe supplies. Once, combined with drink, this was disastrous, causing confusion that was like dementia, but now she is, mostly, calmer. Our blessing is that we are good companions.

25 AUGUST

On a dismal August Bank Holiday Jim & Liz came over for what was intended to be a special lunch, but, after weeks of sobriety, Mieke had made herself ill with drinking and had to stay in bed. So, in the event, Jim and Liz got to work and, with some small help from me, produced a mushroom & ham omelette. I felt angry and disgusted with M., especially with 80-year-old Liz & disabled Jim working in our kitchen. But they set to without fuss, accepting the situation with good humour. What friends they are!

26 August
Having spent the morning recording an interview about Gillian Clarke for a TV programme, I must have been tired by talking so much because when Joe drove me into Merthyr in the afternoon, to have blood tests at the hospital, I felt quite emotional. As he talked, as he does, I felt close to tears, but didn't show my feelings. I was thinking about M. and my fear of losing her. How different our lives together could have been if she had been free of addiction and in good health! I think now of all the things we might have done. Yes, but I have in all honesty to say that I withdraw too easily, so our confined life hasn't been due to M. alone. Now, too, walking & standing with difficulty, I'm more afraid to go into crowded places. And our lives together in one place are good when she doesn't add to our difficulties by making herself ill.

29 August
'Difficulty is the plough,' Yeats wrote; and Geoffrey Hill has eagerly assented. I don't see it like that; for me, poetic art lies partly in the spaces between words – in so placing them that a spirit can breathe. Rilke, I think, spoke of the poems he didn't care for as heated rooms. Edward Thomas spoke wisely of words, 'As the winds use/A crack in a wall/Or a drain, /Their joy or their pain/To whistle through'. Of course, he was artfully rhyming, but his art at best was a channel for the spirit trapped in him through years of self-conscious labouring with prose.

2 October
We face a possibly ruinous situation. Mieke went out in the car last night and will be prosecuted for drink driving. Thank God, she did not hit anyone. But she was witnessed hitting parked cars, and has wrecked our car. The drama began when I shouted at her for causing chaos by drinking, and she shouted at me, and rushed out of the house. She came back before long and seemed calm. Joe then found the state the car was in and talked

to witnesses who had followed Mieke home and called the police. Two policemen arrived, and one of them talked sternly to M. and told her she will lose her license. I realize that, with a court case and findings against Mieke, we may be ruined.

> Why visit again
> that dreadful place?
>
> You have been there before
> and escaped with your life.
>
> Nothing embraces you
> but drear, dark emptiness.
>
> Today, the trees are almost leafless.
> Blackbirds gorge on crab-apples
> on the garden trees –
> yellow beaks pecking bright red fruit.
>
> Light from the white sun
> is a thin smoke.
> It is beautiful, but too gentle
> for late November,
> not kind to the soil
> which needs to be broken.
>
> You, my dear, should wake up
> before the frosts come,
> before the darkest days
> and the nourishing winter sleep.

27 October

Our wedding anniversary: 28 years (31 since we met): a gift of life, at times shaken, but through all a gift.

Leaves are falling on these overcast days. From my desk I can see outer branches of the oak tree in our neighbour's garden, still with a mass of leaves. As I watch, they tremble in a breeze, and, occasionally, one falls. I think of life fallen 'into the seer, the yellow leaf'. How we see ourselves in trees, our flesh in their flesh, budding and decaying!

3 November
Terrible news has come that our beloved friend, Anne Cluysenaar, has been killed by her stepson.

Anne was a wonderful person, kind and attentive and full of curiosity about nature and poetry and ideas. She was my dear poet-friend. We supported each other, sending poems back & forth, criticising, encouraging. Only recently she attended the funeral of Peter Thomas, her co-editor, and wrote a tribute for their *Scintilla*. How much I and other writers owe to both of them! I honestly don't know what I would have done as a writer over the past 15 years if it hadn't been for the welcome they gave my work. If I can do anything for Anne now, it will be for the continuing life of her poetry.

9 November
A lovely message from Elin in response to our grief at Anne's death. 'Friends are our family we choose in life and in some ways more important as we go through stages'. 'Love is forever.'

15 November
A depressing piece in *Planet* about post-devolution English-language poetry in Wales says that most 'new' (i.e., younger) poets follow English models and seek to make names through competitions & prizes. I think of my old friends and their passions – Roland Mathias, John Tripp, Tony Conran with his idea of Welsh 'civilisation' – as well as R. S. Thomas & David Jones. Nigel Jenkins seems to have been one of the last poets to breathe the authentic fire. And Chris Meredith with his sense of 'heartland' and wariness of complicity with the despoilers. Anne, too, who wrote herself into the depth of the country, into its geology & natural history, and through relationships across time. She went back to the first human footprint and beyond; she listened through language to the mind forming. This is what poetry is for, not competitions for prizes within the poetry 'community'. If we can't write ourselves in *deep,* better not write at all.

16 November
Pim van Lommel, in *Consciousness Beyond Life*, doesn't have much to say about language, but I wonder if we can think about transpersonal consciousness without it. Even the shining light of the near-death experience can only be spoken of as a verbal image. So, what happens if death is loss of language?

How should I know!

In actual bodily experience, I confessed my fear of falling to M. A short walk from the car to the doctor's surgery recently was a nightmare. Fear gets into my mind. I totter about quite easily in the house, but have visions of falling over outside. Once, when able-bodied, it was agoraphobia; now, standing up, it's radical insecurity. Here I am, though, still able to think and write.

29 NOVEMBER

Mieke is remorseful and feeling ill. *Why* did she drink, again, during Kay's visit? Because she felt 'inadequate', and because she is 'afraid of intimacy'. But she doesn't really understand. Perhaps Kay comes too close, and M. feels she is a failure compared to the professional therapist she was when she first met Kay. This may not make 'sense', but the problem is emotional not rational, and M., despite appearances, is exceptionally vulnerable in her sense of self. Still, it is a dark mystery to both of us. She *knows* it makes no sense, and is self-sabotage. Once again, we can only feel our way, a day at a time.

> Why go to the dark
> before the dark comes?
>
> We know how it can fall
> without a warning.
> We have seen it take our beloved friend.
>
> Stand beside me as the light fails.
> Add your strength to mine
> as we watch the light go.
>
> See how it shines in our faces.
> What can the dark do
> unless you invite it in?

2 DECEMBER

When I say of Henry Vaughan 'The very air is quicker for his breath' (the allusion is to his poem 'Quickness'), I mean that a true poet quickens us, makes us more consciously alive, and even aware of sharing the sacred breath. It is much to claim! And few in our age would agree. For the few who do, the relationship with the poet is personal, as Anne formed a respectful friendship with Henry Vaughan across the centuries. Poetry thus conceived is a conversation down the ages – words of the dead to which the living respond, as the dead in their lifetime responded to words of the dead: words in every instance with life in them, quick words which enhance our sense of time & place.

19 December
Mieke in drink-obsessed mode. It makes her ill, of course, and it makes me feel ill. She is ruining her life. I wonder what good I am to her; without me I think she would have been dead by now; or perhaps my absence would have forced her to fight harder.

The sun in my eyes is warming and soothing. I've lived long enough with alcoholism to know that I don't understand it. I can't imagine not wanting to be.

23 December
A morning of mist & rain & wind when we struggled to walk from the car park to the bank in Caerphilly. The wheelchair is too heavy for M. to push for any distance, and, mostly, I pushed it, the object to hold giving me stability. But what an effort for both of us! But we did it. Afterwards, though tired, I felt better for the wind & rain in my face.

Christmas Day
M. wiped out. I'd intercepted a bottle of whisky but missed the Cointreau. When we first met, she told me she must never drink liqueurs because they made her 'mad'. Not mad, only asleep or semi-conscious, like a rehearsal for death. I lit the fire, made myself a bowl of tomato soup and sat puzzling over a crossword, cats for company.

> *Christus natus est* but you,
> my love, rehearse for death.
>
> It is not what you want.
> But what is *want*?
>
> A demon that rides the blood
> and seizes pathways of the brain.

>   A fiction that births in the cells.
>   The enemy you kindly welcome in
>   And think your friend.

What a mess of 'ideas' my generation grew up with. I've been working through so much, stumbling, shedding half-truths, sceptical of every position, and sceptical of scepticism. Yet what I live with is a fundamental reverence which takes pleasure in life itself.

For me, the poem that works makes a clear space. It has a light that cuts through: sunlight slanting through forest trees, light illuminating pathways in the mind. Something to see with, not complete vision, but a partial seeing; not self-expression, but opening to a larger self.

All our steps lead to death, but on the way we can come alive.

29 December

Sadly, 'Compulsion' has grown since the first impulse. M. and a few friends have read it and commented. Anne wept. What I feel the need of is some balance. Mieke's drinking bouts are terrible, and a danger to herself. But so much in our life is good. I can't control what any reader now or in the future will think, and I don't know whether it will ever be published. But for the sake of truth, I can't leave it as a desolate recital. Every day of my life testifies to Mieke's love.

9 January 2015

The need now is to go on in the situation in which I find myself. And this means being true to strangeness, not as alienation, but as a sense of the greater, more fundamental reality, which is obscured by a complacent idea of belonging. Looking back, looking forward, being in the present, it is always the narrow mindset I have to resist, the assumption of a fixed knowing. I remember, years back, talking with Anne about this. It was perhaps the deepest ground between us: a sense that life is always more – and stranger – than what we see. This is true, of course, in the land itself, which may at any time look like a finished product, frozen in time, but which, with only a little knowledge of geology and nature and history, we can see as a process, being made and unmade, and really no more permanent or stable than the clouds which draw their changing shadows over it.

25 January

A dull Sunday of unbroken, grey cloud. Mieke is out of it having been on the slide for several days. 'Numb to everything', as Elin says. I've given her soup to eat and yoghurt and bananas, otherwise all she'll do when downstairs is smoke. 'You should write a book about it,' Elin says, 'and make a lot of money.' We share the joke and I feel better for talking to her. Elin thinks Mieke feels sorry for herself – without reason. I don't know; certainly, she's very sensitive, and very stubborn.

How quiet it is here. Quiet in the house with M. in bed. Quiet outside, the day windless, and only an occasional car passing. But life is stirring in the ground and in the trees, and the magpies have been out and about from their home in the fir-tree, preparing for another season, another brood.

5 FEBRUARY

I've come near to despair in recent days. But what is despair? Some final thought that breaks one? I think of running out of the house, rushing a few steps before falling over! And where would I go?

The crisis passes. We talk calmly, we joke and laugh together. Love returns – at dark times its place is taken by anxiety, anger, near-despair. And in its absence, I'm not myself, and nothing but a frightened old man.

11 FEBRUARY

A night with practically no sleep, watching over Mieke, heaving her back into bed when she began to slide out. A dead weight.

I stayed in bed through the morning, as she gradually recovered consciousness.

Going down once in my dressing gown to a knock on the door, I opened it to two well dressed, smiling young people, a man & a woman. They were Jehovah's Witnesses. I sent them politely away.

When M. is like this, I think terrible thoughts, and have sometimes spoken or shouted them. But when she 'comes back', initially not knowing where she's been, she smiles at me so lovingly.

1 MARCH

Mieke is fragile after another day without alcohol. In a way, these are good times. She is herself and we are together. But she can't undertake not to drink again and we both know that soon – in the week ahead – she will be tempted to buy whisky again, and probably succumb. How reasonable I've sounded in talking to her! How clear the solution – not to buy drink – is to me! And yet I know these are only words, and when I see the frailty in the face & movements of this beautiful elderly woman I have to fight down a sense of dread.

How help the people one loves when they have to help themselves but are unable to? However open we may be, we are all to some degree locked in ourselves. No one can be another. Yet we can make spaces for each other. It's what I hope to do

19 March
Alone at night, I talked to Elin on the phone. After some restless nights and days with M., I was, briefly, incandescent with fury. What both Elin & I know is that Mieke with her drinking can be monstrously selfish. It *is* an illness, but her refusal to help herself, from the time when she joined me in England, and for Elin from farther back, in childhood, is unacceptable behaviour. *To say the least*: she is wasting her life and hurting others. For a time last night, I was thinking the unthinkable. Is it possible to kill love? For a person to behave in such a way that love for them dies? I've been through a huge range of emotions with M. What I feel just now is cold anger.

How poignant the thought that non-being will mean that memories of others will be lost. And to waste life! I write for memory and against waste: it's one of the main reasons why I keep a diary. And the more I record, the more I miss. Life is so much more – and other – than the shape of any art.

How all my ill feelings evaporate when *I know* how much we mean to each other. What an emotional roller-coaster our life together has been, and is. But what does one expect of love in a life? Peace? Security? Well, we have always been secure in each other, and when I remember the man I was when we met...

Elin and I both think Mieke's root problem is lack of self-love, and mythmaking about the past. If only she could put all the harm behind her – forgive herself or accept the forgiveness of her Higher Power – and begin to live by releasing her creativity, in whatever form. If only M. could put down the burden of the past, and release in herself the waters of life. She does love others, so how can she not love herself?

23 March
Mieke is in hospital. She was in pain and was coughing blood and vomiting so that I called an ambulance at about 3 in the morning. I've just now been able to talk to her on the phone. She is no longer coughing blood or in

such pain but is being kept in for further examination.

She made such an effort to ensure that I had a happy birthday this year, and I did. I thought she was going to die; and she may. But I hear in her voice on the phone all the old stubborn strength, but exhaustion sounds in it too.

LATER
Waiting for Jim & Liz to come over for lunch. They've been such supportive friends on days when Mieke has been out of it, and I've felt ashamed that Liz, in her eighties, has had to make meals for us in our kitchen. Jim has been my dear friend since we were in our teens. He understands Mieke's problem better than most. Now, I feel flat with tiredness after a night of anxiety & drama, grey in my mind as cloud over the valley.

It's hard not to think M. has brought this on herself. But where do we go from here, if she comes home after treatment? She can't go on poisoning herself. But I know that she can: there's the huge problem we live with – the death she says she doesn't want, doesn't seek. Life for her is such a struggle; but why? Somehow, she can't let herself be with others, as perhaps she can with me. But is that because I'm a simple egotist who accepts her love, and tolerates her behaviour, however much I protest? Is it fear of loneliness that has shaped my life?

These are useless questions. What I want is Mieke well, and back in our home with me. It's difficulty that teaches one about love, not the comfort of having life as one wants it. She was always drawn to the odd ones, the misfits, and I'm one of those. I once looked for a dream, but found instead a woman in the power of a demon. And this has taught me something about love.

1 APRIL
M. continues in hospital undergoing further tests. I am afraid she will die. My secondary fear is that she will come out of hospital and, denying that alcoholism had anything to do with her illness, continue to drink.

Joe brought me a cup of tea in bed and cooked me kippers for lunch. I caught him out with a silly April Fool joke. Later today we'll record poems & extracts for Liz Mathews to use in the film she is making of my work.

8 APRIL
Another lovely spring day, cooler so far, with high, thin cloud. M. is currently in the respiratory ward. In another hour, I'll be able to phone

again to find out how she is. In my mind I see the photo Joe took of Mieke and Anne at The George in Brecon: two beautiful older women sitting side by side. How little we think of the dark when enjoying good days in the light!

Waiting to ring, I take up *Openings,* my journal based on our early years together. For a time, I am *almost* back in those other times & places. I feel again the companionship of life with M. – something so solid but, because past, evanescent: pictures, writing in water. Illusions of the captured moment; but what really matters, growth, a developing understanding. Always partial, but moving to some purpose, within the *home* of our love.

To M. in her sickness
'... a human being is like a half-fragment'

From the hospital
a nurse rings to tell me
you are 'holding your own'.

I look out,
watching a small cloud
shaped like a rowing boat
crossing the blue sky
of an April day.

As I watch
the cloud-boat founders
leaving the sky empty.

Oh, my dear, what if we too
should break apart!

How inadequate my words
freighted with all I cannot say.

14 April
'How old Mieke looks,' Elin said to me as we left the hospital. I remember my father, when he could still see, recognising, as if suddenly, that Mother was old. There's a moment, perhaps, when we're conscious of crossing

over into old age, though others may have seen us as old for some time.

I remember well taking Mother to visit my father in the nursing home. It feels as if it were only yesterday, yet it was some time before my stroke. And now we take the wheelchair in the car, and Elin pushes me – her boys trying to help – through the hospital corridors.

And in my mind, I am still the active man. Until I stand up.

16 April
Leafing time. Blackthorn a light green shower. Oak nubbly with buds showing pressure within. Masses of celandines on roadside banks.

Elin set off to return to the Netherlands this morning. She was wonderful company and a great support to Mieke and to me. In fact, she gave me a holiday.

No one is more aware of the pressure I live under. No one knows Mieke better. She has had her own struggles, and has learnt from her mother's addiction to overcome her own. Her understanding of Mieke, based on longer experience than mine, is a comfort. Not so her belief that M. is unable to change. She counsels acceptance, as Joe does. I find this as hard as detachment. But to accept, continuing to hope: for me, that's probably the better way.

1 May
Mieke came home from hospital yesterday, but after a bad night, when she was shaking and breathing with difficulty, she had to be taken back in today. Of course, she didn't want me to call for medical help but eventually I had to. She had come out of hospital before she should have done, anxious to be home.

As I wait to visit Mieke, I turn to a poem inspired by a painting by Frances Hatch that I attempted the other day. Like Liz Mathews, Frances works with raw stuff. She's very much an artist in the open air who responds to places & conditions by using the materials they provide – in this case, sand, mud, rainwater, blackberry juice. As with Liz, I feel close to this kind of making. At this difficult time, attempting to respond in words is like putting my hand in the soil.

3 May
M. looked much healthier on our evening visit yesterday. She had lost her deathly pallor and flushed look and, with oxygen, was breathing easily. Liquid had been drained from her lungs.

The atmosphere remains heavy. Bluebells and dandelion clocks in smoky light. Hedgerows rich with blossom. Fresh oak leaves almost fully open, on branches trembling and moving slowly up and down. This *flesh of the world*: how it presses to come into being, how its newness flourishes. And out of it, out of the heavy moist atmosphere, the small birds sing. But no cuckoo here, though summer is undoubtedly coming in.

16 May
Sweet-smelling lilac & creamy flowers on the small mountain-ash in the front garden.

M. went out in the car for the first time since coming home and went to the garage where she bought a bottle of whisky, which I intercepted and poured down the sink. Then reasoned with her angrily. To no purpose. It's deeply dispiriting to be back where we were. My life on constant watch.

1 June
M. was so cheerful yesterday morning with a smiling, open face. Later, after she'd been out, she was irritable, depressed, and went to bed. As expected, I found a small whisky bottle, almost empty. Her illness, it seems, is partly a wish to be ill. Hardly a wish, an irrational drive. And then, under the influence, the 69-year-old woman becomes a defiant, stubborn child.

I wonder whether I shall ever complete my book on poetry and the sacred. My energy goes into poetry and shorter critical pieces. The idea of organizing a big book daunts me. I would leave a great deal of work towards the book if I were to die with it incomplete, but would anyone trouble to finish it? Such thoughts occur to me, as they wouldn't have done until recently.

6 June
The death of the politician, Charles Kennedy, at 55, has touched me, as it has many who never knew him. He was an alcoholic who lost the struggle, which is a daily one for an alcoholic, and unimaginable for anyone who is not. One could see at a distance the kind of man he was: intelligent, principled, charismatic – and desperately vulnerable. I see in M., almost daily, the compulsion, which she often succumbs to. Life is so difficult for the drinker, and the very thing taken to ease the way makes it all but impossible, and finally kills. It's the loneliness that strikes me most, in the case of Kennedy, for example, the public man with an inner life he tries desperately to conceal – the private life of the alcoholic that teeters

constantly on the edge of revealing itself, or staggers from exposure to exposure.

Of course, vulnerability goes with being human. We are all, or most of us, not entirely what we appear to be, and some of us are unrecognisable. For this reason, we may be wary of the alcoholic, or react to him or her with revulsion: they show openly the weaknesses we hide. And they remind us how easy self-destruction is, and, however controlled we may be, we are born to die.

SUMMER SOLSTICE
Joe saw the sunrise at Avebury. We saw it here – smoky pink through cloud – after a bad night. Mieke had taken new sleeping pills – four instead of one – on top of alcohol, and become confused. Our days have been shadowed by drink. But I'm not inclined to dwell on it. I'll do what I can to help, but I need to free my mind now. Nothing's to be gained by going over & over this self-destructiveness, which is inexplicable to both of us. We have to live life as we can. For me, this means work, which I've done little of recently – reading, watching TV, struggling with M.'s problem.

23 JUNE
After days of shadow, M. turned such an open face to me last night. At such moments I almost forget the reality of her addiction. Sadly, they are a hiatus not a stop. But they bring to the surface what binds us to each other – not the battle, constantly resumed.

25 JUNE
It was a relief to see Steve, Mieke's care worker, today. M. said: 'His very presence is healing. Because he understands about alcohol.' She had had to drink several beers in the morning, because feeling nervous and lacking in confidence at the visit. The meeting went well. But what neither Steve or I knew was that while sensible resolutions and undertakings were being made, Mieke had another bottle of whisky in the house. At 3 in the morning she woke me up, in panic. I reassured her and eventually we both went back to sleep. Later, I found the bottle, almost empty, in the bed, and had to let her finish it. This is the third bottle hidden in the bed in the past two or three weeks. Each time it seems so demeaning and insulting, but it isn't *meant* to affect me; it's part of this terrible compulsion. In view of Steve's visit, the act of hiding and drinking the whisky seemed defiant. In drink, M. is like a foot-stamping, stubborn little girl: which might be touching if it weren't so dangerous.

5 July

Thunder, heavy rain falling straight down, now finer, cloud lifting a little, hills across the valley faintly green-veiled. Storm in my mind too, but fortunately brief, as I rage at Mieke. Two days ago, it was worse. I shouted things that no one should say or hear. The only redeeming feature is that when she comes to, she has no recollection of what's been done or said. The drinking has steadily got worse since she came out of hospital. I even suspect that attention such as she receives from Steve is a kind of incentive to continue. But as the man in the film – James Cagney – says, *anything* is an occasion for an alcoholic to drink.

When I'm my better self, I realise how lonely Mieke is, how completely locked in herself. I feel with her then, and offer comfort instead of expressing anger and disgust. What the partner of an alcoholic comes to understand is that *everything* he does or says to help is futile. Perhaps this is harder for me, a man of words. But I know that, up to a point, Mieke encourages me to talk, working out some plan or understanding in my mind, which doesn't really touch her. If she doesn't find in herself a way of stopping or controlling the habit, there is no hope. Elin was right: all we can do is love her. But how hard it is when we see the Mieke we love negating herself.

The storm has passed now and a patch of open sky is spreading over from the west. The plants will have drunk up the rain thankfully. I have taken M. something to eat, and can now turn to the third draft of my piece on Aled Rhys Hughes' photographs of Mametz.

6 July

In bed last night I watched a film that I love, John Schlesinger's *Far from the Madding Crowd*. It makes me cry! It reminds me, too, of all that I've loved in Thomas Hardy since I was a boy. And it takes me back to Dorset, to places that I've probably seen for the last time, and if I could visit them, I couldn't walk, and feel the wind over the cliffs and off the sea.

Mieke slept through most of the film. When she woke up, about midnight, she was more ill, more panicky, than I've ever seen her – which is to say a great deal – and stayed awake all night. If I hadn't kept her company, I think she would have gone mad.

11 July

A morning window view: sunlight diffused among trees in the garden and at the quarry edge. A dapple of light shining on individual leaves, leaves in shadow forming a watery green. Indescribable life! The joy of seeing, and being with M., who has been herself since the last episode, purposeful and happy. I've no fear of tempting fate in writing this. It's enough to praise a blessed time.

13 JULY
It's as well I didn't tempt fate. After a bad night, Mieke is out of it. I found three empty whisky bottles in a bag hidden under clothes. How little I know about her drinking! For several days she's been so convincing – until yesterday. Delighted with our win on a scratch card (£100), she went to the shop to cash it, swearing she would not buy anything. But sometime yesterday, and in the night, she drank enough to disable herself.

I watched until I could see she wasn't going to fall out of bed, then went to the computer and continued working on 'Mametz'. Only to lose all the morning's work with a touch of the wrong button. Hey ho, I'm not meant to begin this week positively.

21 JULY
Writing up my paper on Anne's poetry, I find my way back into her mind, and miss her over again. I think of her in her landscape, as she thought of Henry Vaughan: at Little Wentwood Farm, in the fields & woods. I can't imagine the place without her. She made it her world – not possessively, but in a way that makes it more alive for us. As we think of Vaughan's country. It is gratitude that survives.

13 AUGUST
Dog days weather, damp & close, grey sky pressing on dark green vegetation. Mieke feels rotten and is in bed. I've buried myself in my work and have finished 'Henry Vaughan in his landscape'.

I note how age sends me back into the past, as old people have always confirmed. Sometimes I feel I can see my life as a whole – not as in a near-death experience, but in scenes & stretches. These come with some yearning. I would like to be mobile, to be able to move freely and to travel. I would like the fullness of life. Times when M. and I were young lovers. Times when Joe was a boy, and I would carry him on my back into the fields, when he would cry out with delight at simple things.

I think of approaching as near as possible the impossible completion. And it still means newness, the poem that will surprise me, the essay that will turn out differently from what I expected, the unforeseeable journal entry.

15 August

VJ Day remembered after 70 years. What do we know of suffering when we think of those Japanese prisoners of war, and the agony the Japanese powers brought on their people? I have a vague memory of a village party to celebrate the event.

Mieke has made herself very ill. She simply can't stop drinking whisky; nothing else interests her. She speaks to me of love – which I don't doubt – but I want to say: love isn't only what we feel, it's what we do. Feeling can destroy us

As I write, I'm waiting for Jim & Liz to arrive for lunch. I need support; which Elin gives me in abundance, but I am here alone, with a woman who doesn't know how to live.

Later

At my request, Jim brought some beers for M. He discouraged me from talking about her drinking: 'less said, soonest mended'. He was right, and M. joined in and talked quite freely (not about alcohol). But how hard it is sometimes to hold one's tongue! Liz helped me to make a meal and we all enjoyed a good time together.

28 August

M. is bad today. Out for whisky first thing, begging me not to pour it down the sink. I gave her one glass – she would have gone out again and got more if I hadn't. She held herself together when Norman and Deborah visited for coffee, but went out afterwards and came back with strong lagers (and whisky?), and is now in bed. This began again early in the week, when as a result I missed an important hospital appointment. She looks ill and is ill. The contrast with our friends was striking. Norman, at 80, his intelligent, sympathetic self; a life-loving man. Deborah, beautiful & elegantly dressed, now writing her third novel. Both of them with tales of happy visits to Dorset & Edinburgh. Life can be good for older people.

Late afternoon

Mieke is in bed. I wonder how much longer I can go on. Life without her is unthinkable, though she's made me think of it often enough, with bouts of self-destructive drinking. It's terrible to see how completely she negates herself, each time like a rehearsal for death. I look up. Rowan berries on the tree outside the front door are red, like the fuchsias. The beauty of the clouds catches my eye, shape-shifting wanderers, slowly coming apart and dissolving as they drift over. Branches are swaying and leaves shaking in the wind. The whole fir-tree is quivering. It steadies me to look. How many people know, or can imagine, what it's like struggling to keep a bottle from a person who's pleading to be allowed to drink it, though what it contains will disable or kill them?

10 September
Good days with M. followed by dreary obsession. I can't imagine how it must be for her, apparently dead to everything but the need to get drink, then closing down. How lonely she is, I thought yesterday. Later, infuriated by her blind lack of response, I shouted. Then quieted, accepting. But it is a dreadful thing to see.

Today is Elin's 44th birthday. We share fears for her mother, and our extreme feelings. Not today, though.

12 September
When M. is obsessed, as she is now, it's almost impossible to help her to think about anything except drink. The downward spiral has been particularly intense in recent days. Now, at noon, I've persuaded her to drink water and eat half a banana – which is a victory. At the same time, I've turned on the TV and she's shown interest in Jeremy Corbyn's speech following his election as the Labour Party leader.

Elin describes Mieke as a prisoner, and says she has made a prison around me. The idea struck me forcibly. It is true; but in all fairness I must say there isn't much I can do now except work. I may dream of visits to Assisi or India or Australia, which I would have loved to make, but the more realistic dream would be of a walk in Treharris Park, and that would be impossible without assistance.

28 September
Awake, I live more & more in the past. With Mieke drinking or comatose, there isn't much here to rejoice in just now. Yet I've never lost the sense that what I live for is the next step, the poem that's new, however much it draws upon the past. What I want, always, is the next perception – some freshness of word in which the world and its wonder are renewed.

Ill today, Mieke's urge to go out and buy more drink is almost overwhelming. But she holds on. In fact, she is too ill to go out. As she feels better, the obsession will drive her out again. The way addiction works on the mind is terrible. It's what kills people who don't want to die. Mind and body are both in thrall, under compulsion.

18 October
Twenty-three years since my mother died. It was a crisp, starry night. I stepped outside into the garden, and looked through the window into the warm, well-lit house. Everything I had ever known was changed then. From now, life would be different. Mieke was wonderful then and in the days that followed, supporting me and making it possible to grieve openly.

Love will bring grief; it is unavoidable. But when I am most myself, I know how deeply blessed my life has been, and is.

In thinking, in writing, I recognize incompletion. It may be different for a philosopher or a theologian, but for a poet there can never be a final word, in the sense of an absolute truth. A poet's mind is always in process – a puzzle, maybe, confused (in the eyes of others, and often in his own). He's a slippery customer! But in love we can recognize complete being, as I did in Mother, and have done in others, in the unique person, the soul alive. It is a gift to know this, and to hold to the truth.

24 October
Mieke is spending most of the day in bed after going out early to buy beers in order 'to come down', and returning with beers and also, secretly, whisky. It is palpably affecting her mind as well as body. On the phone to Elin, sharing our concerns, I say I could never abandon Mieke, that I'm committed to doing what I can for her lifelong. Elin, worried about me, says Mieke abandoned me long ago, implying that her drinking is all in all. There's truth in this, and last night, waking, the word 'abandoned' echoed in my mind.

25 October
5 p.m. and already the sun has set. What a life this is! Surely, it must end soon. Mieke woke me before 7 this morning, panicking. Was there any drink in the house? What about the small bottle of brandy Joe bought me when I was ill? Then she gets dressed, can't find her bag, finds it and goes out to buy drink. She feels ill. I want her to stay in bed, because Holly, my granddaughter is here, and I don't want Holly to see her like this. Bethan feels the same about her son, and Elin about her boys. How sad that she, who loves children so much, should isolate herself within the family. Sometimes I think she has never learnt to live.

8 November
All praise to the good days & nights, the blessed times of love &

companionship. M., who had scared herself, and felt very ill, stopped drinking several days ago. I take nothing for granted and make no predictions, but I have written so often about the bad times that I must celebrate the joy we have in each other, the deep certainty. Crises may be easier to write about. Certainly, writing at those times is what I'm driven to, and is necessary to survival. But there's a deeper truth than the nightmare we periodically experience: a truth we recognized when we first met, and have proved through all.

20 November
Joe lit the fire and made a good meal for Jim & Liz in mid-week. M. was very ill after several days of drinking. I'd arranged the visit at the time when she was well. Our intention was for her to make our friends a nice meal. They've been so supportive during the period when she's been incapable of hospitality. In the event, Joe stepped in. For some time, he's been good company, and very supportive, my friend as well as my son.

Having expressed my feelings to Liz when we were alone in the kitchen, she said, quietly, 'But it's an illness'. Yes, I know, though I sometimes forget.

Better today, she recognizes my existence. When she's ill, I feel she doesn't really acknowledge the need of anyone else; that she's beyond caring, not selfish, though that's what others feel. She is in another place, a sort of limbo.

12 December
Late afternoon: mist & rain & strong wind, the fir-tree a black figure against failing light, wildly dancing. M. is in free fall again, desperate for whisky. I poured a bottle down the sink this morning, but such gestures are futile. She will buy more. I grasp hopefully at occasional good days, but they are few, and may be deceptive – Just here, M. comes to plead with me. I'll give her some whisky in a cup of milk.

She looks so old and worn when drinking. She who is a beautiful woman when sober. I have to remember the good years with M., when she restored me to life, the companionship. Am I to watch her die or lose her mind?

May God help us.

17 December
R. S. Thomas, the man alone, on his knees in church, praying: I know the

truth of this. But we are not made to be alone; the very language in which we express our solitude has been created by countless generations of men and women, and given to us as our common world. We are intended to be a community, a people, members of one another. In sickness, I have known the distance into and out of which it seems no voice can reach. And what has saved me is human warmth. I can understand how a person in extreme suffering, in desperate loneliness, will cry out to the lonely God. But surely, what we need most, always, is human kindness?

20 December
No one outside can really imagine how life is here. But some try.

M., baffled by her own behaviour, is in bed after drinking a bottle of wine this morning. I spoke to her harshly again, trying to break through. But can I tell her anything she doesn't know? There's nothing I can say or do to stop this descent.

31 December
It has been a year of refugees & migrants, wars & terrorist attacks – aspects of the worst of the Middle Ages. In my small world, I can look back on some objectives achieved: publication of *Scattered Light*, essays on Anne Cluysenaar & Henry Vaughan, and introductions to Aled's Mametz photographs & Tony Conran's *Three Symphonies*. The year has been rich in correspondences too, especially with Liz Mathews & Lindsay Clarke. Sadly, it has witnessed the deaths of fine poets: Lee Harwood, Charles Tomlinson, P.J. Kavanagh, and Christopher Middleton. At times, I know that I am old. It would be truer to say that I am growing into old age.

New Year's Day 2016
At about 4 in the morning M., acting strangely, got out of bed and fell over. After a while she was able to get up. There was little I could do to help. I found a half empty whisky bottle in a drawer, where, days ago, in her presence, looking for something else, I had unexpectedly found 2 empty whisky bottles, and she had expressed surprise and disgust. When I spoke to Jim on the phone and asked what anyone could do to help Mieke, he said: 'Empathize and pray'. He's right. I do, but sometimes forget, and shout or moralize.

Later.
Despite its start, this turned out to be a great day for all of us, Mieke her

good self, Joe coming in from the caravan. Meal, crackers & paper hats, fire, chestnuts, easy conversation, Leonard Cohen… Life on a festive occasion as it should be, which Jim & Liz help to make it, and M. & Joe too when they are themselves.

The winter has been so mild, even warm, that this was the first fire we have had for some time. But what a difference it makes. And I had begun to think the winter would pass without a roasted chestnut!

14 February
I feel lazy at present: a bit of reading, some note taking & journal writing. M. is becoming more mobile after a fall when she twisted her ankle. This morning, on Valentine's Day, she gave me a lovely card of Brancusi's *The Kiss*. In the weeks since she stopped drinking whisky her appetite has much improved and she enjoys my cooking, limited though it is!

When I enter the modern academic thought-world & the speak of authorities I feel I'm being choked mentally, stifled in a small dark airless room. And the thought is so confident. How it piles up abstract terms, building the little room as if it were a model of the world. Systems come and systems go, and one Babel after another houses a generation of academics and students, and totters, and falls, and out of the ruins another is constructed. And life flows on regardless. I am not a total iconoclast. I honour the work of scientists, and of thinkers not bewitched by other thinkers' abstractions. I only feel that reality escapes any system that tries to grasp it. And what are we left with except, perhaps, the freshness of a haiku, or a feather on the stream?

17 February
Yesterday a man from the council came to set up rails in places in the house that are awkward for us, so that we can go on living here as long as possible. I look out on an alien world that's friendly to my eye, not one where I have an illusion of belonging. I can make something of being here, and where I am with M. is home.

7 March
Monday morning. At 7 Mieke pleaded with me to give her a beer, which, reluctantly, I did. The weekend was terrible. As I realized only later, the 'last' drive, following the loss of her driving license, had been to buy whisky. Busy about the cooking and looking after her, I shouted horrible things – to no purpose.

This morning we watched a heron stalking at our garden pond, moving stealthily, long head & beak held like a spear. It was the first thing in days she had shown any interest in. We talked. She spoke of her struggle, and said she didn't know whether she wanted to live. This baffles and infuriates me. I spoke of my hard-won belief that people must sustain one another – that this is what our lives are for. Of course, I can *talk*. Better than shouting.

Over the desolate weekend, when I wasn't cooking (or shouting), I scratched away at poems without much success. There may be something in them, but at present I'm straining and too many of the words are dead on the page.

23 March
Seventy-five years ago, my mother was in labour, in the hospital in Gosport, during an air-raid, when (quoting Hobbes) I and my twin, Fear, were born. Today was a day of messages from family & friends. Joe, cheerful & black-bearded, described himself as our 'slave' for the day and helped with everything. M., though shaky, was in happy mood. In the evening, Chris played his guitar and sang. Jim played and sang, and Jim & Chris accompanied one another. In intervals of music and talk I read poems from *Laureata,* not, alas, Mother's copy from her school days, which is lost, but an identical one. Seeing Mieke's vulnerability, I felt ashamed of the terrible things I've shouted at her. Who am I to judge? Elin is right: all we can do is love her.

Good and bad periods including two falls continued through the opening months of 2016. Once, Mieke said: 'I would chop off my hands sooner than grab a bottle of whisky'. But she went on grabbing bottles, and when our supportive friends, Jim and Liz, came over for a meal, I would help them to prepare it in the kitchen. On one memorable occasion Mieke spoke to me of what had evidently been a rare, happy period during her childhood: a lost idyll, which, as she told me about it, intimated her essential self, and the life she should have been able to enjoy.

4 May
And on a May morning …
Lying in bed with M. looking out on the garden on what promises to be a warm, even hot, day, a breeze stirring leaves & branches of the trees. She says how much she loves this view, which reminds her of life at Epse when she was a girl. Between the ages of 5 and 8, she lived there with

her parents and brother in a grand house in the middle of woods. Prince Bernhard had granted her father the right to live in the house for his work with the underground during the war. M. says that her father, among other deeds, had saved a British airman. Despite the grand house, the family were poor (the father had 'buggered off to France'), the mother making do with little. But for Mieke it was a magical time. She speaks of her sense of wonder at the beauty of nature, of the creatures (deer in the garden, rabbits, hedgehogs, birds), of gathering chanterelles, which she could find by smell. At that time, her eyesight was poor. Later, at Leeuwarden, with her first pair of glasses, it was a revelation to see the details of nature, leaves instead of the green mass of trees. But at Epse she experienced a sense of mystic oneness with nature.

All this she remembered for me this morning, and reflected that the union with nature, without ego, was the opposite of the alcoholic state, when she is trapped inside, in a dark place. Where she was until several days ago, but for now, as her mother said of our relationship, 'all is good'.

8 May
Mieke's 70th birthday. Joe arrived in the morning and together we prepared a splendid meal, which, when our guests arrived in the afternoon, we sat outside to eat. Later, indoors, Jim & Chris played and sang. In fact, it was much like my birthday, but this was for M. and she enjoyed it hugely. Being 70 suits her! She speaks disparagingly of her Sixties, and is of as good a spirit now as I have ever seen her. May this last! There have been times during the past 20 or more years when I doubted she would see this day.

4 June
A terrible day with me shouting horrible things at Mieke. I threw a bottle at her too, not to hit her, it landed beside her, as intended. Some of the cider was lost, which distressed her more than my action. The situation at these times is indescribable. What I witness is a person destroying herself, and completely negating all that she and I value and believe. It isn't Mieke I shout at, but this demonic urge that possesses her.

Summer Solstice
Mieke dreamed that she was carrying a sick child, limp in her arms, and was anxious to get it to the hospital. She understood what the dream meant.

8 July

Worrying with M. over a word in my poem, 'Talking with James Schuyler', we began to talk about life. 'A lifetime has many lives', she said. 'A cat has 7, we have at least 10.' She qualified this: 'The quantity doesn't matter. It's the idea that you have many possible lives – choice makes change possible.' It was lovely to hear her speak like this, her intelligence fully alive, her true beloved self. I felt how lucky I am, and have been.

How difficult such things are to say! Yet they're what we live by – a word, a smile, a sense of deep belonging with another person.

16 July

As I write, Elin & family are on the M1 on the way to spend the weekend with us. M., highly nervous, has gone out to buy drink. She was drinking yesterday and denied it, even when I saw her with the bottle, and she knew that I had seen her! She lies to herself, and may believe her denial – sometimes I think she does.

Writing helps to keep me sane: my daily work, but also writing in this journal. It has become a retreat for me, an asylum. In a more 'normal' household, perhaps, I would need to write less. But, as it is, this is where I can express feelings that are otherwise difficult to deal with, and find a measure of control. I can't hope to change other people but I can help myself.

19 August

To my surprise, the first copies of my new books, *Diary of a Stroke* and *Ancestral Lines*, arrived from Tony Frazer this morning. He has produced them so well: text, cover images, photos in *Ancestral Lines*. I'm delighted with them, and with Tony's promptness in publishing them.

M. was pleased with them, and asked whether I'm pleased. With the productions, yes. With the contents, my answer is more hesitant. Given time after publication, I can always see what could have been done better. But there's no end to this way of thinking, and it risks being a form of vanity. The judgement of quality isn't mine to make.

25 September

The difference between Jim and me must be the incarnational present, which he and Liz experience almost daily at Mass: for them, it underpins everything. I live with a sense of the fluidity of time. For a Catholic time is grounded upon eternity, the one event of Christ's entry into time; in all life's vicissitudes this holds, the Cross is axis of the turning world. My experience is rather of flux, and the production of 'materials' that have constantly to be shaped – as poems make a poetry. I suppose that's it: my work is my life, at any moment partial, and ultimately incomplete, but always *making*. And this must be what I want: not the certainty of a religious faith, however much it comprehends doubt, but creative uncertainty. I don't say this is better, only that it's how my mind works. As we are, so we see, so we make.

8 October

Time becomes incredible as one ages. So does disability to one who was once able. For a split second I think I can jump up and throw off the years, as I do regularly in dreams. But the truth is a life behind me, and in the present a blank sheet, where the struggle always begins.

15 October

With M. agitated, I didn't get to sleep until after 3 this morning, when I dreamt I was at Hayford and my brothers were making coffins for Mother who was either dying or dead, and for Dad. In my dream I felt real grief at Mother's death, and at never again being able to walk with her in the garden. When I woke up, I remained, for a time, in a state of grief.

In such dreams we are again in *the time that was*, which lives in us with the emotion that tells us who we are. I have said the moment is all that exists, and in a sense this is true. But the moment also carries the whole of our past, and, I believe, the life that has made us – the ancestors, the history.

24 October

Lee finds in *Diary of a Stroke* a sadness, a melancholy, and speculates that it is due to my Christian upbringing, and continuing preoccupation with religion. I suppose this does colour my kind of seriousness, and the questions that press on me. His intelligence is more robust – as befits a sculptor, one might say. It may be that I look out more, wondering about death & personal survival, and 'the question of God'. I wouldn't expect Lee to take much interest in Kierkegaard or contemporary theology! But he's far from being a man imprisoned by a glass-walled universe.

27 October

Our 30th wedding anniversary. I took M. for dinner at a country house hotel in the hills nearby, and she enjoyed it immensely, which was my intention. It was good to be out together, but for me sitting and getting up from the chair was a great struggle. That's how it is now; no point in complaining, I simply have to brace myself. '30 years!' we kept exclaiming. Time is simply baffling. In spite of the self-harm, the years together have been a blessing for both of us.

31 October
A still, bright day. Eve of Anne's death-day. What a rent in nature that was – that beautiful woman, alive in mind & all her senses, senselessly butchered. Two years – where? And what she left sustains us, as it will others after us.

5 November
Wind rises and falls. One oak leaf caught on a gossamer shakes outside the window. A bad night with M. saying she was 'manic'. Now, just before noon, she is asleep or resting in bed. In my work on 'Ditch Vision' I have got as far as the essay on Les, remembering that vital man & the good years of teaching we shared at Newton Park.

7 November
Mieke is 'back' after passing most of the weekend practically comatose. Briefly, I was furious, and I felt lonely. But anger is futile, and mainly injurious to me. Over the years, I've come to understand her vulnerability, the damage, however caused originally, that makes her periodically seek oblivion.

Love isn't what we dream about at the beginning of a romantic attachment, though nothing is sweeter. It's what people share together through years that reveal their weaknesses as well as strengths, their ugly sides as well as their charms. My life as a lover hasn't turned out at all what I hoped for when young, but that hope had nothing lasting about it. What I've been given is something more & far other than I could think in those days.

20 December
Early dark of a day when, after my carer had come, I stayed in bed all morning, sleeping or watching birds feeding at the garden table. Mieke is still in bed, recuperating. She was 'out of it' over the weekend, almost having a seizure and begging me to give her whisky. I raged at her, telling her I wanted her out of the house, out of my life, that I wished I'd never

met her. More folly. At the time I can't think and I shout dreadful things. Now, she is herself again, weak, but the M. who is my companion. What I know is that drink, or whatever has caused her alcoholism, has ruined her life, and with me she has a kind of refuge. Outside our life together she could not survive. I feel damaged, not ruined. She brings out in me a terrible fury, and a capacity for saying ugly things I didn't know I had. But at root I care for her, literally, I am her carer. Even at the worst time, I've never doubted that our lives are together, we are each other's home.

NEW YEAR'S DAY 2017
Jim died on New Year's Eve.

> Jesus, be good to him, my dear friend.

We were friends for the best part of 60 years. Our friendship began slowly. He was a popular figure in & around Lymington, and I was shy and on the edge of his circle. Our relationship evolved, we supported each other through difficult times, and by the early 60s we were firm friends. He was deeply kind & generous, a life-loving & life-affirming man, profoundly religious – as he said, not a puritan, but converted pagan. Jim with his mandolin and his songs was the soul of our native area. We were part of each other's lives, and so, for me, he will always be.

Mieke is wonderful in her responses, deeply loving to me and to Jim. At such times, I realize how much I depend upon her and am sustained by her love. In fear of her self-harm, I said she had ruined her life. She knows that I was speaking of her false self, the 'demon' that drives her to negate herself. The truth of what she means to me, and of our love, is deeper than I could say. Jim & Mieke bring home to me the truth of my own words, 'discovered' at another critical moment: 'The only strength is love'.

11 JANUARY
I feel Jim's absence acutely – the world has shifted for me without him. He's in my mind when I wake, and frequently comes into it when I'm working. I think of the places I shared with him, revisiting them. I see us at Pitts Deep, following in the tracks of Forest ponies along the shore; at Ober Water, when acorns were falling explosively into the brown, rain-swollen river; walking on Tennyson Down; in Lymington and Groningen; at Brynbeidog; here and at Tonna. There were few places that we didn't share. In my mind we walk again under the cliffs at Barton and on the

shingle to Hurst. He sings again in The Bugle, The Fleur de Lys, The Red Lion, and people bring him beer, and bring me beer too, because I'm his mate, though I can't sing. This was some of the best of my life. He drew me out; his singing made me feel more alive. And our talk! In a way, we were each other's university. Mieke, observing his expansive gestures when she first met him, saw him as Zorba the Greek. Without his belief in God, the love in which he lived and had his being, he would have been the lost young man I once knew, dragging his feet on Avon Beach and poking a stick into the sand, asking, Why live? And how he lived. He was a blessing to all who knew him.

18 FEBRUARY

Mieke has been drinking regularly in recent weeks, wiping herself out for a day or two of the seven. She will go out to the shops in a taxi, swearing she will not buy alcohol, and return, swearing she hasn't bought any. And later it will become apparent that she is drinking. I fear for her, and I feel the pathos of her situation. But this isn't all my life. It couldn't be. If it were, I would die. Work for ever calls me back. And while I've been working on 'Ditch Vision', thought breaks in of the poems I want to write, or should have written. One life isn't long enough.

I'm pleased with *Ditch Vision*; it's a step forward, a necessary book. But my body aches more these days, my energy for work is less, the big ideas are more daunting. Yet one real haiku is worth infinitely more than making an unproductive fuss.

3 MAY

Looking out of our bedroom window this morning, at all the varied greens, crab-apple covered with blossom, golden yellow kingcups in the pond, Mieke exclaimed: 'This is a little bit of paradise'. It's so good to be with her when she's happy. As she is, she says, when 'looking out'. Looking in, she sees grey, the mistakes she's made, all the bad things. I wish it weren't so, and she could take pleasure in her true self, the loving & intelligent woman she is.

8 MAY

Mieke's seventy-first birthday. She is happy, which makes all the difference to me too. Sometimes (like the other night) I wonder how we've survived. It's the bond that's strong. The feeling of being utterly alone is what I dread – the feeling Conrad may have understood best among writers.

A life without conversation; no voice but one's own! Our very existence depends upon being more than oneself. Mankind without God runs mad, and, with the wrong god, becomes a blight on the face of the planet.

29 May
Jim's birthday: he would have been 77. We grew old together, and in a way that kept us young, or perhaps what it did was give us a sense of continuity, so that we grew old, but through our friendship & shared memories kept in touch with the young men we had been.

2 September
Alone in the evening after M. had gone to bed, I was overcome by a fit of melancholy. *I don't want to be old. I don't want to be disabled.* What brought this on, I think, was the care Elin had shown us during her visit, responding to all our needs and seeing that we were comfortable. Lovingness itself is moving. Such care is also a reminder of how little one can do for oneself.

I'm definitely more aware of aging now. One sign is that I return more often to the past and see my life in stages. A memory or perhaps a dream will surprise me. I will be in another place, with the emotion of another time, and then find myself here, now, a clumsy old man. It was the same with my father: he would wake from a dream of youth to find himself old. This is to be expected. There are still things I can do, and have to do: not work alone, but making life easier for Mieke.

6 October
I wonder how much longer we will be able to live in this house, before death occurs, or infirmity forces us to leave. I am comfortable where we are, and contented with what we have. With her love, Mieke has helped to give me a good life, and I know that I have done the same for her. I still get up each day – if late! – intending to work, and often manage an hour or so, sometimes more. The one thing I always wanted to do most was write. The dream of bringing something back from a dream was more significant than I realized: bringing back, saving from time (if only a note), is a desire that has driven me. It is a form of making: shaping one's understanding of the world, realizing one's being. Subject – place – ground describes my trajectory. A sense of belonging became a question of belonging. It involves one's self, but reaches beyond. What am I part of? What are we part of? How are we connected with one another? The questions aren't abstract, but come with living, and are what we breathe. So, at any rate, I have come to feel.

14 November
These clouded November days have a beauty of their own. Sky, all over grey, brings out the sombre browns & rusty oranges of trees in the valley, and green of the hills beyond. Our young rowan, completely bare, growing straight up, is the very image of aspiring life.

    Mieke has done her 'two bottle trick': one bottle of wine to share in the evening, and one squirrelled away to drink in secret in the night. So, I take a snack to her at midday and she spends the day in bed. I know I can't understand, and I've stopped judging – which was never a benefit to either of us. Other people throw their lives away. This could never be said of M., though she knows how much more she could have made of her gifts. I know that, in a way, she has given her life to me. Sometimes I've felt this as a burden, when she has seemed *only* to live for me, or when it's seemed that I'm keeping her alive. But through all she has never been other than herself, and a mystery. I'm simple by comparison, and she understands me better than I understand her, or she understands herself.

19 December
Days of misery as we approach Christmas, through all the commercial glitz & sentimentality, on a different planet from the birth of a child in a stable. I'm suffering from shingles which is painful & debilitating. Mieke is recovering from a colossal bender that could have killed a strong man. Bright days have alternated with fog in the valley, fog in my mind. England have lost the Ashes seemingly in no time at all: a fitting conclusion to a year dominated by the incompetent & ill-tempered negotiations of our crazy withdrawal from Europe.

11 January 2018
From religious friends I know that it is possible to love God. Indeed, that love of God can be primary, determining the whole shape of a human life. A theologian may ask where love comes from if God, who is Love, does not exist. Watch an animal with her young: love is fundamental to nature; it isn't a human capacity alone. And from nature, and as we are natural beings, it is the female, primarily, that cares and nurtures. Men – I'm tempted to say – learn love from women. This is what I feel; and it is a feeling that should disqualify me from talking about God – the more so in that I regard practically all such talk as absurd. There is a silence at the heart of all things which Eckhart identifies with God. But this is so primal, so utterly beyond all ideas & images… We may sense it as benign; we may

identify it with life, and the meaning of life… This is as far as I can think. I am a man of words. Often, since the beginning of time, love has been wordless. As it often is now.

13 FEBRUARY
M. shaky after knocking herself out with whisky & antibiotics after several good weeks. I was a drinker in my student days – understudy to Jim! – and I thought I knew something about alcohol. But it was nothing like this. Even hard drinkers don't necessarily understand alcoholism, which is like a form of demonic possession. Recovery often seems like a sort of exorcism, when an alcoholic finds God or some 'higher power'. I can't imagine this for M. who is sceptical of all powers except nature. My talk means little. My support means a lot.

24 FEBRUARY
Yesterday I read the first proofs of 'Under the Quarry Woods' and made some revisions in instances where Liz Mathews, very respectfully & hesitantly, had made suggestions. How blessed I am with good readers: Mieke, Liz, Chris Meredith! They make the work itself, the shared work, more real to me, more a living made thing. Liz *lives into* my work – to use an expression Tom Dilworth uses in his biography of David Jones.

We don't understand time because we live in time. In a sense we *are* time, as our bodies grow and our minds develop, and may ultimately become confused or cease to function. And at certain moments we can feel something in us that is beyond time. It may seem like the soul that remains eternally separate, or like a spirit world to which we belong. The one certain thing is that we grow and change.

20 MARCH
What is happiness? It doesn't mean that one lives permanently with a complacent smile on one's face, like a painted egg. Pain & fear & grief are woven into most lives. To me, it means companionship, a deep commitment with another person, together with a sense of purpose. Poetry may be an occasion for joy, but is scarcely a recipe for happiness! It is woven in all the vicissitudes & emotional dramas of a life. It is a habit of Being, not a pastime one turns to on a sunny day, like golf.

It will always be a mystery to me why Mieke returns periodically to her secret vice – for that is what it is, whatever its roots in childhood, and whatever psychological needs it fulfils. It is dark to me, and it is dark to her. She doesn't want to be the person under the influence. A person she dislikes.

Nothing in this world justifies what Mieke does to herself, or excuses the pain she causes others. What I have to admit, though, is that in the very dark of this experience I have glimpsed something I would not have seen without it. With M. I have really known another person's need; felt something of the struggle. It is so easy to be cocooned in complacency, shut in with oneself. But with M. I have known – I know - life, shared life, with its interwoven light & dark.

5 MAY
Johan, Mieke's beloved brother, died today. She wasn't able to be with him, but Elin sat beside him in the hospital. As children, close to each other in age, M. and Johan supported each other in the difficult, M. says 'abusive', family situation. We all spent time together in Beverwick & Amsterdam, and enjoyed his company here on one occasion. But Johan was a recluse in later years, and only contacted M. twice recently, the last time when he was dying.

10 JUNE
Mieke had been drinking heavily while I had been away attending my friend Stephen Batty's funeral in Sherborne. Today, after secretly drinking a bottle of vodka, she was completely out of it, lying across the bed. Coming to later, she said she could not bear to be in the house without me. Recently, with Joe, we have devised a strategy of white wine only, one bottle a day, which has worked quite well – except on such occasions. The great sadness is that we can no longer share adventures together, such as my trip to London to launch *Under the Quarry Woods*, or an experience such as the funeral, because M. can no longer travel far.

On 27 August, Mieke was taken into hospital, where Elin and I visited her over the following days. She was on oxygen and obviously very poorly, but she smiled at us bravely through her oxygen mask and we hoped she would recover sufficiently to have the operation on her hiatus hernia which was long overdue. When we returned from a hospital visit on the evening of September 1, I received a call from a nurse at the hospital to tell me my beloved wife had 'gone'.

Repetition helps to show what Mieke's life as an alcoholic was like, but doesn't help to explain it. Among all the things she said to me, it is her dream of the sick child, limp in her arms, with her anxiety to save it, that has stayed in my mind as the most significant. Mieke loved and had a special understanding of children. She was a consummate professional in her treatment of disturbed children, but the key to her understanding was love. She was most herself with children, who released the child in herself. This was beautifully observed by the poet James Simpson, who wrote to me after Mieke's death, remembering an occasion when he had visited us with his two young girls: 'They were quite little, and Mieke presented them with a wooden bowl full of cherries. There was nowhere to put the stones so she encouraged my little ones to spit them back into the bowl. What a glorious mess of saliva and juice, stones and spit there was. I remember very strongly Mieke's sense of glee at their abandon, but there was also a sense of longing from her, to be on her knees dribbling and spitting juice alongside them. I will miss her wild wounded soul.'

As I read back over this tragic narrative, wondering whether I should make it public, I am acutely aware of all that it omits. I know how little this record is true to Mieke and the fullness of our life together. It risks diminishing both of us, as if the mystery of Mieke's being could be ascribed to addiction, and my life could be summed up as that of the bewildered man who tried to help her. After reading the first draft, Elin said to me: 'Remember, Jerry, you weren't only Mieke's husband, you are a poet'. In order to correct the balance a little, I have included passages from my diary that record my thinking and natural observations. Ostensibly, these have nothing to do with our struggle with alcoholism. But it would be a lie not to include them, for it was Mieke who set me free to be myself in my poetry and thinking. It was my life as a writer that Mieke encouraged and nourished. She was my keenest, most astute critical reader. When she was well – between illnesses – she read my work, and told me – as I asked her to – whether it was alive or not, whether it had the 'quickness' which I seek above all. Any maturity I have achieved as a human being and as a writer I owe in large measure to Mieke. This is one way in which there was so much more in our life together than a bare record of addiction could suggest.

I set out to make this record in an attempt to understand the woman who, in her compulsion, was such a stranger to me. What have I understood? Principally, how much she suffered. She was almost constantly in pain, and one of her reasons for turning to alcohol was certainly to dull the pain. I have now lived long enough with ill health to know how wearing the daily struggle, for one's own sake and for other people's sakes, to maintain an appearance of 'normality' can be. Mieke once shocked me by claiming she had no inner life. She also once said: 'I find being so difficult'. How could I believe that she, who was such a vital person, had no sense of self? I didn't believe it, but I have seen truth in something Elin has recently said *to me: that Mieke could not live for herself, but stayed alive out of her love for us. Elin also says: 'There is only love'. Words which chime in my mind with something I wrote in the state of desolation from which Mieke originally saved me: 'the only strength is love'.*

In the Rumoured Place

At dusk, trees at the edge
of the woods bristle
with darkness.
Another winter night is coming on,
another night we will not share,

end of another day,
countless lone hours.

There is no word like this –
alone – to bring on
the dark and the cold.

*

Sudden on a dull day
sunlight on the wall,
unexpected, yet
as if it has always been there
waiting for cloud to pass.

How words will say more
than we mean, or less,
more than we can know.

The light was like dawn
in the middle of a dark day.

As I saw it, the word
in my mind was 'passing'
in a friend's message
speaking of you.

Jeremy Hooker

What did it mean?
What does any word point to
that we can say is real?

*

Poetry is a thing
I've never understood,
the art I've loved
since I was a boy,
and with which I've sought
to shape a life.

What use to me
if I cannot reach you
and a single word –
passing –
leaves me speechless?

*

Light of another day fades
sharpening the edge of the hills
darkening the dark form
of the fir tree, that stands
like a figure of myth.

Are we the stories we tell ourselves?
Do we make them of such things –
trees streets fields light on a wall?

And you, my love, what was the story
that came to you in a bottle
washed up on the shore
of your loneliness?

You, who meant life to me,
how, even in the depths
of intimacy, could I know
the story that you told yourself?

*

One crocus on a leaden day
under cold rain,
one yellow flower
as we saw it together
last year, this
little flower
spiky with life.

*

First, after months
of silence, it was the owls
calling to each other
again in the night.

Today, snow,
an unexpected brilliance
across the garden,
and sun that dazzles
when I draw the curtains.

Welcome, I say,
thankful for these voices
in the night,
glad of a wintry sign
in this all too human world
which is mine, but no longer yours.

*

Jeremy Hooker

I too have valued the little words
that speak of being,
like *breath* and *earth* and *love*.
But what, now, can I make
of these – *gone*, and *never again*?

I can find no simile
that isn't a lie, no metaphor
to break through the air
that has become a wall,
a sky that binds the world,
in which I cry to you,
and know there can be no answer.

*

Not yet the blackthorn,
but a milder air,
light cloud softening the hills,
a change you would remark on.

And what I think of
is your whole life,
the little girl you were
on your father's boat
sleeping to the sound
of water lapping
against the hull,
the years of springs
bringing the crocus,
you growing to be
the woman you were,
with a self unknown.

*

Smoky warm blue days
that bring pleasure
and a touch of fear…

Sunlight, blue sky, space –
it begins again, season
I love most, flowers
on the blackthorn,
blossom white as an old man's hair.
It begins, and the leafless space
opens to the blue sky,
the mountain across the valley.

It begins, and the world opens
and you,
in all this space, cannot be found.

*

Is this where being ends?

Wind begins to sing
on silence
in the back yard.

The cat lying on the bed
begins to purr.

A depth of silence settles in.
But what do the words mean?
What is the worth of a word
spoken with no one to hear?

The wind will not answer.
Whatever the cat understands
it isn't this.

Night, I say. *Wind*. Silence.
May sleep take me soon.

*

A voice that breaks in on me,
or breaks in me,
as days pass, singing
Fields of Gold.
Your funeral song
to accompany the coffin
decorated with sunflowers.
A breath of the west wind.
What is more angelic
than the human voice?

With my father, it was the last
of the man. And it was the man.

With you, too, I hear
you speaking and calling.
A voice that has gone
and will be with me always.

*

Dead, gone: words
stark with absence.

Words are what we build with
fluid as water, light as leaf,
more adamant than stone,

constructing meaning
to live by, or raising
a babel of the mind.

And when words fail?
Poetry, mouthless,
dumb as the dead.

*

Close the window, shut out
the great absence
that presses against the pane.
My heart is with the ash
that was your beauty.

*

Sun rising
through the woods,
at first, bright rays
of a halo, but soon
dazzle,
obliterating the winter trees.

All gone in light,
but not as I wish –
the distinctness
of things –
a black branch

Jeremy Hooker

a bird chasing a bird
the day springing.

*

Blackthorn ivory
against slate cloud.

Snowfall on the black bough.
I would watch for days,
waiting to call you to see
the beauty of the simple fact
which, now, I see alone.

*

There is no place now
where you are – the globe
is a desert.
     Grief
would empty the universe
of all but itself, paint
with a black egotism
you would not allow –
     you,
my woman of the sunflowers
who touched them
with a living hand.

*

Being nowhere
     in no place
among the billions
on Earth – nowhere,

everywhere un-being
  non-being –
nowhere, but the city
of Brahman within the heart.

*

Woman of Vincent's country
who knew the dark
of clogging clay
and sought the sun.
Daughter of the land
of Hieronymus Bosch
familiar with creatures
of the watery grave
who knew the need
to heal the broken mind
who gave her life to others
and could not heal her own.

*

I know what the philosopher meant
who saw the soul
in expressions of the human face.

A face that lingers in the air.
A face that is carried in the heart.

But where in this world
or out of it
is the face that bore your smile?

*

What is a man crying
for his dead mate
but a stricken animal?

A man without science
who shakes a corpse
or scrabbles at the earth
with bare hands and broken nails.

A man lifting up rocks
weeping
crying out
to whatever gods
smiting the air
hammering his head
against a sky that has turned to stone.

*

Lear, howling
over his daughter
dead in his arms –
I thought in my ignorance
Shakespeare nodded.
Now I know he did not.

•

Room within rooms
dark behind light
lone in company –
    this is the place
my old friend spoke of

after his wife died
when he was living:
'half in the other world'

It is the distance I saw in his face
the voice I heard behind his voice

It lay between us
shadow in sunlight
    this rumoured place
far off
yet close as breath
    somewhere
I heard of, but did not enter
until now

*

Oblivion
was what you sought,
a day out
with no care, no pain.

Oblivion,
but not like this,
the eternity
that we call rest.

Look: night ends
that was like a corpse.

Mist lifting reveals
buds on the pear tree
breaking into leaf.

Life comes back
with the light, wind
rustling the leaves
and small birds twittering.

Is oblivion better than this?

*

Unhappy child,
I would change the world
for you, if I could.

The war is over; your father
wounded by what he has seen
emerges from hiding.
He will not settle again.

Is this where the damage began?
Was this the source of your pain,
the wound you bore life-long?

Let the day last for you
that begins on the boat
near the water-line, where
you hear small waves whispering,
where you listen in perfect peace.

*

That quiet man, buried
in a corner of Dorset
as he wished,
what he called death
was oblivion.

And wished for?
Who can say?

What haunts me
 is the idea
of non-being, the fear
that your spirit died
with your body, and when
I cry into silence
there is no one to hear.

*

They call these the small hours
when I lie in bed, watching
one star
visible through the window
scintillating
one fiery spot
in all the dark
	As I watch,
absence expands
rushing like a wind
through the universe
leaving only this spark

If there are beings on other worlds
do they die, as we do?
Do they grieve
and look with longing
at our dot in space
imagining paradise
where they walk again with the dead?

If they do not,
how could we speak with them?

*

West wind, west wind,
bringing the Atlantic
over the hills, visiting
with a kiss of rain

Blow me fresh air
into the cobweb corners
of my heart and mind.
Be lyric, wind,
breath of life, messenger,
carry me again
into the shared land
where my hand meets a hand
and the voice that answers
when I call is the voice I love.